JUSTICE
and CHARITY

JUSTICE
and CHARITY

An Introduction to Aquinas's
Moral, Economic, and Political Thought

Michael P. Krom

Baker Academic

a division of Baker Publishing Group
Grand Rapids, Michigan

© 2020 by Michael P. Krom

Published by Baker Academic
a division of Baker Publishing Group
PO Box 6287, Grand Rapids, MI 49516-6287
www.bakeracademic.com

Printed in the United States of America

Library of Congress Cataloging-in-Publication Control Number: 2019048613
ISBN 978-1-5409-6224-9
ISBN 978-1-5409-6316-1 (casebound)

Scripture quotations are from The Catholic Edition of the Revised Standard Version of the Bible, copyright © 1965, 1966 National Council of the Churches of Christ in the United States of America. Used by permission. All rights reserved worldwide.

20   21   22   23   24   25   26   7   6   5   4   3   2   1

To my students

Contents

Acknowledgments

I have dedicated this book to my students because they both inspired this project and assisted me in its execution. Were it not for the opportunity to teach Thomistic Philosophy each fall, and for the kinds of discussions their interests generated, I would never have gone down this path. This book, then, is an attempt to charitably render a debt of gratitude, and I hope I have been successful in this. Many of them read earlier versions of this book; their critical feedback helped me to clarify my own thought as well as provide a clearer presentation to future readers. If my students are to be thanked for their assistance, it is only just that I take responsibility for any of this book's shortcomings.

The monks of Saint Vincent Archabbey have provided me with the opportunity to teach the seminarians and collegians under their charge, and for this I thank them. In addition to their leadership roles in the college and the personal encouragement many of them have given me, their commitment to a life of prayer and work has been a witness and reminder to me of what academic life is all about. While I cannot thank them all, I should especially mention Archabbot Douglas Nowicki as chancellor of Saint Vincent College, Br. Norman Hipps as president, Fr. Rene Kollar as the dean who supported this project, Fr. Pat Cronauer as dean of Saint Vincent Seminary, and Fr. Andrew Campbell as my spiritual director. More importantly, the monks of Saint Vincent are to be thanked for reminding me that the purpose of writing is *Ut In Omnibus Glorificetur Deus* (so that in all things God may be glorified).

I am blessed to work in a collegial environment, and with this in mind I should especially acknowledge the members of the philosophy department, George Leiner, Eric Mohr, Sr. Mary Veronica Sabelli, Gene Torisky, and Margaret Watkins. Sr. Mary Veronica is to be especially thanked for our many conversations over lunch on topics ranging from Thomistic metaphysics to Italian pronunciation. In addition, I should thank those who have helped me by patiently reading parts of the manuscript or at least hearing out some of the ideas: Jerome Foss, Jason Jividen, Matthew Minerd, John Martino, Stephen Little, Kody Cooper, Adam Tate, and the blind reviewers. Further thanks go to Jonathan Sanford, Monte Brown, Chris Edelman, Daniel Kempton, Steve Cortright, Graham McAleer, and Grattan Brown for inviting me to give lectures to students at their respective colleges and universities. Finally, the editorial staff at Baker Academic has been wonderful to work with; I should especially thank Dave Nelson for his support and advice along the way, and Eric Salo as well as the rest of the editorial team for helping to make this work presentable.

In all of this, I have tried to keep in mind that my primary vocation is to my family, and I thank them for letting me slip away more often than I would have liked to see this project to completion. My wife, Jessica, loves and supports me in spite of my tendency to unleash philosophical ramblings when I should be doing more important things like helping get kids to bed or putting the groceries away. My children are fortunately too unworldly to realize that it is not normal to engage in platonic dialogues while doing yardwork or playing Frisbee, and so James, Isaac, Henry, Margaret, Malcolm, and even little Evelyn have been great partners in pursuit of Wisdom.

Abbreviations

CAP	Aquinas, *Commentary on Aristotle's "Politics."* Translated by Richard J. Regan. Indianapolis: Hackett, 2007.
Catechism or CCC	*Catechism of the Catholic Church.* New York: Doubleday, 1995. Available at http://www.vatican.va/archive/ccc_css/archive/cate chism/ccc_toc.htm.
Compendium	*Compendium of the Social Doctrine of the Church.* Washington, DC: USCCB Publishing, 2009. Available at http://www.vatican.va /roman_curia/pontifical_councils/justpeace/documents/rc_pc_just peace_doc_20060526_compendio-dott-soc_en.html.
CST	Catholic social thought
DR	Aquinas, *De regno.* Translated by R. W. Dyson. In *St. Thomas Aquinas: Political Writings.* New York: Cambridge University Press, 2002.
SCG	Aquinas, *Summa Contra Gentiles.* Translated by Anton C. Pegis, FRSC. Notre Dame, IN: University of Notre Dame Press, 1991.
Summa or *ST*	Aquinas, *Summa Theologiae.* Translated by the Fathers of the English Dominican Province. 2nd ed. Available at http://www.new advent.org/summa.

References provide the relevant division within the text. For example, *ST* II-II.25.3ad1 refers to *Summa Theologiae, Secunda secundae* (second part of the second part), question 25, article 3, reply to the first objection. I have used translations that are widely available so that the nonspecialist reader can easily access them. In the case of *ST*, more recent translations are available, but readers would most likely be working with the online version. In places where I amend the translation for my purpose, I indicate this with a bracket and provide a note justifying the change.

Chapter Guide

St. Thomas Aquinas follows the Aristotelian tradition of dividing practical philosophy, or the "philosophy of human affairs," into (1) moral philosophy, (2) economics, and (3) political philosophy. In addition, he distinguishes between the truths we can know via reason (philosophy) and those we can know via revelation (theology). After exploring Aquinas's teachings, we will look at the relevance of Aquinas today in light of Catholic social thought (CST). Thus, the book is divided as follows.

Part 1: Moral Theory

Chapter 1: The Natural Desire for Happiness (Moral Philosophy)

Outline: the goal of moral philosophy is to promote a proper understanding of natural, imperfect happiness and the means to obtaining it; in particular, natural happiness requires the formation of the cardinal virtues, of which *justice* is the most important; the natural desire for happiness leads one to recognize the limitations of acquired virtue, thus pointing to the need for grace.

Chapter 2: Grace and Perfect Happiness (Moral Theology)

Outline: the goal of moral theology is to promote a proper understanding of perfect happiness and the means to obtaining it; in particular, perfect happiness requires the infused virtues, of which *charity* is the most important, in conjunction with the fruits and gifts of the Holy Spirit; knowing the person and life of Christ is central to living rightly, and one grows in virtue via participation in sacramental life.

Part 2: Economic Theory

Chapter 3: The Goods of the Earth and the Good Life (Economic Philosophy)

Outline: while the goods of the earth should be used so as to promote the happiness of all, this is best achieved by a system of private ownership; yet the owners of the goods of the earth have a moral responsibility to use them for the good of others; most importantly, *justice* is the virtue by which one determines the proper ownership and use of such goods.

Chapter 4: The Goods of the Earth and Perfect Happiness (Economic Theology)

Outline: in theological tradition, to be rich means to be in least need of the goods of the earth, and thus, to the extent that one owns such goods, to be most ready to share them with others; doing so requires following the order of love and grasping the theological meaning of value; *charity* guides one in such acts of giving.

Part 3: Political Theory

Chapter 5: The Common Good in the Earthly City (Political Philosophy)

Outline: political philosophy's aim is to promote life in accordance with the acquired virtues, and thus human law must be rooted in natural law as applicable to the particular circumstances of the community; this is what it means to promote the common good; put differently, the law must determine how *justice* can be best served in the lives of the citizens; this chapter concludes with a discussion of the just limits of obedience to political authority.

Chapter 6: The Twofold Citizenship of the Christian Wayfarer (Political Theology)

Outline: political theology's aim is to promote perfect happiness in the Body of Christ, the Church; this requires determining the best relationship between the Church and the state in particular circumstances, pointing all people toward God as the fount of justice; put differently, the Church promotes *charity* among Catholics, and by Catholics toward all others; this chapter concludes with a discussion of the charitable limits of obedience to political authority.

Part 4: The Perennial Teaching of the Angelic Doctor

Chapter 7: Aquinas's Moral, Economic, and Political Theory Today

Outline: Aquinas must be "updated" so as to apply his insights to the questions of our times; in this chapter we see how Aquinas is compatible with CST but also helps us to understand and articulate it; in morality our focus is on sexual ethics; in economics we look at our wage-based, globalized economy, as well as at care for creation; in politics we look at key concepts that arise due to the dominance of modern liberal democracies.

Appendix: Schema of the Virtues

The schema in this appendix provides the principal distinctions between the types of virtues discussed throughout the book.

Introduction

Finally, brethren, whatever is true, whatever is honorable, whatever is just, whatever is pure, whatever is lovely, whatever is gracious, if there is any excellence, if there is anything worthy of praise, think about these things.

—Philippians 4:8

Even as regards those truths about God which human reason could have discovered, it was necessary that man should be taught by a divine revelation; because the truth about God such as reason could discover, would only be known by a few, and that after a long time, and with the admixture of many errors. Whereas man's whole salvation, which is in God, depends upon the knowledge of this truth. Therefore, in order that the salvation of men might be brought about more fitly and more surely, it was necessary that they should be taught divine truths by divine revelation. It was therefore necessary that besides philosophical science built up by reason, there should be a sacred science learned through revelation.

—St. Thomas Aquinas, *Summa Theologiae* I.1.1

Peace is not merely the absence of war, nor can it be reduced solely to the maintenance of a balance of power between enemies. Rather it is founded on a correct understanding of the human person and requires the establishment of an order based on justice and charity.

—*Compendium of the Social Doctrine of the Church* 494

One of the central aspects of Christianity is its conviction that discipleship requires some form of separation from the world. The Christian is to be "in the world but not of it." While this pithy adage can be interpreted in a variety

1

of ways, we could say generally that it contains a twofold teaching: on the one hand, Christians seek the peace from on high that the world cannot give; on the other hand, Christians are sent forth into the world to evangelize those caught up in worldliness. Christians see themselves as "the light of the world" (Matt. 5:14), called to live among those dwelling in darkness so that the lost too may come to glorify God.

There is no doubt that the world today labors under darkness and that it needs a great light. We live in a time of ideological conflicts, in which the citizens of the nations of the modern world seem incapable of agreeing upon even the most basic of moral, economic, or political principles. Civil discourse has been replaced with violent protest, and reasoned dialogue with character assassination. It seems clear enough to the Christian that even the modern world, despite all of its self-proclaimed greatness, has proven itself incapable of establishing the peace that is the desire of the nations. Political parties and philosophical theories have shown themselves to be all too human and only remind us of the world's own pithy adage: man is a wolf to man. The Church, then, the "city set on a hill" (Matt. 5:14), continues to stand today as a refuge for those who recognize that no earthly city can provide a lasting peace and that true citizenship is from on high.

Sadly, this conception of the Church as the alternative to the world would hardly be evident to those outside the Church today, and even to many within it. While Catholics have often seen the two-thousand-year unity of the Church as a response to the problem of exponential divisions within Protestantism in its five-hundred-year history, even the most ardent defender of Catholicism cannot deny that the Church today looks very much to be *both* in and of the world. Lay Catholics publicly deride one another (often for the benefit of their respective political parties), and clergy at the highest levels engage in nasty public battles over central teachings of the Church. Even those within the Church self-identify using political terms, calling themselves conservative or liberal Catholics as if to suggest that their highest allegiance is to party politics rather than to the Body of Christ. Catholics appear to be quite comfortable in the world, giving the impression that they are Republicans or Democrats first, and Catholics second. For all too many, being Catholic is like retaining an old-world ethnicity in the US: one privately celebrates feast days and one's cultural heritage but in public speaks and thinks in the terms dictated by the nation. While the Church does not force us to reject political citizenship, she demands that we direct it to the heavenly, and we can do that by heeding her call to engage the world rather than conform to it.

I wrote this book out of the conviction that those who want to heed the Church's call to engage our culture need to look to the past; in particular, they should familiarize themselves with the writings of St. Thomas Aquinas, the Church's Angelic Doctor. This book sets before itself the task of introducing the reader to Aquinas's moral, economic, and political theory both because he is a superb teacher and because his system of thought provides an interpretive key to the Church's engagement with contemporary society.

While some have seen Pope Francis as a harbinger of a new way of engaging the world that looks less to Christian patrimony than to new modes of thought, he himself has never challenged an oft-repeated teaching issued from the highest levels of Church authority: those who want to think with the Church must have "St. Thomas as a teacher."[1] As a matter of fact, the Holy Father once responded to his critics by saying, "*I want to repeat clearly that the morality of* Amoris Laetitia [one of the central documents of his pontificate] *is Thomist, the morality of the great Thomas.*"[2] Whether or not one sees Pope Francis as advancing the Church's teaching or departing from it, the point here is that the writings of St. Thomas Aquinas are still relevant to those who want to speak or think with the Church today and join in her new evangelization to the modern world.

Further, in addition to Aquinas's influence *within* the Church, many a convert to Catholicism has read his or her way *into* the Church thanks in no small part to Aquinas. For both Catholics and non-Catholics, despite the cultural and historical distance that separates us from him, Aquinas continues to be seen as a guide to living well, to living in the truth in the face of the complex moral, economic, and political issues that we face each day.

Admittedly, the lamentable divisions within the Church are at least in part a result of disagreements over the value and centrality of Aquinas for us today, and thus it is unclear how Aquinas can help us foster charitable dialogue within a fractured Church. As a Byzantine Catholic myself and thus one who sees tremendous value in retrieving other voices within the Church, I am wary of giving the impression that we should only listen to Aquinas. Byzantine Catholics have often been the victims of a narrow-mindedness among their Roman brethren, and those within the Roman rite who have tried to bring voices other than Aquinas's to the dialogue have sometimes been met with the same kind of treatment.

---

1. Code of Canon Law 252, §3, available at http://www.vatican.va/archive/cod-iuris-canonici /cic_index_en.html. See also United States Conference of Catholic Bishops, *Program of Priestly Formation*, 5th ed. (Washington, DC: NCCB Publishing, 2006), 157.

2. Pope Francis, quoted in Antonio Spadaro, SJ, "Grace Is Not an Ideology: Pope Francis' Private Conversation with Some Colombian Jesuits," *La Civiltà Cattolica*, September 28, 2017, https://laciviltacattolica.com/free-article/grace-is-not-an-ideology-a-private-conversation-with -some-colombian-jesuits (emphasis added).

The riches of the Church are vast, and there is a veritable cloud of intellectual witnesses to whom we could turn, but we must be aware that Aquinas is a central voice and one which the Church has consistently asked us to heed. The goal is not to close off thinking but to open it up, to understand what the Church is teaching and to equip ourselves with a vocabulary as well as formation that will allow us to dialogue more effectively. Studying Aquinas's moral, economic, and political theory gives one who wants to think with the Church a critical vocabulary and intellectual formation. As an important voice within the Church who has helped shape her teachings, Aquinas continues to be a guide to living justly and charitably in the face of whatever controversies we may encounter.

St. Thomas Aquinas (1225–74) was born into a wealthy Italian family and could have let its influence purchase for him a life of relative ease. Instead, against his family's wishes he followed his calling with an unestablished order of preachers known as the Dominicans. His brilliance was soon discovered, and he embarked on an all-too-brief professorial career at the University of Paris and in his native Italy. He left behind for posterity an incredible variety of works, most importantly (especially for our purposes) an introduction to theology called the *Summa Theologiae*. Thanks to his encyclopedic memory and zeal for careful argumentation, he was in an ideal position to help synthesize Catholic theology with the newly rediscovered works of the pagan philosopher Aristotle. While he generated controversy of his own, and some of his teachings were condemned by the bishop of Paris shortly after his death, he quickly was recognized as a doctor of the Church. In more recent times, he was given the title of Common Doctor, in light of his centrality to Church teaching.

With all of this praise for a medieval churchman, one may wonder how his thought is applicable today: What could a thirteenth-century friar have to tell us about how to live well in the twenty-first century? How could he help us address the challenges posed by modern views on human sexuality or by technological advances in the field of human reproduction, the difficulties of making morally responsible economic choices in a globalized free market economy, or the problem of being a conscientious citizen in a secular nation? Aquinas's premodern, feudal, and thoroughly Catholic world would seem to make him of limited value in speaking to our modern, postindustrial, and pluralistic world.

Aquinas can still speak to us because our common humanity unites us more than our respective positions in time and space divide us. We cannot return to the past, but we can look to the same goal of union with our Creator; we cannot turn a blind eye to the incredible advances in science, technology, economics, and political organization since the thirteenth century, but we can place these on the same foundation of human nature informed by revelation that we share with Aquinas. To learn from Aquinas is not to accept the flawed science he relied upon or to take everything he said as if it were gospel. Rather, to learn from Aquinas is to allow the perennial truths that he unearthed to inform the way we approach the questions posed by life in the twenty-first century.

As a matter of fact, Aquinas's centrality to the Church today at least in part stems from this desire to speak to the modern world. The body of teachings that has come to be known as Catholic social thought (henceforth CST) was initiated in the late nineteenth century by a pope who, inspired by a revival of Thomism in his times, devoted an entire encyclical to this subject. In *Aeterni Patris* (1879), Pope Leo XIII exhorted Catholic teachers "to implant the doctrine of Thomas Aquinas in the minds of students, and set forth clearly his solidity and excellence over others."[3] In his landmark encyclical *Rerum Novarum* (1891), Leo provided a model of applying Aquinas's insights to the "brave new world" of modern politics and society. And that encyclical set in motion a series of documents from the Church in which she engages contemporary issues with the wisdom of the past. More recently, while in 1998 John Paul II's *Fides et Ratio* opened the door to the study of other philosophical schools besides those of the Thomists, in it he still emphasized the Church's wisdom in "proposing Saint Thomas as a master of thought and a model of the right way to do theology."[4] As Pope Francis seems to be telling those caught up in recent controversies, any development in Church teaching must be built upon this veritable foundation. Thus, CST is both a decidedly new approach to talking about moral, economic, and political life and at the same time an opportunity for retrieval. It is as part of this tradition that Pope Francis's teachings, and those of his predecessors as well as successors, should be read.

Of course, not everybody reads CST through the lens of Aquinas, and to prove that the popes are right to ask us to do so would be a formidable task indeed, one that exceeds our introductory purposes. I hope that a work such as this one can provide some assistance in seeing why the popes have insisted on the value of reading St. Thomas. A colleague of mine once exasperatedly remarked that CST "can mean whatever you want it to mean," and the claim

3. Leo XIII, *Aeterni Patris* (August 4, 1879), §31, website of the Holy See, http://w2.vatican.va/content/leo-xiii/en/encyclicals/documents/hf_l-xiii_enc_04081879_aeterni-patris.html.

4. John Paul II, *Fides et Ratio* (September 14, 1998), §43, website of the Holy See, http://w2.vatican.va/content/john-paul-ii/en/encyclicals/documents/hf_jp-ii_enc_14091998_fides-et-ratio.html.

here is that studying Aquinas can help us remove this perception. Admittedly, even well-intentioned and informed thinkers will disagree as to how to apply CST to the concrete situations of daily life and public policies, but at least they will be guided by the same fundamental principles and vocabulary as is the Church rather than those provided by the political parties of their nation. As an introduction, this book presents Aquinas's moral, economic, and political thought as clearly as possible with the goal that the reader will let the Common Doctor's illuminative mind shed light on whatever difficulties he or she may face on the road ahead.

As is appropriate for our introductory purposes, the focus here is on moral, economic, and political teachings that can be gleaned from Aquinas's *Summa Theologiae* (*Summa* or *ST*), which he wrote "to instruct beginners" (*ST* introduction). And, to be clear, we are not following the structure of the *Summa* but are instead selecting those passages that address our respective topics. Further, on occasion it will be necessary to use his other writings to complete our understanding. And, again in keeping with our purposes, the engagement with Thomistic interpreters is kept to a minimum. Hopefully this does not lead to a distortion of these basic points or to not giving credit to the scholars where it is due. I write this book more as a teacher than as a scholar, readily admitting that this forces me to only gloss over issues that one could spend years studying. I acknowledge throughout the extent to which I am indebted to the ideas of others, and I generally try to stick to what scholars broadly agree upon as well as encourage the reader to go to the secondary sources for a deeper understanding of the various topics. That being said, there is no doubt that I am taking stances on debatable points throughout; whenever possible I refer the reader to the works of scholars who in my mind make convincing arguments for the position in question. Most generally, I would extend what Jeffrey Hause says about Aquinas's relationship to Aristotle's moral philosophy to Aquinas's economic and political theories: "When he formulates his own Christian ethics, Aquinas does not repudiate this improved Aristotelian ethics [that he had developed in his commentaries on Aristotle's works], but adapts it for inclusion in his theological system as an ethics transformed. . . . The result is a dramatic and powerful illustration of the Thomistic theological thesis that grace does not destroy nature but builds on it."[5] In each of the chapters on Aquinas's philosophy we will see how his Aristotelian approach to the study of human nature points toward

5. Jeffrey Hause, "Aquinas on Aristotelian Justice: Defender, Destroyer, Subverter, or Surveyor?," in *Aquinas and the "Nicomachean Ethics,"* ed. Tobias Hoffmann, Jorn Muller, and Matthias Perkams (New York: Cambridge University Press, 2013), 163–64.

the need for grace to perfect the human desire for true wisdom, and thus to philosophy's status as a "handmaid" to theology. In the concluding chapter we take Aquinas himself as a handmaid to CST, showing how his insights can be brought to bear on a variety of contemporary issues.

I urge you to study carefully the suggested background readings from Aquinas at the beginning of each section and see for yourself how this master of philosophy and theology uses the adage "When in doubt, make a distinction." The time you put into reading them for yourself is well worth it, as they provide a veritable school for the mind and for daily life. If you take my word for it, you make me rather than Aquinas your guide: what I provide here only introduces you to your teacher so that you can gain more fruit from his lectures. You will also find an appendix at the end of this book containing a schema of the virtues that are discussed throughout the book. Further, a bibliography for this introduction (at the end of the book) includes works that can tell you more about Aquinas's life and thought and the general framework upon which his moral, economic, and political theory rests. That being said, I do not presuppose any familiarity with these works, and so those for whom this will truly be an introduction to Aquinas should not feel unprepared for what lies ahead. Finally, for the reader with a more scholarly purpose (or with a professor who expects him or her to have such a purpose), I provide a bibliography for each part for further study at the end of this book.

PART 1

Moral Theory

1

The Natural Desire for Happiness (Moral Philosophy)

Happy is the man who finds wisdom,
    and the man who gets understanding,
for the gain from it is better than gain from silver
    and its profit better than gold.
She is more precious than jewels,
    and nothing you desire can compare with her.
Long life is in her right hand;
    in her left hand are riches and honor.
Her ways are ways of pleasantness,
    and all her paths are peace.
She is a tree of life to those who lay hold of her;
    those who hold her fast are called happy.
                —Proverbs 3:13–18

But how can a man be just before God?
If one wished to contend with him,
    one could not answer him once in a thousand times.
He is wise in heart, and mighty in strength
    —who has hardened himself against him, and succeeded?—
he who removes mountains, and they know it not,
    when he overturns them in his anger;
who shakes the earth out of its place,
    and its pillars tremble;

>who commands the sun, and it does not rise;
>   who seals up the stars;
>who alone stretched out the heavens,
>   and trampled the waves of the sea.
>
>   —Job 9:2–8

1. Introduction

As we begin our study of moral philosophy, we must address a popular mis-conception about ethics: in our society we often think of the moral life in terms of rule following, of doing one's duty without regard to one's own well-being. On this conception, ethics is not about our own happiness but about obedience to a moral code regardless of our own interest or desires. Think, for example, of that moral exemplar, Superman. Superman was just "doing his duty," he tells those he helps; he is the super cop who perfectly serves and protects the human race simply because it is the right thing to do. On our understanding, ethics forces us to choose between what we ought to do and what we want to do. Doing the right thing is like dieting: it does not satisfy our desire for a tasty meal, but we should do it in spite of this.

Aquinas's moral philosophy is much richer than this: ethics is not so much about doing good as it is about *being* good, and being good is about satisfy-ing our natural desire for happiness; ethics, then, is the study and pursuit of happiness. Our rule-following, duty-based understanding of ethics is not so much false as it is incomplete. Ethics *is* about doing what we ought to do, but it turns out that this is what we really want anyway. Doing the right thing is more satisfying than betraying and hating our fellow human beings; friend-ship and love are naturally pleasant and good, even if we do not recognize this initially. Dieting is initially painful and leaves us dissatisfied with our meal, and yet those who stick with it end up finding delight in eating nutritious foods. Aquinas inherits from the Greek philosophical tradition the recognition that ethics is for the soul what medicine is for the body. We can no more be happy without being just than we can be healthy without a good diet and exercise. Happiness does not come to us accidentally, nor can it be achieved by acts of wickedness. Rather, happiness is achieved through ethical living, and we must choose not between serving others and our own interest but between hope and despair, love and hate.

In addition to this false dichotomy between ethics and personal happiness, another common ethical position in our culture is relativism, the view that nothing is truly good or evil. Maybe in movies there are superhumans who choose good over evil, but in real life this is not and could not be so, for good and evil are relative to cultures and to perspectives. One person's freedom fighter is another person's terrorist, and so on. According to the relativist, ethics is not like mathematics, where there are objective answers to our problems, but like taste, where there are only subjective likes and dislikes. Ethics is not objective and absolute, but subjective and relative.

One often hears today that the Catholic position on so many matters is not "either/or" but "both/and," and this is a good example of this approach: since ethics is rooted in our shared human nature from which we can derive natural laws,[1] ethics is objective and absolute; since ethics must consider the particular circumstances of each person and since every moral situation is different, ethics is subjective and relative. While (as we will discuss shortly) some actions such as killing the innocent are intrinsically evil and thus can never be done, the right thing to do in any situation will depend upon a variety of unique circumstances. Let us consider again the example of diet: all humans share in common the need for basic types of foods, and also the inability to digest certain objects. In this sense, a good diet is fixed for all of us; however, our height and weight, allergies, available resources, cultures we live in, and so forth will dictate the particular way that each of us will achieve our own individual good. It is objectively the case that none of us can drink motor oil as part of a healthy diet, and yet it is subjectively the case that some of us can handle an occasional milkshake whereas others, due to lactose intolerance or obesity, would be harming their health by partaking of such a delight. Relativism posits just another false dichotomy, for it assumes that ethics must be subjective because it is not objective in the way that mathematics is. Rather, the objective given of human nature is compatible with the subjectivity of human persons, called in their own unique way to live out lives of friendship and love.

This chapter outlines Aquinas's moral philosophy, or the study of what reason and nature tell us about how we should live. Our study will be divided into the following sections: (1) our last end, (2) human acts and passions, (3) virtues and vices, and (4) the best way of life. We will revisit these topics when discussing moral theology, which incorporates faith and revelation. In general, we are following Aquinas's maxim that grace perfects nature: moral philosophy points us toward what by nature we are seeking in our quest for happiness; moral theology shows us how what God has revealed to us provides the grace necessary to achieve our goal. As we will come to see by the end of

---

1. Given the centrality of natural law to political theory, we will hold off until part 3 to more fully discuss Aquinas's natural law theory. Here we will simply note its centrality to moral life.

this study, there is no such thing as "an autonomous Thomistic philosophical ethics," for those who pursue happiness within the limits of nature alone come to see how confining these limits are.[2] Before launching into the particulars of Aquinas's moral philosophy, a more general discussion of the workings of creation will be helpful, and we will use Aquinas's discussion of good and evil in the third part of *Summa Contra Gentiles* to do this.

2. Called Forth to Share in God's Goodness: Good and Evil in Creation

Background Reading: SCG 3.1.1–4, 7, 16–20, 25

Not only are "good" and "evil" important ethical terms, but they are fundamental aspects of creation as a whole. God is Goodness itself, creation is an image of this Goodness, and humans are that part of creation that can share uniquely in this Goodness through acts of intellect and will.[3] This section works through these points in order to ground our discussion of moral theory on a proper understanding of the good as what all created things seek, and evil as the failure to obtain the end, union with God.

In Homer's *Odyssey* there is an important scene early on in the story that establishes a vision of the created order as intrinsically purposive. The wicked suitors are plotting the demise of our hero, Odysseus, when suddenly a pair of eagles descends upon them, "wielding their talons, tearing cheeks and throats." The old lord Halitherses correctly interprets this as a sign from Zeus that Odysseus will return. Yet one of the brazen suitors, Eurymakhos, shows his foolishness by declaring, "Bird life aplenty is found in the sunny air, not all of it significant."[4] Homer's lesson in all of this is that everything that happens under the sun is meaningful, for the events of the natural world are signs pointing to divine realities. As the philosophers would put this point, nature does nothing in vain, for there is a reason for every action under the sun. The whole created order exhibits purpose by acting for an end, and this end the wise man knows to be the God who instills this natural order in his creatures.

---

2. This term comes from Denis J. M. Bradley's seminal work, *Aquinas on the Twofold Human Good: Reason and Human Happiness in Aquinas's Moral Science* (Washington, DC: Catholic University of America Press, 1999).

3. Let us not forget the angels here. They, too, bear God's image in a unique fashion, though this is not the place for a discussion of their important role in creation, nor of their differences from humans. See *ST* I.50–64 for a detailed discussion of the angels.

4. Homer, *Odyssey*, book 2, trans. Robert Fitzgerald (New York: Farrar, Straus and Giroux, 1998), 155–93.

Every action, even that of the unthinking creature, is for an end, an example of which is the tadpole acting so as to become a frog. This may sound anthropomorphic to us: surely the tadpole does not "seek," "desire," or "will" to become a frog. Every action is goal oriented, yet in the case of the tadpole this involves no conscious determination but rather a natural inclination toward that which fulfills its nature. As Aquinas puts it, using one of his favorite examples, "As far as this point is concerned, it makes no difference whether the being tending to an end is a knowing being or not. For, just as the target is the end for the archer, so is it the end for the motion of the arrow" (*SCG* 3.1.2). In more contemporary terms, the tadpole's DNA dictates how it will act and directs it to the end or goal of becoming a frog. The end is that which fulfills the nature of a thing and is also its good.

We tend to think of "nature" as the beginning or as that which is prior to reason and reflection rather than as the end that a being seeks. For example, we often think of primitive humans as more natural than modern humans given that they live off the land whereas we live "away" from the land. But nature is more properly understood from the end which something seeks, from its perfected state. The frog, in this sense, reveals the nature of the tadpole; the frog explains why the tadpole does what it does.

To put this distinction between the beginning and end state of a creature somewhat differently, we could think of this in terms of "what happens" as distinct from "what things seek." If we understand nature as "what happens," in many cases we would be forced to say that it is more natural for tadpoles to die before becoming frogs, that becoming a frog is *un*natural, for the majority of tadpoles in a given pond may get eaten or otherwise die before metamorphosis takes place. On the other hand, if we understand nature as "what things seek," then we can always and everywhere say that it is natural for tadpoles to become frogs, for that is their end state. In this more fundamental understanding of nature, it is natural for beings to achieve their respective end, even if we must acknowledge that they do not always, or even usually, do so.

Finally, the terminus or end of natural inclination is a good: "That toward which an agent tends in a definite way must be appropriate to it, because the agent would not be inclined to it except by virtue of some agreement with it. But, what is appropriate to something is good for it. So, every agent acts for a good" (*SCG* 3.3.2). By nature, then, each creature seeks a proper good, and this can be described in another way as seeking perfection or the fullness of its own capacities: "Every action and movement are seen to be ordered in some way toward being, either that it may be preserved in the species or in the individual, or that it may be newly acquired. Now, the very fact of being is a good, and so all things desire to be" (*SCG* 3.3.4).

In seeking its good, a thing seeks being; there is a profound metaphysical point to all of this: *to be is to be good*. This insight helps us to grasp the next point: since being is good, evil is not a being but a privation or a turning away from being. Every intention is for some good, and yet defects prevent the achievement of the good: "That which follows from an action, as a different result from that intended by the agent, clearly happens apart from intention. Now, evil is different from the good which every agent intends. Therefore, evil is a result apart from intention" (*SCG* 3.4.2). We do not want to think of evil, then, as some opposing force or existing being that must be resisted. Rather, "evil" is the term we use to designate something missing or lacking, such as the situation of a tadpole that lacks the necessary environment in which to flourish.

Since all creatures are interrelated, the good that each creature seeks and the evil it avoids must be coordinated with the good of other creatures. Every nature, every act of seeking, works together into a whole that imitates the goodness and being of God. Reason itself tells us that there must be a cause of causality, a Goodness of which the universe's goodness is but an image, a Creator of creation; this Cause of causes, Goodness itself, and Creator, we call "God."[5] What is the universe but God's image? What is the diversity of things, the multiple ways and gradations of beings, but the image of a Being that in its simplicity and unity brings forth this wondrous variety as an ordered approximation of Itself? As Aquinas puts it, "It pertains to divine providence that the grades of being which are possible be fulfilled" (*SCG* 3.72.3); and, again, "The large number and variety of causes stem from the order of divine providence and control" (*SCG* 3.74.4). Similarly, in the *Prima Pars* of *Summa Theologiae*, he states, "For goodness, which in God is simple and uniform, in creatures is manifold and divided and hence the whole universe together participates [in] the divine goodness more perfectly, and represents it better than any single creature whatever" (*ST* I.47.1). Variety and diversity, ordered toward one and the same ultimate Good, is itself a good, for it is the way that creation imitates its Creator.[6]

---

5. It is not surprising that the entirety of Aquinas's moral theory rests on God as the Cause of all things. However, it is important to emphasize here that *reason* reaches this conclusion independent from *faith*. Aquinas begins the *Summa* with five ways to prove that God exists, and to the reader who does not believe in God my response is to ask him or her to read *ST* I.2, which covers philosophical arguments for the existence of God. In fine, Aquinas would assume that anyone who studies moral philosophy would have previously come to see the necessity of a Cause of causes, and thus can here assume this knowledge.

6. All of this might lead one to ask why there is evil at all given that everything God created is good. For a thorough Thomistic treatment of the problem of evil, see John F. X. Knasas's *Aquinas and the Cry of Rachel: Thomistic Reflections on the Problem of Evil* (Washington, DC: Catholic University of America Press, 2013).

God created variety and diversity as the means by which his creation would reflect his undivided Goodness; so too he brought into being a terrestrial creature that, while merely a small part of creation, is capable of grasping its beauty, goodness, and truth. Through acts of intellect and will, the human being transcends the created order, recognizing creation as an image of the God whom he desires to know, love, and serve. Humans uniquely participate in the Good to the extent that they rule themselves in accordance with God's providential order.

Whereas most created things seek their good unknowingly, the dignity of the human creature consists in its ability to rule itself via intelligence and will. Humans "are not only ruled but are also rulers of themselves, inasmuch as their own actions are directed to a fitting end" (*SCG* 3.1.4). While it is necessary that we seek our own good, it is up to us to determine how to achieve this; faulty reasoning and disordered acts of will prevent us from achieving our good, rendering us vicious and wounded. Through actions proper to us as free, intelligent creatures, we achieve a wondrous unity with God. We do not seek just to be like him, but to know him: "A thing is more closely united with God by the fact that it attains to his very substance in some manner, and this is accomplished when one knows something of the divine substance, rather than when one acquires some likeness of Him" (*SCG* 3.25.2).

Put in the ethical language that is familiar to us today, humans are willed by God for our own sake, not as slaves; we are rational and free and, in seeking our own good, simultaneously seek to enter into union with God (see *SCG* 3.112). Yet this yearning cannot be satisfied through reason alone, and thus, as shall be clear by the end of this chapter on moral philosophy, we need some communication and assistance from God in order for what St. Augustine called our "restless hearts" to find rest.

3. Happiness, Our Last End

Background Reading: ST I-II.1–4

While all things seek their own proper good, humans are distinct from the elements, plants, and irrational animals in that humans seek their good via reason and will. Whereas the good of the frog consists in certain bodily satisfactions such as health and reproduction, these goods for humans are only means toward further ends such as friendship, leisure, and love. Think of a dog, for example: when its bodily needs are satisfied, it either plays or sleeps; while we humans find delight in such things as well, they do not satisfy our desires but merely keep them at bay. As much as we love sports, we must admit that Aquinas has a point about them when he says, "If sport were an end in itself, the proper thing to do would be to play all the time, but that is not appropriate" (*SCG* 3.25.9). Sports are for the serious business of living, and there is something inappropriate about the life of the woman who works hard all week so that she can play soccer on Saturday and watch soccer matches on Sunday morning. Soccer should be played because it promotes health, friendship, and love toward God and neighbor. The term "happiness" is used to indicate this human good that goes beyond health and amusement. If happiness is the good that we are seeking, before we set sail on the journey of ethical living, it is important for us to answer an initial question: "In what does happiness consist?"

We have already established that bodily goods and play or amusement will not suffice for happiness. More systematically, let us turn to Aquinas's own answer to this question. In *ST* I-II.2, Aquinas works through the many contenders, and, in addition to bodily goods and pleasures, rules out (1) wealth, for this is not an end but a means to an end; (2) honor, for we give this to people as a sign of their excellence, and yet happiness is not a sign of excellence but the excellence itself; (3) fame or glory, for this too we give to people because we consider them to be happy, and, in addition, happiness should depend on us, not on the fleeting opinions of others; (4) power, for this, like wealth, is a means to an end, and also can be used for evil, whereas happiness is always a good; (5) any created good whatsoever, for our desires cannot be satisfied by anything less than the unrestricted, eternal good-in-itself which we call "God."

Humans are rightly called "dissatisfied animals" in that we always want more, for neither bodily goods or pleasures, wealth, honor, fame, power, nor any other created good can truly satisfy us. Infinite are the desires of the human heart, and thus the finitude of these goods will not do. This limitless desire leads us to create art, invent an endless variety of things, and improve upon our personal, social, political, and religious lives, but it also makes us dissatisfied with anything other than God. Blaise Pascal, a sort of modern Augustine, points out that our art, technological devices, jobs, and games are just so many forms of diversion unless we root them in God; whenever we try to pursue means as if they were ends, we set them up as false gods, worshiping the creature rather than the Creator.[7]

---

7. As Pascal puts it in a passage entitled "Diversions": "Being unable to cure death, wretchedness and ignorance, men have decided, in order to be happy, not to think about such things." Blaise Pascal, *Pensées* §133, trans. A. J. Krailsheimer (New York: Penguin, 1995), 37.

Happiness consists in the perfection and even surpassing of our nature as knowers and lovers. J. R. R. Tolkien created a delightful creature that illustrates this, the hobbit. As he tells us in the beginning of *The Hobbit*, the hobbit-hole "means comfort," and yet we come to discover that the greatest hobbit of all was the one who gave this up for the adventure of a lifetime, gaining thereby something much more precious than a ring of power or worldly fame: knowledge and love. To paraphrase Pope Benedict XVI, we are not satisfied with mere comfort; only greatness will do. Our highest faculties, reason and will, seek rest in knowledge and love. But to say this is to say that only God can provide us with happiness: "Final and perfect happiness can consist in nothing else than the vision of the Divine Essence" (*ST* I-II.3.8). As Tolkien recognized, Frodo Baggins could not be happy in the Shire, but had to end his middle-earthly adventure by sailing into the Western beyond, into a sun that never sets.[8]

In this life we get only a foretaste of the goodness we seek, for "we see in a mirror dimly" (1 Cor. 13:12). As Aquinas points out in question 5, article 3, we can only imperfectly achieve happiness in this life, for this life is always mixed with evils such as the death of loved ones, but perfect happiness dispels any shadows. Further, the more of the good we have, the more we want; yet "the goods of the present life pass away; since life itself passes away" (*ST* I-II.5.3). Imagine a man who has lived a beautiful life and is surrounded by his loved ones on his deathbed. His granddaughter asks him if she will ever see him again; for him to answer anything other than "yes" would be to indicate either that he is not happy or that he does not desire to continue in his happiness, and if the latter, he is clearly not truly happy. There must be life beyond the grave in which the Perfect Good, God, will be known, or we cannot be perfectly happy; those are the only options.

One might respond to all of this concern about the perishability of earthly goods by arguing that, if we have God in our lives, we need nothing else. We can be happy in this valley of tears because we know that our God is "the living God" (Jer. 10:10), who gives us everything that is good. To some extent Aquinas would agree, for God alone can make us happy. What need have we to fear evils or the death of a loved one (see question 4)? Yet Aquinas points out that "God cannot be seen in His essence by a mere human being, except he be separated from this mortal life" (*ST* I.12.11). Even if God is in our hearts, he is so only imperfectly in this life. As we work through the means

---

8. Even if you are not a lover of all middle-earthly things, I encourage you to read Tolkien's "On Fairy Stories," which is readily available online, for his reflections on how a good fairy story plays upon our natural desire for happiness.

to achieving happiness, we will see how humans seek to climb the mountain of perfection, achieving thereby an imperfect happiness, and yet themselves come to see that the mists block their view of the peak.[9]

4. Assessing Moral Situations: Human Acts and Passions

Background Reading: ST I-II.6–8, 18–20, 23, 24

When we say of a creature that it is good, what do we mean by this? Returning to the tadpole-filled pond, we would find that some get eaten by insects, fish, or other predators; some succumb to disease; some have genetic abnormalities that make development impossible; and still others end up in an inhospitable environment such as a part of the pond that dries up. A good tadpole, then, is one that, despite all of these obstacles, achieves the perfected state of the frog. More generally, we can say of any creature that its goodness consists in the perfection of its nature, the actualization of its potentials, or the fullness of its being. This general statement about goodness is true when applied to humans, though incomplete.

In some sense humans are just like any other creature in that they are good when they achieve the perfection of their species. Yet something must be added to this general notion of perfection given that their nature is both rational and free: it is not enough to perform the actions that lead to the physical perfection of the species, for a human must achieve an interior perfection that gives purpose to the physical development. The tadpole is entirely ruled by its nature, whereas the human has a nature that gives it a share in rule. For the tadpole, the good life consists in being ruled by its instincts and thereby directed to its end; for the human, the good life requires ruling over these instincts (the passions) so as to freely take up the difficult task of joining together the goods of body and soul.

Body and soul are not two separate substances (contra Descartes), nor are they natural enemies (contra Plato). We are the composite union of soul and body and must achieve our good as rational, free, bodily creatures. Further, we are naturally social and political creatures, and so our actions must be compatible with promoting the good of others, despite difficult situations where this might require sacrificing our time and talents or, as other occasions

---

9. This issue opens up a host of questions regarding the relationship between nature and grace, the natural desire to see God, etc. For a recent introduction to the history of such discussions and for understanding on just what is at stake, see Lawrence Feingold, *The Natural Desire to See God according to St. Thomas Aquinas and His Interpreters* (Naples, FL: Sapientia Press of Ave Maria University, 2010).

may demand, inflicting harm on one who threatens our life or livelihood. Thus we enter into the realm of moral philosophy, for we are daily put into situations in which we must determine how to achieve our perfection under the guidance of reason. Yes, there is a goodness in doing the right thing, but the fullness of being and goodness requires doing it for the right reasons, with the right desires, and so forth; in a word, we cannot really be good unless we perform human and not just physical acts. What do we mean by moral situations, then?

Whereas in our discussion of the goodness of the tadpole we are primarily interested in external actions, with humans we must consider motives or intentions as well. To consider another example: if a rabid dog kills a child, this is a misfortune and a tragedy, but there is little in the way of moral assessment to do here. Unless the dog escaped from the care of an inept owner, there is no one to blame. While we can still describe the action as evil in a certain sense in that innocent human beings should not be killed, and in that the dog suffers from a disease that makes it act contrary to its own nature, moral situations are not just about actions but also about reasons and intentions. Aquinas begins his analysis of moral life with this central point, that "those actions are properly called human which proceed from a deliberate will. And if any other actions are found in man, they can be called actions 'of a man,' but not properly 'human' actions, since they are not proper to man as man" (*ST* I-II.1.1). While the physical actions we perform can be good or evil in one sense, we cannot analyze them as moral, human actions until we regard them as arising from reason and will.

In question 18, Aquinas begins by noting that an action is good or evil to the extent that it has or lacks being (article 1); for example, a girl throwing a Frisbee is performing a good action inasmuch as she actualizes a power to perform it; on the other hand, if her friend has a broken arm and is therefore unable to play with her, while we might hesitate to call her friend's inability an "evil," we recognize that a defect is preventing her friend from performing an action and that this lack of action is a kind of evil. But in order to analyze this as a human or moral action we must add three considerations: (1) moral action or object (article 2); (2) circumstances (article 3); (3) intention or end (article 4). Thus, as Aquinas puts it, "A fourfold goodness may be considered in a human action. First, that which, as an action, it derives from its genus; because as much as it has of action and being so much has it of goodness. . . . Secondly, it has goodness according to its species; which is derived from its suitable object. Thirdly, it has goodness from its circumstances, in respect, as it were, of its accidents. Fourthly, it has goodness from its end, to which it is compared as to the cause of its goodness" (*ST* I-II.18.4). After explaining what Aquinas means by these three additional criteria for analyzing a moral situation, using the girl throwing a Frisbee as an example, let us discuss two of Aquinas's own examples as aids for developing one's moral judgment based on the four criteria: (1) a man unknowingly committing adultery and (2) a man killing another in self-defense. The first example helps illustrate the relationship between object, circumstances, and end; the second introduces the rudiments of what is today called the principle of double effect. After examining these four criteria, this section concludes by examining the role of the passions in moral life.

We have already seen that the genus of an action has to do with how it exhibits the actualization of a power. The second criterion of a moral situation is the object. And here we must be careful, for here we refer not to the purpose the agent has in performing the action (which is actually the fourth kind of goodness—namely, "end") but to the action itself as assessed by reason in terms of its suitability for human agents seeking the fulfillment of their nature as rational beings. Thus, at least in the abstract, actions themselves can be evaluated in terms of their appropriateness for the "objective" of living well apart from whether or not the agents performing them do so with the right motives. Much like contemporary biology analyzes nature in terms of genus and species (e.g., the poison dart frog is a species of the genus "frog"), Aquinas analyzes human actions into genus and species. In terms of its genus, the girl throwing the Frisbee is performing a good action whereas the girl with the broken arm is unable to act at all. In terms of its species, we would have to know more about the situation before determining whether or not the action of throwing the Frisbee is a good *human* action.

As Aquinas points out, "Although external things are good in themselves, nevertheless they have not always a due proportion to this or that action. And so, inasmuch as they are considered as objects of such actions, they have not the quality of goodness" (*ST* I-II.18.2). For example, let us assume that she has borrowed the Frisbee from a friend without asking permission. In terms of the object of this action, what previously seemed like an innocent and even good action now turns out to be evil, for using what belongs to another without permission is contrary to reason and thus evil. Thus, some "external" actions are either good (e.g., giving alms) or evil (e.g., adultery), for they either do or do not conform to reason's reflection regarding what actions are appropriate to the end of human perfection. On the other hand, other external actions are neither good nor evil: "It may happen that the object of an action does not include something pertaining to the order of reason; for instance, to pick up a straw from the ground, to walk in the fields, and the like: and such actions are indifferent according to their species" (I-II.18.8). If we now assume that the Frisbee does indeed belong to her, this external action is indifferent in its species and thus we cannot at this point say whether her action is moral or immoral.

In addition to the object of an action, another factor one must consider in moral evaluation is the circumstances in which it takes place. In the concrete situation, we must consider what other activities the Frisbee player could or should be engaged in. For example, perhaps she should be doing her chores. While it is true that some actions are morally indifferent in terms of their species, individual, deliberate actions always involve a moral component because reason must be brought to bear in every situation of our lives to help us determine what we should be doing (see article 9). Thus, the circumstances of actions provide an important moral consideration.

In some cases, the circumstances only add to or detract from the goodness or evil of the object (see article 11); for example, if the Frisbee player does not have permission to use her friend's Frisbee, her action has the species of wrongful use. However, if we add the circumstance that her friend needed the Frisbee for an important activity, the evil of the action would be increased. On the other hand, if her friend were out of town and would have no occasion to use it, the evil would be diminished.

In other cases, "whenever a circumstance has a special relation to reason, either for or against, it must needs specify the moral action whether good or bad" (*ST* I-II.18.10). Imagine that our Frisbee player is playing with the Frisbee in the dining room when she should be doing her homework *and* that her mom has set the table with her finest dishes and crystal. In this case an action that is indifferent in its species, due to a change in the circumstances of place as well as time, has as its object something repugnant to reason (e.g., disobedience, negligence) and thus takes on the characteristic of an evil species. As her mom would say in good Thomistic fashion: "This is neither the time nor the place for that." Similarly, had the girl already done her homework, though at this time of day her mom would generally be happy to see her playing Frisbee, the daughter would still be engaged in a thoughtless and possibly even disrespectful act: "Dear, this *is* the time but *not* the place."

In addition to the genus of goodness and being, the species or object, and the circumstances, the fourth and final consideration is the end intended by the will. It is because our actions can be voluntary, because we can "tend" toward certain goals and pursue determined means to those goals, that they can be considered moral or immoral. Recall the rabid dog: its actions can bring about evil in the world, and yet we cannot assign praise or blame to the dog itself, for it simply does what its diseased nature directs it to do. The end is the most intimate, or in Aquinas's terminology, "formal," aspect of a moral situation: "The species of a human act is considered formally with regard to the end, but materially with regard to the object of the external action" (*ST* I-II.18.6). Thus, while we will qualify this below, it would appear that the goodness of an action depends upon the will and that the will's intention determines the action's moral species, even to the point that an action with a good object loses its moral status as a good action if it is done with an evil intention. Aquinas's own example is of a man who "wills to give an alms for the sake of vainglory," thereby performing a good action that, "as willed by him, . . . is evil" (*ST* I-II.19.7ad2). In such a case, the external action is in itself good (giving alms), and yet the interior action of the will (self-glorification) renders the human action performed evil.

Similar to the case of a circumstance specifying the object of an external action, an external action that is indifferent in its species can become morally good as a result of a good intention. Our little Frisbee player is not yet doing something morally good simply by playing with her friend, but if she does so because her friend is low in spirits and she wants to cheer her up, she now wills a good deed and renders the action itself morally good as well (see *ST* I-II.19.7 and 20.4). Frisbee playing is indifferent in its species, yet the human action in this case unites this external action to a good interior action (friendship) and thus renders it morally good.

To be clear, though, we must add that one cannot make an evil action good simply by willing a good end. We are speaking here of external actions that are either good or indifferent in themselves. External actions that are evil in their species cannot become good simply because they arise from a good intention, for actions themselves have objectives or ends that can be morally evaluated apart from the personal intentions or ends of those performing them. More simply, the ends do not justify the means in such cases. As Aquinas says in regard to the case of giving alms out of a desire for vainglory, "If we consider the goodness of the external action, in so far as it comes from reason's ordination and apprehension, it is prior to the goodness of the act of the will: but if we consider it in so far as it is in the execution of the action done, it is subsequent to the goodness of the will, which is its principle" (*ST* I-II.20.1). The will only intends rightly when it directs external actions that are in accord with reason to fitting ends. Again, "that which is in respect of the order to the end, depends entirely on the will: while that which is in respect of due matter or circumstances, depends on the reason: and on this goodness depends the goodness of the will, in so far as the will tends towards it" (20.2). In order to clarify this, we will introduce Aquinas's distinction between what he calls *per se* and *per accidens* causes.

Some actions are "in themselves" (*per se*) ordered to good or evil consequences. On the other hand, other actions only "accidentally" (*per accidens*) bring about good or evil consequences. In the case of giving alms for vainglory, one performs an external action that *per se* is ordered to a good, and yet, since he who performs it does not intend it as a good (interior action), the human action is rendered morally evil. Yet in the case of the Frisbee player trying to cheer up her friend, it is only *per accidens* that the action in question takes on the species, for it is her intention that orders it to a moral good (an act of friendship). As Aquinas explains,

> When the external action derives goodness or malice from its relation to the end only, then there is but one and the same goodness of the act of the will which of itself regards the end, and of the external action, which regards the end through the medium of the act of the will. But when the external action has goodness or malice of itself, i.e. in regard to its matter and circumstances, then the goodness of the external action is distinct from the goodness of the will in regarding the end; yet so that the goodness of the end passes into the external action, and the goodness of the matter and circumstances passes into the act of the will. (*ST* I-II.20.3)

Conversely, one cannot cause a *per se* evil action to become good simply by intending it as a good, and yet an action that *per accidens* results in an evil consequence can be good due to intention. As we will see, this distinction helps us to analyze the situation of a person who kills another in self-defense.

While the will initiates human actions and directs them to the end, the will itself is only good when it conforms to reason. Thus, the good will is one that takes its starting point from reason's determinations. And the universal principles derived by practical reason for determining which actions will bring about the human good, happiness, are called natural laws. As Ralph McInerny puts this, "The principles of practical reason are what Thomas calls the precepts of natural law. . . . Since reason regulates, guides, rules the will, it is not surprising that the principles whereby this regulating is achieved receive the name law."[10] While we will devote more space to natural law in the context of political philosophy in chapter 5, for now suffice it to say that (1) reason is capable of determining whether or not various actions are suitable to human living and (2) the will is good both by intending what reason has proposed as being in accordance with natural law and by executing the appropriate external action.

The end intended is an interior act of the will and explains why the person in question is performing the external action. Most basically, intention unites

---

10. Ralph McInerny, *Aquinas on Human Action: A Theory of Practice* (Washington, DC: Catholic University of America Press, 2012), 108.

multiple external actions into a whole: the Frisbee player is taking up a particular stance, gripping a disk, bending her elbow, and so forth, yet these all constitute one single action of "playing Frisbee" due to her intention to do so.[11] Further, if the mother were to approach the daughter with a stern look on her face and angrily ask, "What are you doing?" it would be one thing for her daughter to say, "Using someone else's Frisbee without permission," and quite another for her to say, "Playing Frisbee." Assuming that she answers the latter and that she had good reasons to think that she was permitted to play with the Frisbee, while her action still is not in accordance with the moral order, she is not intending a moral evil, and thus wrongful use does not factor into explaining the "why" of her action. Since the species is derived from intention, morally speaking we could not characterize this as a human act of theft. More broadly, while ignorance does not necessarily excuse one's evil actions, as Aquinas puts it, "Ignorance of circumstances excuses malice of the will" (ST I-II.19.2ad3).

Our will seeks happiness *of necessity*, and every intentional action seeks some good as a means to this highest end, yet through (1) misapprehension, (2) a failure to determine the appropriate actions for seeking this good, or (3) seeking a lower good over a higher good, evil is the result. Aquinas's example for a case of misapprehension is a man "intend[ing] to eat honey, but he eats poison, in the belief that it is honey" (SCG 3.4.5). As for the failure to determine the appropriate actions for seeking this good, Aquinas uses the example of a man who steals from another in order to give alms to the poor (see ST I-II.18.8); while this is not quite the situation of Robin Hood, this is the popular understanding of his actions.[12] As for seeking a lower good over a higher, let us return to the girl playing Frisbee when she should be doing her chores; she is seeking a good, though because she should be willing a higher good, her action is evil. As Aquinas puts it, "It is impossible to will something good when one ought not to, because one ought always to will what is good: except, perhaps, accidentally, in so far as a man by willing some particular good, is prevented from willing at the same time another good which he ought to will at that time" (ST I-II.19.2ad2). In general, this is a twist on the old adage: good intentions can pave the way to an evil will.

If we fail to develop our rational faculties, our will lacks guidance, and our good intentions can lead us further and further down the wrong path. Socrates

11. For a more thorough discussion of the different acts of will that constitute and execute human actions, and of will's relationship to reason in the acts of deliberation, consent, and choice, see McInerny, *Aquinas on Human Action*, chap. 3.

12. We will return to the complicated story of that most famous of archers and merry men in chap. 5, for the political situation in which he acts is most intriguing.

is famous for having claimed that vice is simply ignorance, but Aquinas heavily qualifies this by explaining that one can have (1) a general knowledge of moral principles without grasping their applicability to a particular situation and (2) a "habitual" knowledge that one fails to consider due to some distraction or hindrance (see *ST* I-II.77.2). An adulterer, falsely thinking that the pleasure of being with his lover is good for him, may be ignorant in either or both of these senses, but unless he is utterly depraved there are at least sober moments in which he reflects on and condemns himself for his acts.

Our actions cannot be considered *human* actions unless we intend them, and yet Aquinas considers actions to be voluntary even when the agent is in some sense ignorant of their immoral character. The man who intends to obtain pleasure by pursuing the *per se* evil act of adultery cannot simply redescribe it as "making a new acquaintance." Even if he acts out of what Aquinas calls "ignorance of evil choice," his action is still voluntary: whether he is in the grips of a perverse passion or habit or is simply ignorant of the universal law that prohibits adultery, he is responsible for this ignorance and so performs a human action. After a brief discussion of conscience, we will consider a case in which ignorance does excuse from culpability.

Our conscience should guide our intentions, even if this does not necessarily prevent us from performing evil actions. Conscience is that act whereby we (1) recognize what we have done (witness), (2) judge what we should or should not do (incite or bind), and (3) judge that we have done well or ill (excuse, accuse, or torment).[13] In another way, we sometimes use the term "conscience" to refer to the natural habit whereby we know the fundamental principles of natural law, though Aquinas uses the term "synderesis" to designate this (see *ST* I.79.12). Since conscience provides us with our moral judgments, it is always wrong to act against our conscience, to voluntarily do something that our judgment tells us to be wrong.

Even though we must always act in accordance with our conscience, it is possible for our conscience to err, to form a mistaken judgment, and in a situation where this occurs the old adage "Damned if you do, damned if you don't" applies: on the one hand, if we follow our conscience, we are performing an evil action; on the other hand, if we do not follow our conscience, we are willing evil insofar as we are deciding not to do what conscience tells us to be good (see *ST* I-II.19.5–6). To use an analogy: we are born with a general ability to see but must hone our vision, perhaps with the help of corrective lenses, in order to see the subtleties of the truth. Similarly, it is our responsibility to form our conscience so that its judgments conform to reason and prepare

13. See *ST* I.79.13.

us to discern good from evil in the complex situations that we all must face. The adulterer may be ignorant of the moral law, and yet he is responsible for this ill-formed conscience. While it is conceivable that this conscience is so warped that he does not violate it when he cheats on his wife, he still damns himself by his actions.

We are now ready to consider two moral situations that help illustrate and clarify certain aspects of Aquinas's ethical theory, (1) the case of the unwitting adulterer and (2) that of the man killing in self-defense. And this is the appropriate place to point out that our account of the fourfold goodness of moral actions is only a first pass at all of this. In *simplifying* Aquinas's analysis we hopefully have not *oversimplified*. Scholars of Aquinas have staked out a bewildering array of positions on his moral theory and have devised fascinating moral situations in order both to illustrate the ambiguities in Aquinas's account and to defend their own interpretations. The examples we highlight here go some of the way toward indicating how nuanced Aquinas's account is and where some of the interpretive questions arise, but they only show the tip of the iceberg.[14]

First, as surprising as this may seem, Aquinas himself provides us with this rather risqué example: How should we assess the moral situation in which a man unknowingly has sex with a woman who is not his wife? And let us add something of our own to this: What if she gets pregnant as a result?

One must wonder where Aquinas came up with such an example. Here is what he says: "If a man's reason errs in mistaking another for his wife, and if he wish to [satisfy her] when she asks for [the marital debt], his will is excused from being evil: because this error arises from ignorance of a circumstance, which ignorance excuses, and causes the act to be involuntary" (*ST* I-II.19.6).[15] First, in its genus, a sexual act that leads to pregnancy is good, for the purpose of the sexual act is procreation, and to achieve this is thus a perfection and a good. Second, in its species or object and thus in terms of the order of reason, the external act is evil, for there is no other way to describe it but as an act of adultery. Third, however, as Aquinas himself indicates, the circumstance is crucial here in that it makes an act that is evil in its object excusable; note that the object is still evil (after all, it is still adultery), but the human act is

---

14. For a thorough treatment of moral actions that explains some of the principal interpretations and articulates a thorough defense of his own view, see Steven J. Jensen's *Good and Evil Actions: A Journey through Saint Thomas Aquinas* (Washington, DC: Catholic University of America Press, 2010).

15. I have changed the translation to better reflect the Latin text: Aquinas calls what the woman asks for her *debitum*, and this I am translating "marital debt" in order to avoid the misleading use of the term "right" here (which will be discussed in chap. 7) and in order to bring out the biblical roots of Aquinas's language (see, e.g., 1 Cor. 7:3).

not necessarily evil: he unwittingly committed adultery, even if he is not an adulter*er*. While we can only use our imagination here, let us say that he is either blind or married to a woman with a wicked twin sister.[16] Fourth and finally, as we have noted already, the moral character of our acts must be rooted in freedom. In this case the legitimate ignorance of this man is of such a character as to make his action "involuntary," for he intends an act of love for his wife and through no fault of his own does otherwise.

Summing up, the action in question (1) is evil in its species in that adultery is against the order of reason, yet (2) is not an evil human act since it stemmed from a good interior action (the intention to render the marital debt) marred by excusable ignorance (see *ST* I-II.21.2), and, due to the goodness and being that the sexual act itself has, is "the cause of human generation" (18.1ad3). This helps clarify that one cannot pursue an evil means to a good end (in this case, adultery that leads to a baby), for it is only the man's ignorance of what he is doing that makes his actions excusable. And, speaking about the child that results, this distinction between the physical goodness of the woman getting pregnant and the involuntary moral evil of adultery helps us to speak delicately about his or her existence: dad made a mistake, but the child is not a mistake. Dad intended an act of love, and there is no mistake but rather success when sex leads to a child. Yes, dad is a fool, but this child is good. As they say, "God writes straight with crooked lines."[17]

Our second example is killing in self-defense, an issue taken up by Aquinas himself (*ST* II-II.64.7); his treatment of it is generally considered to be the origin of the principle of double effect, or the principle that one can, in certain situations, perform an action that will lead to evil effects provided one does not intend them.[18] Aquinas does not provide a specific example of this, so let us provide one ourselves: a man is awakened by the sound of his front door opening in the middle of the night and goes downstairs to investigate; upon reaching the kitchen, he sees a burglar in the dining room and yells, "Get

---

16. I have to imagine this was a well-known example, or perhaps from a play, fable, etc. In addition, it is a variant on the situation Jacob found himself in on his own wedding night (see Gen. 29:16–31).

17. Imagine that the unwitting adulterer, upon discovering what he did, secretly rejoices in his good luck. He has often fantasized about sleeping with this other woman, and now he got what he wanted. This is a third category of ignorant action between the voluntary and involuntary: an action can be called "nonvoluntary" when one is justifiably ignorant of the evil one commits and yet would have done it even had one known (see *ST* I-II.6.8).

18. The principle of double effect is often invoked in biomedical ethical issues. For a good introduction and resource, see Benedict Ashley, OP, Jean deBlois, and Kevin O'Rourke, *Health Care Ethics: A Catholic Theological Analysis* (Washington, DC: Georgetown University Press, 2006).

out of my house!" The burglar runs at him, knife in hand; the homeowner, intending nothing other than to defend his own life, grabs a kitchen knife, counters the burglar's attack, and delivers a fatal stab to the heart. How do we assess this moral situation?

First, in its genus, death is an evil, a negation of being. Second, in its species, Aquinas is careful to distinguish between the death of the burglar, which is not intended, and the act of self-defense, which is: the homeowner did not intend to kill him; rather, he intended to defend himself. In a case like this, the action takes its species from intention; it is the action of self-defense that is morally significant and the cause of the goodness of the action. Thus, the moral object of this action is not *per se* "killing another" but "doing what is necessary to preserve one's life." Third, in its circumstances, what legitimates the death of the burglar is him forcing the homeowner to defend himself in a manner that led to the burglar's death. The word "led," which suggests passivity, is being chosen carefully: the homeowner did not intend to kill the burglar; rather, he intended to save his own life and stabbed at him in order to prevent the burglar from killing him. Most fundamentally, the burglar is the cause of his own death, for he forced the homeowner's hand. Thus, we are not speaking about an evil species (taking someone's life) being directed to a good, but about an indifferent action (wielding a knife) that, due to the circumstances, takes on a good species (self-defense). This is a *per se* good action that has *per accidens* the evil consequence of the death of another. That being said, it is worth pointing out that the homeowner had other options prior to the stabbing and may, in hindsight, realize that he could have avoided this altogether: Why didn't he stay in his room and call the police? Why not shout out from his bedroom, "Who's there?" Fourth and finally, we have already stated that the intention of the homeowner was to save his own life and that this makes his action good; let us also clarify that he used only the amount of violence necessary to preserve his own life: for the sake of argument, let us assume that he was aiming for the burglar's shoulder, intending to disable his assailant. Had he intended to kill the burglar out of anger, or stabbed him in the back as he attempted to flee, he would have intended evil.

While it is clear that the homeowner must intend self-defense, does this mean that he cannot also intend to kill the burglar as the necessary means to preserve his own life? What if he is forced to choose between his own death and the death of the burglar? Aquinas is unfortunately unclear regarding this last point. One possible interpretation refers to principles that we will introduce in our study of economic and political theory, respectively—namely, that necessity can sometimes "override" laws (see chap. 3, §2) and that public officials have the authority to intentionally kill in pursuit of the common good (see chap. 5, §6). On this account, the homeowner temporarily becomes a public official and thus can intentionally kill the burglar if forced to do so. Yet Aquinas never says this, and good arguments can be mounted to the effect that in such a case the homeowner cannot even as a last resort intend to kill; on this "weaker" view of how the principle of double effect applies, self-defense may *risk* the death of an assailant but never bring it about *intentionally*.[19]

Lest all of this violence leave a bad taste in our mouth, it is worth mentioning that Aquinas returns in this context once again to his favorite example of vice, adultery. Before concluding his treatment of killing in self-defense, Aquinas points out that one cannot commit adultery in self-defense (see *ST* II-II.64.7ad4); it would seem that even the imagination of Aquinas could not come up with a situation in which this would be justified.

Now that the factors that must be weighed in a moral situation have been discussed, we need to turn to a consideration of moral character: If the goal of moral life is to be happy, is it enough to do the right thing, or must we also desire to do the right thing? In other words, what is the role of the passions in all of this? When it comes to the relationship between the passions and the moral life, we can find two extremes: on the one hand, the passions can be seen as irrelevant for moral assessment or even as inherently evil; on the other hand, the passions can be seen as the only guides to moral life, as the rightful masters that reason must serve. In the ancient world, even if this is somewhat misleading, we could see these as the respective positions of the Stoics and the Epicureans; among the moderns, this is analogous to the respective positions of Kant and Hume, at least as they are popularly understood. Throughout human history, as Nicholas E. Lombardo puts it, "There is one view that is suspicious of human emotion and seeks to guard against it, restrain it, and prevent it from taking control. Then there is another view that exults in emotion and desire and glorifies following wherever it might lead."[20] While Christianity seems obviously opposed to the position that the passions should rule over reason, there is much to recommend the view that the passions are inherently evil, that they are the result of our fallen human

---

19. See Jensen, *Good and Evil Actions*, chaps. 2.2 and 6.4, for a good introduction to the various interpretive positions, the difficulties each faces, and the larger questions at stake here regarding Aquinas's overall theory of moral action. For a defense of the "stronger" version of the principle of double effect against "weaker" versions, see Edward L. Krasevac, "Can Effects That Are Inevitable and Instrumental Be *Praeter Intentionem*?," *Angelicum* 82 (2005): 77–88.

20. Nicholas E. Lombardo, OP, *The Logic of Desire: Aquinas on Emotion* (Washington, DC: Catholic University of America Press, 2010), xii. We are glossing here the relationship between a host of terms such as "emotion," "desire," "affection," and "passion." Lombardo's work provides a helpful background on how scholars have tried to parse these and provides his own compelling, original reading.

condition. The general thrust of Byzantine Christianity is to see overcoming passion as an important step toward theosis (union with God), and the fruits of this position are manifest in the rich spiritual life of the Christian East.[21] In between these two extremes is the Aristotelian position that moral action is not simply about reason and will, but must include the proper bodily desires and aversions.

Aquinas takes up this Aristotelian position and sees the passions as the natural consequence of bodily existence.[22] The body is naturally inclined toward or away from certain objects depending upon whether they are perceived to be good or evil. These inclinations are called "appetites," and motions of the sensible appetite (toward or away) are called "passions."[23] When a man sees a woman whom he finds to be beautiful, he is naturally attracted, and in him arises the passion of love, which moves him toward her. As Aquinas explains in *ST* I-II.24.1, considered in themselves, the passions are neither morally good nor evil; in this case, it is good according to nature for a man to feel passion for a beautiful woman. Yet, insofar as the passions must come under the guidance of reason and will, they can be morally good or evil; so, if this man is married to another woman, such a passion is inappropriate and, if commanded by or not prevented by the will, and thus voluntary, morally evil.[24] There are two general types of passions, concupiscible and irascible.

Aquinas follows a long tradition that originated in the Stoics of enumerating four principal passions: joy, sadness, hope, and fear (see *ST* I-II.25.4). More specifically, these passions are divided into two groups: joy and sadness are concupiscible (see article 2); hope and fear are irascible (see article 3). The concupiscible passions are more basic to the soul in that "the object of the concupiscible power is sensible good or evil, simply apprehended as such, which causes pleasure or pain" (*ST* I-II.23.1). In addition to joy and sadness, other concupiscible passions include love and hatred. The irascible passions arise when the sensible good or evil cannot be achieved without "difficulty or

21. Kallistos Ware offers an edifying reflection on this question, showing that there is a lesser tradition within the Christian East of viewing the passions positively; see his "The Passions: Enemy or Friend?," online or in *In Communion* 17 (Fall 1999).

22. *ST* I-II.24.2 provides a great example of Aquinas's charity in interpretation, his effort to show in most cases that those who seem to hold unsound positions really do not. Regarding the Stoics' difference from the Aristotelians, he says, "This difference, although it appears great in words, is nevertheless, in reality, none at all, or but little, if we consider the intent of either school."

23. As we discuss below, sensible appetite is contrasted with intellectual appetite, or the faculty of the will.

24. See *ST* I-II.17 and 24 on the question of to what extent passions can be voluntary.

struggle"; thus, in addition to hope and fear, we find despair, daring, anger, and so on. Returning to our attractive woman, an unmarried man who feels love for her, and yet despairs of being loved in kind, is in a pitiful condition indeed. His love must be supported by hope if he is to profess it to her.

Moral excellence is not simply about reasoning and willing correctly, for one must also feel correctly in order to be good. It is one thing to *do* good, another to *be* good. The good person is the one whose passions are ordered properly: "Just as it is better that man should both will good and do it in his external act; so also does it belong to the perfection of moral good, that man should be moved unto good, not only in respect of his will, but also in respect of his sensitive appetite" (*ST* I-II.24.3). This position respects the goodness of the body, for being good as a human is a matter of body and soul: "In God and the angels there is no sensitive appetite, nor again bodily members: and so in them good does not depend on the right ordering of passions or of bodily actions, as it does in us" (*ST* I-II.24.3ad2). The necessity of having proper passions in order to be good seems obvious in the case of courtship: How could we call a man who seeks to marry the beautiful woman a true lover unless he had the proper passions? He could not *be* a good husband without the passion of love even if he could *do* what reason and will demand. Yet what if he does not experience the proper passions? How can he address this situation? For it would seem that passions are not really up to us; we either feel them or we don't.

When we speak of being good, of having good character, we have in mind the one who has a fixed disposition to do the right thing. As pleasant as it may make us feel to think about "random acts of kindness," such an approach to morality would be disastrous. On the other hand, moral life is not about generating a list of rules and consulting it when the appropriate situation arises. The first approach is irrational, the second is dispassionate. The moral life is not about arbitrarily deciding to do good on this occasion because I am in the mood or about reasoning out moral principles in every new situation as if starting from scratch; rather, it is about forming a fixed character that allows me to do what is good in whatever situation life gives me.[25]

We have a tendency to think of moral life as going out and doing some kind deed or mapping out a course of actions based on moral principles, but

25. In contradistinction to those who would emphasize the freedom to choose what one does in each individual situation independently from one's character, Aquinas insists upon the role of the virtues in freeing us to do what is good. See Servais Pinckaers, OP, *The Sources of Christian Ethics*, trans. Sr. Mary Thomas Noble, OP (Washington, DC: Catholic University of America Press, 1995), for a solid introduction to the history of this debate between the "freedom of indifference" and the "freedom for the good."

this exaggerates our importance to the world: the world is not populated by so many passive people who need my assistance. Moral life is more often about responding to a situation than creating one. Remember the homeowner example: he responds to the burglar breaking in, and while few of us will be faced with such an extreme situation, we daily encounter the beggar, the elderly woman struggling to get up the steps, the friend who asks for advice. Put differently, we must avoid our culture's overemphasis on choice and its tendency to think of moral life in terms of the freedom to decide what one should do today. This is the point of the classic example of the baby at the doorstep: I would not choose to find a baby at my door, but if I have the virtues, I will be disposed to do the right thing in such a situation. My moral character is not so much about what I choose to have happen, but what I choose *to do* and *to be* given the contingencies that brought me into the world with these particular circumstances.

5. Virtues and Vices

Background Reading: ST I-II.49, 55–61, 64

The virtues are what allow us to both reason rightly and possess a firm resolve to act rightly in any situation; the vices thwart our natural desire for our own good. The burglarized homeowner must be virtuous in order to overcome the fear that would debilitate most of us. In order to calmly decide what to do in the heat of the moment, he must have prepared himself for just such a situation: "The brave man chooses to think beforehand of the dangers that may arise, in order to be able to withstand them, or to bear them more easily" (*ST* II-II.123.9). For him it is as if time slows down so that he has more time to think and act; by contrast, for the coward in such a situation the clock seems to tick as fast as his pounding heart, leaving him so little time to deliberate that he can hardly be said to think or even act. Whereas the brave man uses his passions in order to act rightly, the coward is overcome by them (see *ST* II-II.123.10; 125.4). Similarly, the adulterer has passions so "loud" and demanding that he can only with difficulty "hear" the voice of reason. Further still, his reason has become so corrupted that he may even believe his own lies, so to speak. The virtues, then, allow our reason and will to benevolently rule over the passions in the pursuit of happiness; the vices enslave reason and will to the tyranny of the passions in pursuit of ever more perverse and dissatisfying "delights."[26]

26. I am reminded of the sixth chapter of Oscar Wilde's *The Picture of Dorian Gray*, where Lord Henry attempts to persuade Dorian Gray to take up smoking: "You must have a cigarette. A

In discussing the essence of virtue, Aquinas begins with St. Augustine's definition: virtue is "a good quality of the mind, by which we live righteously, of which no one can make bad use, which God works in us, without us" (*ST* I-II.55.4obj1). While Aquinas does not want to criticize Augustine here, he does add some clarification. First, he explains that a better, or more specific, term than "quality" would be "habit," for habits determine the powers of the soul to act in particular ways (see *ST* I-II.49–55).[27] Second, habits can be either good (e.g., generosity) or evil (e.g., stinginess), and virtue denotes good habit, vice bad habit. Third, virtue exists in a subject, in a person, as denoted by "the mind." Fourth, virtue is a habit that is always used for good, and this is why, for example, we do not call the intelligent burglar "prudent" but rather "crafty"; thus, it is by virtues that "we live righteously." Fifth and finally, Aquinas qualifies the definition by pointing out that not all virtues are "work[ed] in us [by God], without us," for we obtain some virtues by our own power (acquired virtues), and others by God's grace (infused virtues). We will return to these infused virtues that God works in us in chapter 2; here we are concerned with the acquired virtues, for these are the subject of moral philosophy.

The acquired virtues are of two general types, moral and intellectual. Since our soul has different powers that make possible the various activities humans must perform, and since virtues are habits that perfect those powers so that they can pursue appropriate objects, the virtues can be categorized in terms of the powers that they perfect. In terms of the virtues, the three chief powers of the soul are (1) the intellect, (2) the will (intellectual appetite), and (3) the passions (sensitive appetite),[28] which, as noted, are divided into the concupiscible and irascible.

The virtues by which the intellect is perfected are called "intellectual," and here Aquinas makes a distinction: Aristotle had determined that there were five intellectual virtues—namely, wisdom, science, understanding, art, and prudence. Aquinas notes that the first four of these are only virtues "in a relative sense" (*ST* I-II.56.3) and that prudence alone is a virtue strictly speaking. The reason for this distinction is that, whereas wisdom, science, understanding, and art provide "an aptness to act," prudence alone confers

---

cigarette is the perfect type of a perfect pleasure. It is exquisite, and it leaves one unsatisfied. What more can one want?" *Picture of Dorian Gray* (New York: Dover, 1993), 58.

27. While the English word "habit" is derived from the Latin *habitus*, the very word Aquinas is using here, there is no doubt that this word has a different meaning in common speech than the more technical meaning here. Yves Simon provides a helpful discussion of what it means to call virtue a "habit" in *The Definition of Moral Virtue* (New York: Fordham University Press, 1986).

28. See *ST* I.77–83 for Aquinas's treatment of the powers of the soul.

"the right use of that aptness" in that it is directly related to rectitude of will. Aquinas is pointing here to the distinction between the theoretical intellect, which pursues truths concerning the nature of things, and the practical intellect, which pursues the truths of right living. Returning to our Frisbee player, she may possess great understanding and may have the scientific knowledge that would allow her to do her homework well, but she is not making the right use of these talents. Without prudence, she is not, strictly speaking, a good person, for she may *know* the universal principles of the practical intellect or natural law, but she does not determine the appropriate means to achieve the ends specified by reason.

The will does not need specific virtues in order to guide us as individuals in seeking our own good; for this, reason suffices and the will can simply adhere to reason.[29] However, our good must be in conformity with the good of others, for we are social creatures and must live in peace with the members of our community. The virtue that perfects the will in regard to "the good of one's neighbor" (*ST* I-II.56.6) is justice, and it is a moral virtue in that it is perfective not of the intellect but of the intellectual appetite. Returning to the burglarized homeowner, we can see how Aquinas's understanding of justice makes this situation so challenging: How can someone will his neighbor's good while lunging at him with a knife? If he wills the death of this man, it is hard to see how he is looking out for his good; thus, Aquinas demands, even when one's life is at risk, that one wills to defend one's life and not to harm one's neighbor.

Like the will, the passions (concupiscible and irascible) are perfected by moral virtues. Whereas the intellectual virtues are about knowing, the moral are about doing; the moral virtues ensure that we feel or will appropriately in a moral situation and that we have a promptness to obey the voice of reason (see *ST* I-II.56.4). The chief virtues of the passions are temperance, or moderation (concupiscible), and fortitude, or courage (irascible). Notice that this relationship between reason, the will, and the passions indicates the necessity of possessing both intellectual and moral virtue in order to be and do good. Without prudence (and understanding), we cannot decide what is the right thing to do (see I-II.58.4); without temperance and fortitude, our reason will be distorted by the sway of passion (see I-II.58.5); and without justice, we cannot coordinate our own good with the good of our neighbor. Again, this is why we cannot speak of a good burglar or a good Nazi, for it is not an act of true courage to harm the innocent; a courageous action must

---

29. On this point, see *ST* I-II.56.6. It is worth noting, though, that Aquinas does acknowledge a metaphorical sense in which justice applies to the whole soul: in the virtuous soul reason rules and the passions obey (see *ST* II-II.58.2).

also be a just action. If virtues perfect us, then they are not true unless they allow us to do the right thing.

To bring together these various points concerning the virtues, the principal, or "cardinal," virtues are prudence, justice, temperance, and fortitude. It is worth quoting Aquinas in full here before defining each of these virtues separately:

> For the formal principle of the virtue of which we speak now is good as defined by reason; which good is considered in two ways. First, as existing in the very act of reason: and thus we have one principal virtue, called "Prudence." Secondly, according as the reason puts its order into something else; either into operations, and then we have "Justice"; or into passions, and then we need two virtues. For the need of putting the order of reason into the passions is due to their thwarting reason: and this occurs in two ways. First, by the passions inciting to something against reason, and then the passions need a curb, which we call "Temperance." Secondly, by the passions withdrawing us from following the dictate of reason, e.g. through fear of danger or toil: and then man needs to be strengthened for that which reason dictates, lest he turn back; and to this end there is "Fortitude."
>
> In like manner, we find the same number if we consider the subjects of virtue. For there are four subjects of the virtue we speak of now: viz. the power which is rational in its essence, and this is perfected by "Prudence"; and that which is rational by participation, and is threefold, the will, subject of "Justice," the concupiscible faculty, subject of "Temperance," and the irascible faculty, subject of "Fortitude." (*ST* I-II.61.2)

Of the cardinal virtues, prudence alone is an intellectual virtue; justice, temperance, and fortitude are moral virtues. Prudence is that intellectual virtue by which reason determines the means to acting in conformity with the ends of the moral virtues, thus dictating to the will what is to be chosen in the concrete situation;[30] the object of prudence, then, is not theoretical truth but truth concerning "things done" (see *ST* II-II.47). Justice is "a habit whereby a man renders to each one his due [*ius*] by a constant and perpetual will" (*ST* II-II.58.1), thus coordinating one's own good with the good of others as its object. Temperance is the moral virtue by which an "object of desire," and specifically pleasure concerning touch, is brought under the control of reason (see *ST* II-II.141). Fortitude is the moral virtue by which the "fear of difficult things" is brought under control, thus empowering the will to pursue the good (see *ST* II-II.123).

Regarding the point concerning means and ends, prudence does not determine *that* one should exercise fortitude, but rather *how* fortitude is to be

---

30. See *ST* I-II.13.1 on the relationship between reason and will in the act of choice.

exercised in bringing about its object: imagine how ineffective a soldier in battle would be who spends time asking himself if he should be brave. He must act, and act now; the virtue of fortitude allows him to spring into action, whereas prudence directs him to engage the enemy in this or that way, or even fall back when necessary. As Aquinas says, prudence "applies universal principles [as determined by natural reason] to the particular conclusions of practical matters. Consequently it does not belong to prudence to appoint the end to moral virtues, but only to regulate the means" (*ST* II-II.47.6). Thus, practical reason works out the principles of right action or object to be pursued, prudence determines the means to this end, and fortitude ensures that our appetite is rightly ordered in performance of the action so dictated.

Further, we should notice here that acting under the guidance of the virtues ensures that it is not just my actions that are good, but it is *I* who am good. I can do what virtuous people do, and thus perform virtuous actions. Unless I have the virtues, though, I cannot do virtuous actions with the right intention and desire. For example, imagine I go to a grocery store and am given too much change by the cashier. Upon realizing this, I ask myself, "Should I give the excess back?" As I look around the store, I notice video cameras, I notice the cashier eyeing me as if she is testing me, and I also notice that she is rather attractive. In light of these considerations, I decide to give the excess back because I do not want to get caught stealing and because I might thereby gain her affection. Clearly such an action is just, and yet I am not just. Unless I give her back the excess simply because it is owed to the store, I am not good; rather, I use the good action as a means to my own advantage rather than perform it as a good in itself.[31]

One final point about the virtues: connected with these cardinal virtues are a variety of secondary virtues, each of which plays a specific role in bringing reason, will, or passion to bear on the various objects of human life. The cardinal virtues are so named (from the Latin *cardo* or "hinge") because they are those virtues on which the other virtues depend. To the cardinal virtues are "annexed" such virtues as *eubolia* or "deliberating well" (prudence), religion (justice), magnanimity (fortitude), and humility (temperance), each of which has a role in directing human action to particular situations. We will take up points concerning the secondary virtues as needed; for now, suffice it

---

31. We could also add that, at least to some extent, the very asking myself of the question "Should I give back the excess?" indicates that I am not a just man: the just man does not decide to be just, but uses his prudence to determine how he can be just in any given situation. If I ask myself if I should be just, I reveal to myself that I am not just. See Glaucon's opening speech in book 2 of Plato's *Republic* for the famous "Gyges' Ring" example illustrating, he thinks, that people do not want to be just.

to say that the variety of moral situations demands a multiplicity of virtues for the art of living well.[32]

Before turning to the question of the best way of life, a few words about vice and sin are in order. Following Aquinas, we will briefly discuss (1) vice in general (*ST* I-II.71–74), (2) the causes of sin (*ST* I-II.75–84), and (3) the effects of sin (*ST* I-II.85–89). First, just as in intellectual matters there is only one truth and an infinite number of falsehoods, so in moral matters is there only one good for each situation and an infinite number of evils. Let us use the classic image of an archer shooting for a target: there is only one bull's-eye; every other shot would be in some way off the mark. More specifically, for every virtue there are two extremes, for the archer can aim too high (excess) or too low (deficiency), and between the extremes and the mean (virtue) there are an infinite number of more or less bad shots to be made. The burglarized homeowner could have rushed down the stairs without any thought for his own safety (excess: fearlessness) or hidden under his covers in bed (deficiency: fear or timidity), but instead he confronted the burglar (mean: fortitude). Thus, vice refers to a disordered habit such as fearlessness, and sin to an inordinate act such as unnecessarily risking one's life (see *ST* I-II.71.1).

Second, when attempting to analyze the causes of one of his own transgressions, St. Augustine exasperatedly and rhetorically asks, "What was my feeling in all this [sinful activity]? Depraved, undoubtedly, and woe is me that I had it. But what exactly was it? *Who can understand sins?* . . . Who can unravel that complex twisted knottedness?"[33] Aquinas wrestles with the same issue, using examples to illustrate the oddity of sin as a cause: the absence of light as a cause of darkness, or the presence of fire as the cause of a privation of cold. He concludes as follows: "The will lacking the direction of the rule of reason and of the Divine law, and intent on some mutable good, causes the act of sin directly, and the inordinateness of the act, indirectly, and beside the intention" (*ST* I-II.75.1). This brings us back to the adulterer who knowingly cheats on his wife: even if he does not intend to be a sinner, his seeking the good of pleasure without the guidance of reason is the cause of his sin.

Third, although we are naturally inclined to virtue, sin weakens this inclination, making it harder for us to attain the happiness we desire. Individual sins become habitual, which is to say that they lead to vices, and these vices distort our self-understanding and our ability to seek the Truth. While we often think of sin as something desirable that, unfortunately, God forbids us from seeking, this view is based on a flawed conception of freedom: "Sin is

---

32. See the appendix for a schema of all the virtues discussed throughout the book.
33. Augustine, *Confessions* 2.9–10, trans. F. J. Sheed (Indianapolis: Hackett, 2006), 33–34.

contrary to natural reason," and thus "freedom from sin is true freedom" (*ST* II-II.179.4). Aquinas's example illustrates both the darkness under which the sinner labors and the fact that sin can never efface the divine image and likeness: "A transparent body . . . has an inclination to receive light, from the very fact that it is transparent; yet this inclination or aptitude is diminished on the part of supervening clouds, although it always remains rooted in the nature of the body" (*ST* I-II.85.2). Sin places obstacles before our reason (ignorance), will (malice), irascible (weakness) and concupiscible (concupiscence) passions,[34] and still the eyes of our soul are always receptive to light, even if it may take a miracle for the sun to pierce through the clouds.

6. The Best Way of Life

Background Reading: ST II-II.58.12, 81.6, 123.12, 141.8, 179

One aspect of the cultural relativism that dominates even many Catholic communities is the insistence that there is no best way of life. "Who are you to judge?," "Celebrate diversity," and "Do your own thing" are so many catch-phrases of our culture. As distortive as this attitude can be, let us return to what we said at the beginning of this chapter: since ethics is rooted in our shared human nature, ethics is objective and absolute; since ethics must consider the particular circumstances of each person and each moral situation, ethics is subjective and relative. Every moral situation is different, and every person is unique in his or her own way of being made in God's image and likeness; thus, what is best for me is not necessarily best for you. "I've gotta be me" is not incorrect; it is just that we need to emphasize how difficult it is to gain the self-knowledge that will allow me to truly *be* me. When we speak of the best way of life, then, we must always bear in mind that what is best absolutely is not necessarily best for me: I may not be called to be the head of the nation, and so it would be wrong for me to act as if I can direct my fellow citizens, and yet I am called to be a good citizen and promote the common good in the ways appropriate for me. And, as we will see, the best way of life has a twofold meaning, for our intellects are what is best in us, but what is best for us as humans is to live out our vocations as embodied creatures.

The best way of life would initially appear to be the one that actualizes what is best in us, and this is our intellect. Strictly speaking, the intellectual virtues are more excellent than the moral virtues in that they perfect our highest power, the intellect (see *ST* I-II.66.3). Further still, wisdom, or the

---

34. See *ST* I-II.85.3.

knowledge of the highest causes of all things and of God as the Supreme Cause,[35] would seem to be the greatest virtue. Our greatest power is our intellect, and its perfection consists in knowledge, specifically knowledge of God as the Cause of Causes; therefore, the best way of life is the contemplative, not the active, life, or the life of wisdom.[36]

Following this line of thought, the moral virtues are certainly important, and yet they are "dispositive" in that they serve as the means to the formation of the intellectual virtues rather than exist for their own sake. As Aquinas says, "Now the moral virtues curb the impetuosity of the passions, and quell the disturbance of outward occupations. Hence moral virtues belong dispositively to the contemplative life" (ST II-II.180.2). The demands of the moral virtues seem to distract us from the contemplative life, and thus are a hindrance to it. If not for the frailties of the human body and its need for material things, if not for our troublesome neighbors who need our help, we would devote our lives to study, contemplation, and the joy of knowing the Truth.

Yet, as great as the life of the mind is, we are human beings, bodies and souls, and the best life for us must be one that incorporates our whole person into virtuous activity. Our passions and will are not slaves to the intellect but friends, sharers in the fullness of a life lived well. As discussed earlier in our initial treatment of the virtues, the moral virtues are more properly called "virtues" than wisdom is. As Aquinas says in this context, "If we consider virtue in its relation to act, then moral virtue, which perfects the appetite, whose function it is to move the other powers to act, as stated above [ST I-II.9.1], is more excellent" (ST I-II.66.3). The intellectual virtues may be more excellent as habits insofar as they perfect that which is best in us (our intellect), but since we are earthly beings called forth to both think and act well, moral virtues are more perfective. In addition, we must examine the limits of the contemplative life as it can be lived within the bounds of philosophy; put differently, we must ask what can be known about God within the limits of natural reason and whether such wisdom is sufficient for a truly contemplative life.

Without revelation, very little can be known about God, and the more one reflects on this, the more insufficient wisdom turns out to be for happiness. As Aquinas explains, reason can discover *that* God exists but not *what* God is.[37] Thus, the God of the philosophers is always seen, as it were, from a distance, with no means of penetrating into his essence. The contemplative life

---

35. See *ST* I-II.57.2, 66.5.

36. On the distinction between the active and contemplative life, see *ST* II-II.179.

37. See *ST* I.2–43 for Aquinas's discussion of what can be known about God through reason and what can be added to that knowledge through revelation.

that lacks grace turns out to be rather unsatisfying, then, for the wise pagan discovers the vast divide between himself and the God his intellect seeks. Socrates was right to call himself wise in this sense, that he knew himself to be ignorant when he reflected on his inability to obtain the wisdom of the God.[38] What is the wise pagan to do, then, when he discovers the minimal value of human wisdom? His natural desire to know the essence of the God who is the Cause of all things cannot be satisfied, and he realizes that his supposed wisdom is a knowledge of his own ignorance.

This is where the moral virtues can come back into play, for there is another virtue that has the potential to open the path to the God glimpsed by wisdom: justice. As Aquinas argues when making the point that the moral virtues are more perfective of our being than intellectual virtues,

> The subject of a habit which is called a virtue simply, can only be the will, or some power in so far as it is moved by the will. And the reason of this is, that the will moves to their acts all those other powers that are in some way rational, . . . and therefore if man do well actually, this is because he has a good will. Therefore the virtue which makes a man to do well actually, and not merely to have the aptness to do well, must be either in the will itself; or in some power as moved by the will. (*ST* I-II.56.3)

Notice the emphasis here on the will as that power which makes us and our acts good. Among the moral virtues, then, that which gives us "a good will" is most perfective. Thus, justice is the greatest moral virtue and the greatest virtue in perfecting our being, in that it is "most akin to reason" and also in that it is that virtue "whereby man is set in order not only in himself, but also in regard to another" (*ST* I-II.66.4). Whereas fortitude and temperance perfect me *for myself*, justice perfects me *for others*; it is by justice that I am able to place my own good within the context of the common good.[39] Justice is the greatest moral virtue in itself, and yet, relatively speaking, one of the secondary virtues turns out to be greater still: religion.

As is made clear by claiming that justice is the greatest virtue in directing our actions, happiness turns out to be about serving rather than being served. This is especially true in regard to God, for religion, a secondary virtue annexed to justice, demands acknowledging my inability to "pay back" the gift of existence itself. When discussing the virtue of religion, Aquinas makes a

38. See Plato, *Apology* 23a–b.

39. It is worth noting that Aquinas makes this claim before distinguishing between general and particular justice. Since the common good is greater than the good of the individual, I would argue that he means that general justice is the greatest virtue (for it is "virtually" all virtue), and in a secondary sense particular justice is the greatest virtue.

surprising claim in light of what he said before concerning the ranking of the virtues: "Religion approaches nearer to God than the other moral virtues, in so far as its actions are directly and immediately ordered to the honor of God. Hence religion excels among the moral virtues" (*ST* II-II.81.6). Religion turns out to be the greatest of the moral virtues because it directs us to the object that alone can make us happy. And, further, as Kevin E. O'Reilly points out, "The exercise of all the virtues allows the human agent to participate in the divine goodness. This participation is greatest in the case of the exercise of the virtue of religion."[40] To sum up: while our natural desire for happiness cannot be satisfied without knowledge of who God is, reason tells us that our rational power is too weak to give us this knowledge; this points us toward the need to seek him by some other means, which is where religion comes in, for it alone of the moral virtues can direct us to God.

Before we conclude, we must point out the difficulties here. First, religion does not have God as its object but as its end: "God is related to religion not as matter or object, but as end: and consequently religion is not a theological virtue whose object is the last end, but a moral virtue which is properly about things referred to the end" (*ST* II-II.81.5). Religion cannot "reach" all the way to God, for it merely prepares us for union with God; it is like knocking on a door that we cannot ourselves open. As Mary C. Sommers puts it, "Religion . . . is not *about* God, although it is *for* God."[41] Second, for reasons that will be clearer in chapter 2 when we discuss the infused virtues, it is not entirely certain that we can even have the virtue of religion without revelation. The good pagan will come to realize the need for religion (as Plato's Socrates seems to acknowledge on his deathbed as shown in *Phaedo*), but it may be that he is incapable of acquiring this virtue.

Given the experience of humans who have tried to come to God without revelation, it would appear that the natural desire to enter into a relationship with God would, without grace, lead to one of two vices: either the excess of superstition (see *ST* II-II.92–96) or the deficiency of irreligion (see *ST* II-II.97–100). Suffice it to say for now that moral philosophy points to the need for moral theology, though it cannot see the way to it without the grace given by the God who became Man.

40. Kevin E. O'Reilly, OP, "The Significance of Worship in the Thought of Thomas Aquinas: Some Reflections," *International Philosophical Quarterly* 53.4 (2013): 461.

41. Mary C. Sommers, "He Spak to [T]hem That Wolde Lyve Parfitly": Thomas Aquinas, the Wife of Bath and the Two Senses of 'Religion,'" *Proceedings of the American Catholic Philosophical Association* 65 (1991): 148.

2

Grace and Perfect Happiness (Moral Theology)

My son, if you receive my words
and treasure up my commandments with you,
making your ear attentive to wisdom
    and inclining your heart to understanding;
yes, if you cry out for insight
    and raise your voice for understanding,
if you seek it like silver
    and search for it as for hidden treasures;
then you will understand the fear of the LORD
    and find the knowledge of God.
For the LORD gives wisdom;
    from his mouth come knowledge and understanding;
he stores up sound wisdom for the upright;
    he is a shield to those who walk in integrity,
guarding the paths of justice
    and preserving the way of his saints.

—Proverbs 2:1–8

If I speak in the tongues of men and of angels, but have not love, I am a noisy gong or a clanging cymbal. And if I have prophetic powers, and understand all mysteries and all knowledge, and if I have all faith, so as to remove mountains, but have not love, I am nothing. If I give away all I have, and if I deliver my body to be burned, but have not love, I gain nothing. . . . Love never ends;

as for prophecies, they will pass away; as for tongues, they will cease; as for knowledge, it will pass away. For our knowledge is imperfect and our prophecy is imperfect; but when the perfect comes, the imperfect will pass away. When I was a child, I spoke like a child, I thought like a child, I reasoned like a child; when I became a man, I gave up childish ways. For now we see in a mirror dimly, but then face to face. Now I know in part; then I shall understand fully, even as I have been fully understood. So faith, hope, love abide, these three; but the greatest of these is love.

—1 Corinthians 13

1. Introduction

We saw in the first chapter that, while there is a natural law (reason as applied to human action) that objectively determines how we must act, moral philosophy is not simply making a list of rules for what we should and should not do. Moral life is not so much about doing our duty but about being good: moral philosophy is the human attempt to determine how we should live given our natural desire for happiness in the concrete circumstances of our lives. Like the tadpole "seeking" to become a frog, we seek our end; unlike the tadpole, we are not like arrows shot from a bow but rather rational, free creatures who must rule ourselves in accordance with the good, the true, and the beautiful. Philosophically speaking, a good life is not a gift to us, for it is the result of nobly taking up the challenge of pursuing excellence. By forming our character via the four cardinal virtues and the virtues annexed to them, we take upon ourselves a "second nature" that allows us not just to do what reason or natural law demands but to delight in doing so; in a word, the virtuous person is the good and happy person.

We also saw that moral philosophy points to the limits of the merely human attempt to procure our own happiness. The more we cultivate our intellects, the more we become aware of the unbridgeable gap between who we are and who we want to be: our desires are infinite, but the objects of the world are finite, and we are mortal. Human wisdom tells us that there is an infinite object, a Supreme Cause, a final goal for our lives, and yet this God of the philosophers is unapproachable and unknowable. We cannot bring him down to us, nor can we propel ourselves up to him. Human wisdom, then, directs us to cultivate a relationship with God through acknowledging our inability to "pay back" the gift of existence; thus, we attempt to acquire the virtue of religion. As we concluded, though, it is unclear if this is possible, and even if we could acquire the virtue of religion, this would not bridge the gap but merely dispose us to cry out for mercy: come to us, for we cannot come to you.

It is only natural, then, that we turn to moral theology, to the study of how revelation cooperating with reason can answer to our natural desire for happiness. And, again, we begin by recognizing that the Catholic Church is often seen as a rigid enforcer of rules rather than a loving Mother who wants her children to be happy. Those who tell us that being a Christian is not about following rules but about forming a relationship with Christ are for the most part right, and yet they miss the mark: it is because Holy Mother Church loves us that she give us rules, and it is because she wants us to be perfect that she constantly goads us to grow in life with Christ. We form a relationship with Christ *as* members of his Body, the Church, and through the sacraments receive the grace that purifies us as we grow ever closer to the God who is Perfection itself. Here we anticipate our respective studies of economic and political theory, for moral theology exhorts us to seek the good in concert with one another: "The fulness of grace, which is centered in Christ as head, flows forth to His members in various ways, for the perfecting of the body of the Church" (*ST* II-II.183.2).

This chapter outlines Aquinas's moral theology, or the study of what reason cooperating with revelation tells us about how we should live. Our study will be divided into the following sections: (1) our last end revisited; (2) the infused virtues; the gifts and fruits of the Holy Spirit; the Beatitudes; (3) the best way of life revisited; (4) Christ as the exemplar of human life, and the sacraments as the instruments of life in Christ.

2. Our Last End Revisited

Background Reading: ST I.1; I-II.5, 109

The first question, first article of the *Summa Theologiae* establishes the central point that we have been driving toward—namely, that the perfection of human nature requires revelation. The question with which Aquinas opens his study of theology is whether philosophy is sufficient for bringing humans to the happiness they seek, and initially it seems that philosophy can do this, for "everything that is, is treated of in philosophical science—even God Himself; so that there is a part of philosophy called theology, or the divine science, as Aristotle has proved" (*ST* I.1.1obj2). In response to this, Aquinas makes two points. First, "man is directed to God, as to an end that surpasses the grasp of his reason: 'The eye hath not seen, O God, besides Thee, what things Thou hast prepared for them that wait for Thee' (Isaiah 64:4). But the end must first be known by men who are to direct their thoughts and actions to the end. Hence it was necessary for the salvation of man that certain truths which exceed human reason should be made known to him by divine revelation" (ST I.1.1). As we saw in chapter 1, reason can only glimpse the God who alone can satisfy the desire for wisdom. Were it not for revelation, our restless hearts could never find rest; the question "Why?" that drives us deeper into the mystery of existence could never be answered. The end of moral philosophy turns out to be an imperfect end, or a means to the supernatural end of the beatific vision.

Second, even those truths about God that reason can discover would only be known by those few philosophers among us who were gifted with penetrating intellects and lives of leisure that would allow for such profound inquiry. Yet revelation tells us that our God is a loving God, that he "desires all men to be saved and to come to the knowledge of the truth" (1 Tim. 2:4). Therefore, "in order that the salvation of men might be brought about more fitly and more surely, it was necessary that they should be taught divine truths by divine revelation" (ST I.1.1). Philosophy is not sufficient to bring us perfect happiness, and still our desires are not in vain, for through revelation the clouds are opened, the Light can be seen. Despite the joy that these words should bring us, that our hearts will find rest in God, we must remember that the fullness of this Truth cannot be known in this life.

As Aquinas says in his *Commentary on the Apostle's Creed*, "After the arrival of Christ any old woman knows through faith" (translation mine) more about God and what is necessary for salvation than any philosopher ever could. And even what this old woman, the wise theologian, or the fiery mystic can know in this life is only a foretaste of what will be known in the world to come. Only union with the Divine Essence will do, and, to revisit a point we made in chapter 1, "God cannot be seen in His essence by a mere human being, except he be separated from this mortal life" (ST I.12.11). Let us be mindful of this point as we turn to the life of grace, for the graces we receive in this life and the charity that is at the root of life in Christ will be brought to perfection through the death that has no victory, the death that is the door to new life.

3. The Infused Virtues; the Gifts and Fruits of the Holy Spirit; the Beatitudes

Background Reading: ST I-II.62–70; II-II.4, 8, 9, 17, 19, 23, 45, 46

Moral philosophy tells us that it is by activity in conformity with virtue that we are made happy, that virtues are either moral or intellectual, and that the good life is built upon the four cardinal virtues (prudence, justice, temperance, and fortitude) as well as their annexed, secondary virtues. Does this become false or distortive from the perspective of moral theology? Truth cannot contradict truth, and grace perfects nature; thus, this depiction of the moral life is not inaccurate but only incomplete. To say otherwise would be to reject the goodness of our natural faculties, to accuse God of deceiving us by giving us a nature that, in seeking him, of necessity goes against him. The natural virtues (moral and intellectual, cardinal or secondary) are truly, though imperfectly, virtues, and they are perfected by being incorporated into the infused virtues (see *ST* I-II.65.2). As Tom Osborne explains, only the *acquired* virtues can be formed without grace, and this formation is always imperfect insofar as it fails to fully direct the agent toward the true good, God.[1]

If performing virtuous actions makes us happy and the natural virtues are imperfect, it is necessary that God bestow upon us certain virtues that guide us as we live in Christ. As Aquinas says, "Because such [perfect] happiness surpasses the capacity of human nature, man's natural principles which enable him to act well according to his capacity, do not suffice to direct man to this same happiness. Hence it is necessary for man to receive from God some additional principles, whereby he may be directed to supernatural happiness" (*ST* I-II.62.1). To use an analogy: a pitcher of water is sufficient to quench our daily thirst, but with a squeeze of lemon and a few leaves of a tea tree or mint plant, this nearly flavorless liquid is *infused* with a pleasing aroma and flavor down to the last drop; further, the infused water now has nutrients in it that can improve this already healthy beverage. So it is with the infused virtues, for they both (1) give new purpose and delight to the actions the natural virtues enjoin and (2) push us on to still greater actions that we could not otherwise perform. Only by these virtues can we enter into union with God, and only he can make this possible, though it is important to point out that they are *not imposed* upon us: "Infused virtue is caused in us by God without any action on our part, *but not without our consent*" (*ST* I-II.55.4ad6; emphasis added). Virtue is a perfection of free will such that we can use it rightly (see *ST* I-II.55.1), and with the infused virtues God does not interfere with but enhances our freedom to pursue our own good.

In order to understand the nature and purpose of the infused virtues more fully, we must follow Aquinas's distinction between three types of infused

---

1. See Thomas M. Osborne Jr., "Perfect and Imperfect Virtues in Aquinas," *Thomist* 71.1 (2007): 39–64; another helpful source on the development of and relationship between acquired and infused virtue is Reginald Garrigou-Lagrange, OP, *The Three Ages of the Interior Life: Prelude to Eternal Life*, trans. Sr. M. Timothea Doyle, OP (St. Louis: Herder, 1951), 1:57–66.

virtues: (1) theological virtues, (2) infused cardinal virtues, and (3) infused secondary virtues.

First, the theological virtues take us to the summit of moral life. These are the primary infused virtues in that they answer to the purpose of God working virtues in us that surpass our capacity. As Aquinas says, they "are called 'theological virtues': first, because their object is God, inasmuch as they direct us aright to God: secondly, because they are infused in us by God alone: thirdly, because these virtues are not made known to us, save by Divine revelation, contained in Holy Writ" (ST I-II.62.1). These are the virtues spoken of in Scripture as the marks of the Christian—namely, faith, hope, and love or charity. Let us discuss each of the theological virtues in turn, and then compare them; as we shall see, Aquinas firmly roots his treatment of the theological virtues in the teachings of St. Paul, who tells us that "if I have all faith, so as to remove mountains, but have not love, I am nothing," and, again, "faith, hope, love abide, these three; but the greatest of these is love" (1 Cor. 13:2–13).

Aquinas follows and unpacks the definition of faith found in the letter to the Hebrews: "the assurance of things hoped for, the conviction of things not seen" (Heb. 11:1). First, faith is that habit whereby the will conforms itself to God as its object and end. Second, faith conforms the intellect to God as Truth despite lack of proof. Third, the effect of conforming intellect and will to God is to open up the path to eternal life with him. Bringing these together, Aquinas provides a more "scientific" definition of faith: "Faith is a habit of the mind, whereby eternal life is begun in us, making the intellect assent to what is non-apparent [as commanded by the will]" (ST II-II.4.1), thus perfecting both the intellect and the will (see 4.2).

Let us distinguish faith as a theological virtue, then, from the more ordinary use of the word "faith": when I have faith in something that other members of my society tell me, I mean that I take them to be reliable sources of truth and so hold to be true what they have related to me. Yet to have faith in this sense is to take something as true that might prove to be false: sometimes they are wrong, and, worse still, sometimes they deceive me. For clarification we could call this "belief" rather than faith and recognize it as a sort of substitute for knowledge: given that we cannot know all things ourselves, we must take others at their word even though we know that this might lead us into error.

Unlike belief, the theological virtue of faith gives us knowledge, for God does not deceive: "In order that men might have knowledge of God, free of doubt and uncertainty, it was necessary for Divine matters to be delivered to them by way of faith, being told to them, as it were, by God Himself Who cannot lie" (ST II-II.2.4). Admittedly, faith only gives imperfect knowledge, but it is knowledge nonetheless.[2] Further, while many people believe true things concerning God (e.g., that God is one), unless they are in the state of grace this would be true belief rather than faith.

As intimated in our discussion of faith, the next step in adhering to God is to place our hope in him as our supernatural end. Let us return here to the passions and recall that hope is one of the four principal passions, that its opposite is despair, and that it arises in us when we perceive a good to be possible, though difficult, to achieve (see chap. 1, §4). When discussing the theological virtue of hope, Aquinas makes an important distinction: this good can be acquired either by our own efforts or by assistance from another. When this assistance can only come from God, then we must be graced if we are to acquire it. And, further, since it is by faith that we know that God will help us and bring us into union with him, hope depends on faith.

The theological virtue of hope, then, is that virtue by which one "attains God by leaning on his help in order to obtain . . . eternal life, which consists in the enjoyment of God Himself" (ST II-II.17.2). Whereas faith "makes us adhere to God, as the source whence we derive the knowledge of truth, . . . hope makes us adhere to God, as the source whence we derive perfect goodness [i.e., happiness]" (ST II-II.17.6). Lastly, the theological virtue of hope is distinguished from the passion of hope not only in terms of its object or cause (both of which are God) but also in that it resides in the will rather than in the irascible appetite (see ST II-II.18.1). This means that hope is compatible with the passion of fear and even of despair, for there may be times, even for the ardent believer, when "the spirit indeed is willing, but the flesh is weak" (Matt. 26:41). Even if we cling firmly to God, we may find times when we wish that he would make it clearer how he is going to guide us safely home.

The third and final theological virtue, charity, brings about our perfection, for by it we cling most fully to God. Whereas faith and hope unite us to God for our sake, "charity makes us adhere to God for his own sake, uniting our minds to God by the emotion of love" (ST II-II.17.6). We can think here of the distinction between imperfect and perfect contrition: it is one thing to repent of one's sin because one fears punishment, quite another because one hates to offend God. A man who had faith and hope but lacked all charity could still repent given that he wants to regain the good of eternal life he knows God will give to the believer; however, he would repent *for himself* and not *for God*. Charity allows us to act selflessly, to do what is good simply because God is goodness itself. And yet, it turns out that the charitable soul also loves

---

2. See ST II-II.4.8 for Aquinas's detailed comparison of the knowledge of faith with other kinds of knowledge.

itself, for it is by loving God that we are made capable of loving ourselves *in* God (see *ST* II-II.25.4), and our neighbors as ourselves. "Charity is the friendship of man for God" (*ST* II-II.23.1) and, as an act, includes within it love of neighbor (*ST* II-II.25.1).

Since charity seeks to direct all things to the glory of God, it is the greatest of all the virtues (see *ST* II-II.23.6) and also their form, for "it is charity which directs the acts of all other virtues to the last end, and which, consequently, also gives the form to all other acts of virtue" (*ST* II-II.23.8). Strictly speaking, though I do great deeds, though I help the poor and overcome injustice, if I do not do them out of love for God, I am not virtuous (see *ST* II-II.23.7). Aquinas, citing Augustine, goes so far as to say that "the actions which an unbeliever performs as an unbeliever, are always sinful, even when he clothes the naked, or does any like thing, and directs it to his unbelief as end" (*ST* II-II.23.7ad1). By way of analogy, a husband who takes his wife out on Valentine's Day, puts on his best attire, buys her beautiful flowers, and says all the right things, but does not love her, only *appears* to be a true lover. Unless he loves her for her own sake, he cannot be united to her in body and soul even if he does what lovers are supposed to do. To return to the words of St. Paul, if I have "not love, I am nothing" (1 Cor. 13:2). As Aquinas puts it, the action of one lacking charity can "be generically good, but not perfectly good, because it lacks its due order to the last end" (*ST* II-II.23.7ad1). Those with the acquired or even infused virtues who perform acts of courage, of friendship, of justice, or of faith certainly do good deeds, but they are imperfectly good insofar as they are not done for the sake of love.[3]

While faith and hope can be had without charity, "without charity, they are not virtues properly so-called" (*ST* I-II.65.4), for only the lover of God is pleasing to him. Similarly, since mortal sin destroys charity in the soul, and since all of the other infused virtues depend upon charity, "charity being banished by one act of mortal sin, it follows that all the infused virtues are expelled 'as virtues'" (*ST* I-II.71.4). We do not have the infused virtues in the way that we have the acquired virtues, and thus we must always be mindful of the fact that spiritual life depends entirely upon our cooperation with God.

In light of what we have said, the theological virtues can be ordered in two different ways. First, in terms of acquisition or generation: we have already stated that faith must come before hope, for we cannot hope for eternal life unless we first believe that God will grant this to us. Similarly, hope must

---

3. A more detailed treatment of this topic would take us into the distinction between actual, virtual, and habitual ordering to an end. See Thomas M. Osborne, "The Three-fold Referral of Acts to the Ultimate End in Thomas Aquinas and His Commentators," *Angelicum* 85 (2008): 715–36, for a study of this distinction.

come before charity, "for just as a man is led to love God, through fear of being punished by Him for his sins, . . . so too, hope leads to charity" (*ST* II-II.17.8). Second, in terms of perfection: all of the virtues other than charity, even faith and hope, imply a certain distance from God. Thus, charity is the most perfect of the theological virtues, "since faith is of what is not seen, and hope is of what is not possessed. But the love of charity is of that which is already possessed: since the beloved is, in a manner, in the lover, and, again, the lover is drawn by desire to union with the beloved" (*ST* I-II.66.6). Conversion to Christ, then, is an ongoing process, a continuous growth in virtue and, more specifically, in love. In chapter 4 we will examine more fully what charity entails in terms of love for neighbor in the context of economic theology. For now we are concerned about the general framework of the virtues, and this requires looking at the other infused virtues that apply charity to daily life—namely, the infused cardinal virtues and the infused secondary virtues.

The infused cardinal virtues allow practical reason, the will, and the concupiscible as well as irascible appetites to come under the guidance of charity and thus direct our actions to our supernatural end of life with God. Like justice, charity resides in the will. Yet charity most fully perfects the will, for it goes beyond justice in willing not just another's good but the will of God. Thus, while many of the actions that the moral life enjoins could be pursued both by the good pagan and by the good Christian, others are distinctly Christian. For example, the husband taking his wife out on Valentine's Day ought to love her whether or not he is a Christian, for the intimate friendship between husband and wife is natural: "There seems to be the greatest friendship between husband and wife, for they are united not only in the act of fleshly union, . . . but also in the partnership of the whole range of domestic activity" (*SCG* 3.123). While it is true that a Christian would have a deeper motive for loving her in that his charity calls him to love her in God, the way he would treat her in this instance would be the same. In such cases, from the outside the good pagan and the good Christian "look" the same, even if their intentions differ. To use the formal language for assessing moral situations (see chap. 1, §4), both the good pagan and the Christian have the same object, an act of marital love, but the Christian has a more final end—namely, union with God.

Christians are called upon to go beyond what human reason demands and measure their actions by what Aquinas calls "the Divine rule" (see *ST* I-II.63.4); in certain situations this will mean performing actions that go beyond human reason. In such cases not only does one intend the love of God that only grace can give us; in addition the moral object is known to be good only because of the Divine rule and can only be pursued by one who has the virtue of charity willing the supernatural end of the beatific vision. Aquinas's own example regards the cardinal virtue of temperance: "In the consumption of food, the mean fixed by human reason, is that food should not harm the health of the body, nor hinder the use of reason: whereas, according to the Divine rule, it behooves man to 'chastise his body, and bring it into subjection' (1 Cor. 9:27), by abstinence in food, drink and the like" (*ST* I-II.63.4). To abstain from food and drink goes beyond simply being healthy with respect to them. So, imagine that Valentine's Day falls on a Friday during Lent. In addition to celebrating the feast of St. Valentine by attending Mass with his wife, he could suggest that they eat a vegetarian meal without dessert and that they offer up this sacrifice for struggling married couples. In this case such a meal would "look" different, though we should be quick to point out that the food can still be delicious, and their conversation filled with mirth.

The four cardinal virtues are now doubled, for there are four *natural* and *acquired* cardinal virtues, and four corresponding *supernatural* and *infused* cardinal virtues. Aquinas uses the same term for each one; for example, whether we moderate food and drink according to reason or according to the Divine rule, the virtue is called "temperance," and so one must judge in context which one he has in mind. Two other points to make regarding the infused cardinal virtues: First, their presence does not necessitate or require possession of the corresponding acquired cardinal virtues. This, among other things, helps us make sense of the experience most adult converts have—namely, that baptism does not necessarily remove bad habits. While this "doubling" of the virtues might seem unnecessary, Michael S. Sherwin uses the real-life conversion of a notorious alcoholic named Matthew Talbot to illustrate the point that "even though one may still struggle with the remaining effects of one's acquired vices, in the grace of conversion we have the infused capacity to live a life directed to a higher goal."[4] The alcoholic who converts does not necessarily become temperate in the sense of having a proper desire for moderate alcohol consumption. Rather, usually such a person finds that she is still an alcoholic, even if one who now has the grace to overcome her vicious desires so as to avoid mortal sin. At baptism she does not receive the acquired virtue of temperance, but rather the infused, and this only allows her to combat her disordered passions, not necessarily remove them. Second, since the acquired virtues are habits, they are not lost by a single sinful act; yet, since mortal sin and charity are incompatible, and since charity is the "root" of the theological virtues, a single sinful act that is mortal removes the infused virtues (see *ST* I-II.71.4).[5]

---

4. Michael S. Sherwin, OP, "Infused Virtue and the Effects of Acquired Vice: A Test Case for the Thomistic Theory of Infused Cardinal Virtues," *Thomist* 73 (2009): 36–37.

5. This is one reason to think that the acquired and infused virtues "coexist" such that, for example, the adult convert who already had the acquired virtue of temperance now has both

In addition to theological virtues and infused cardinal virtues, the third and final type of infused virtue is infused secondary virtues. Just as the infused cardinal virtues allow charity to guide the four faculties of the human person to the supernatural end, so the infused secondary virtues guide the infused cardinal virtues to act under the guidance of charity in the more particular situations of daily life. While this much is clear, Aquinas leaves us with an interpretive difficulty, for he tells us that "infused and acquired temperance differ in species; and *the same applies to the other virtues*" (*ST* I-II.63.4; emphasis added). What "other virtues" does he have in mind here? All of them, or just the cardinal virtues? In other words, is it the case that every virtue, be it moral or intellectual, cardinal or secondary, is bifurcated into acquired and infused, or is this only true of the cardinal virtues?[6] The context in which he makes this claim does not decisively answer this question, though I would argue that the preponderance of the evidence favors reading him as meaning only the cardinal virtues. This interpretation can be confirmed by two considerations.

First, consider the greatest of the intellectual virtues, wisdom; Aquinas's account of the contemplative life suggests that the purification the acquired intellectual virtues must undergo in order to contemplate God comes from the infused moral and theological virtues coupled with infused prudence and the gifts of the Holy Spirit (see *ST* II-II.180, 182). Thus, there is no such thing as the virtue of infused wisdom, for acquired wisdom is completed via the theological virtue of faith and the Holy Spirit's gift of wisdom.

Second, if we look at Aquinas's discussion of the secondary virtues in the *Secunda secundae*, it is clear that some of them only exist in an infused form. For example, patience and perseverance are secondary virtues to infused fortitude, and there is no acquired form for them (see *ST* II-II.136 and 137). The reason this would make sense is that, as Aquinas explains in *ST* II-II.63.4, the acquired and infused virtues of the same name nonetheless differ in species, and thus under them would fall different secondary virtues. To use an analogy, just as one can be a defensive player in European football (soccer) as well as in American football, despite the fact that the type of defensive players in each sport differs, so would there be different secondary virtues for natural

---

acquired and infused temperance. This is a contested issue in current scholarship; for a cautious defense of the "coexistence view," see Angela McKay Knobel, "Can Aquinas's Infused and Acquired Virtues Coexist in the Christian Life?," *Studies in Christian Ethics* 23.4 (2010): 381–96.

6. The fact that Aquinas does not specify for each virtue whether he is discussing it as acquired or as infused is puzzling and lends evidence to the position that Aquinas is generally concerned only with the infused virtues. For an example of how scholars engage this question, see Andrew Pinsent's argument that most of *ST* II-II is about infused virtues in his *The Second-Person Perspective in Aquinas's Ethics* (New York: Routledge, 2012), 66–67.

and infused temperance, respectively. These secondary virtues help perfect our desire to live a life of perfect charity, and yet even actions done in accordance with the infused virtues do not suffice. We must complete our discussion of the life of the good Christian by discussing the final components of living out the call to holiness.

The gifts and fruits of the Holy Spirit work with the theological virtues to bring about perfect incorporation into the Body of Christ, and the Beatitudes enumerate the virtuous actions by which one achieves this perfection. Let us discuss these in order. First, the prophet Isaiah relates that there are seven gifts of the Holy Spirit: "And the Spirit of the LORD shall rest upon him, the spirit of *wisdom* and *understanding*, the spirit of *counsel* and might [*fortitude*], the spirit of *knowledge* and the *fear* of the LORD. And his delight [*piety*] shall be in the fear of the LORD" (Isa. 11:2–3; emphasis added). According to Aquinas, the fact that Isaiah refers to "Spirit" rather than "gift" indicates that, like the infused virtues, the gifts of the Holy Spirit are "in us by Divine inspiration" (*ST* I-II.68.1). He goes on to define gifts as "perfections of man, whereby he is disposed so as to be amenable to the promptings of God" (*ST* I-II.68.2), and by doing so indicates that the gifts do not direct us to different actions than those that the infused virtues enjoin, but rather provide us with a habit that makes us more docile and receptive to God's guidance (see *ST* I-II.68.3). The seven gifts of the Holy Spirit "are in all who are possessed of charity" (*ST* I-II.68.5), for, even though the theological virtues are more excellent than the gifts (see *ST* I-II.68.8), the gifts are necessary for perfection. As John Capreolus, an important fifteenth-century defender of Aquinas's moral theory, puts this: "Besides the inclinations given by the virtues, which are, as it were, in an active state, we need a movement that is passive on our part and active on the part of the Holy Spirit, in order to be directed to the supernatural end."[7]

Next, in addition to the virtues and to the gifts of the Holy Spirit, the fruits of the Holy Spirit are a central part of the life of the believer. In Galatians 5:16–23, St. Paul contrasts desires and works of the Holy Spirit with the fruit of the Holy Spirit.[8] Aquinas connects these fruits to the twelve fruits of Revelation 22:2 found in "the holy city Jerusalem coming down out of heaven

---

7. John Capreolus, *On the Virtues*, trans. Kevin White and Romanus Cessario, OP (Washington, DC: Catholic University of America Press, 2001), 310.

8. It should be noted that the Greek text only lists nine fruits and that the listing of twelve is found in the Latin Vulgate, which Aquinas relied upon. The Church follows the tradition on this point, and so contemporary Church teaching is compatible with Aquinas's claims (see CCC 1832). Another issue to note is that St. Paul speaks of the "fruit," not "fruits." One way to resolve this apparent disagreement is by pointing out that one speaks of the fruit of the tree when speaking of all of its fruit collectively. For example, the owner of an orchard would say, "The fruit are usually ripe in September."

from God" (Rev. 21:10). Whereas the gifts are habits, both the Beatitudes and the fruits of the Holy Spirit are acts. The term "fruits" refers to the fact that the believer delights in the virtuous actions that grace allows him or her to perform, and in this sense all of the Beatitudes are also fruits, but not all fruits are beatitudes: "For the fruits are any virtuous deeds in which one delights: whereas the beatitudes are none but perfect works, and which, by reason of their perfection, are assigned to the gifts rather than to the virtues" (*ST* I-II.70.2). Aquinas sees a threefold division between the fruits, based on "the various ways in which the Holy Ghost proceeds in us: which process consists in this, that the mind of man is set in order, first of all, in regard to itself [charity, joy, peace, patience, long-suffering]; secondly, in regard to things that are near it [goodness, benignity, meekness, faith]; thirdly, in regard to things that are below it [modesty, contingency, chastity]" (*ST* I-II.70.3). When we recall that the infused virtues allow us to conform our actions to the Divine rule but do not remove the desires of the "old man," we can see why the fruits would be necessary for happiness. By the infused virtues cooperating with the gifts, we know and will the good, and by the fruits we delight in doing God's will.

Finally, in the Sermon on the Mount as recounted in the Gospel of Matthew, Jesus speaks of eight beatitudes: poverty of spirit, meekness, mourning, hungering and thirsting for justice, mercy, purity of the heart, peacemaking, and endurance of persecution (see Matt. 5:3–12).[9] Happiness or beatitude consists in virtuous action, and hence "the Beatitudes" refers to those acts that follow from possession of the virtues and gifts (see *ST* I-II.69.1). Aquinas sees in the enumeration of the beatitudes a proper account of the path to happiness: the first three beatitudes (poverty of spirit, meekness, and mourning) prevent us from falling prey to "sensual happiness," a false way of life that seeks fulfillment through bodily goods. The next two beatitudes (hungering and thirsting for justice, and mercy) push beyond this, helping us to acquire the happiness found in the active life, specifically in giving others their due and, further still, exercising "spontaneous gratuity" for those in need. Third, the perfection of man consists in the beatific vision, and thus the next two beatitudes (purity of heart and peacemaking) refer to "the effects of the active life, which dispose man for the contemplative life" (*ST* I-II.69.3). "The eighth beatitude is a confirmation of all the beatitudes" (*ST* I-II.69.3ad2), for the perfect lover will endure any persecution rather than lose his beloved. Thus, the order of the beatitudes corresponds to the growth in virtue that guides the wayfarer to his or her heavenly home. The Beatitudes, then, are

9. The reader may notice that mourning is found before meekness in the list of beatitudes in contemporary Bibles. The Latin Vulgate translation of the Bible that Aquinas used has the order found here, and I retain this order so as to follow his presentation.

not a separate grace bestowed on the believer, but rather a list of the virtuous actions that lead to perfection.

This is not the space to work through all of the details concerning how the virtues, gifts, fruits, and beatitudes are interrelated, for this would involve working through the *Secunda secundae* as a whole, focusing specifically on questions 8, 9, 19, 45, 52, 121, and 139, where Aquinas takes up the seven gifts of the Holy Spirit in connection to specific virtues, fruits, and beatitudes. Suffice it for now to say that Christian life is an ongoing conversion to the God who asks much of us but who gives us both the native faculties and the grace to delight in doing his will; through this joyful service our hearts will find rest in him, the giver of all good things (see James 1:17).

Summing up all of this, we could say, first, that those who practice the acquired virtues achieve an imperfect happiness that acknowledges its own inability to achieve the final end of human existence.[10] There is only one final, perfect end of human existence, the beatific vision, and the good pagan, as aware as he is of the limits of his knowledge, is not even in a position to hope for what God promises us through revelation: participation in his trinitarian life of knowledge and love (see 1 Cor. 2:6–13). Second, in this life, the Christian in the state of grace participates imperfectly in the perfect happiness that can only be found in heaven. Third and finally, those who have passed through the death of our mortal flesh and delight in the beatific vision have perfect happiness. In short, Aquinas distinguishes between the virtues that one can acquire and which fit one for social life (the good pagan), the "perfecting" virtues of the pilgrim (the Christian in this life), and the "[perfect] virtues attributed to the Blessed, or, in this life, to some who are at the summit of perfection" (*ST* I-II.61.5).

4. The Best Way of Life Revisited

Background Reading: ST II-II.171, 175, 180–184

In our attempt to answer the question "What is the best way of life?" in chapter 1, we made two points that we should return to here: (1) the best way of life *in itself* is not necessarily the best way of life *for me*; (2) while generally the contemplative life is higher than the active life since the intellect is what

---

10. Another point to add is that, as a result of the fall, we cannot even possess the acquired virtues perfectly. The disorder in the human soul that the fall brought on means that the passions cannot be brought under the perfect control of reason (see *ST* I-II.109.2). Only in the beatific vision can this be removed. I encourage the reader to spend some time thinking through all of these points by studying Aquinas's *Disputed Questions on the Virtues*.

is best in us, given the frailty of merely human wisdom and the fact that we are both bodily and spiritual, having a virtuous will (i.e., justice and, more specifically, religion) is best *for us* (see chap. 1, §6); simply put, the active life would seem to be more perfective of our persons than the contemplative life. How does the presence of grace, building upon nature, affect our answer in light of these points?

Regarding the first point, in some sense grace negates this distinction between the best in itself and the best for me, for the life of charity is both best in itself and best for everyone. As Aquinas points out, even faith and hope "have not the perfect character of virtue without charity" (*ST* I-II.65.4). Strictly speaking, one cannot be virtuous without charity, and the good and best life *is* the life of charity. That being said, since charity calls each of us to different degrees of perfection, the distinction between the best in itself and the best for me is retained; to put this point in contemporary language: I am called to become the best version of me, though what is best for me may not be best for another. Once again, ethics is both objective and subjective: while we are all called to the same end, the beatific vision, God calls us as unique persons with our own particular calling.

Regarding the second point (that the intellect is best in us and yet the active life of conforming the will to justice and religion is best), in a qualified way it retains its validity: on the one hand, because we are wayfarers or pilgrims on this earth, our intellects are limited to the imperfect knowledge given by faith coupled with the gifts of the Holy Spirit, and yet our wills can be conformed ever more perfectly to him in charity; on the other hand, when we pass through stingless death, our knowledge and love will perfectly correspond, for we will be wise lovers of the God who is Truth and Love. Let us develop both of these points in order to gain a deeper understanding of what moral theology has to teach us about the best way of life.

There is a wonderful passage in St. Thérèse of Lisieux's *The Story of a Soul* where she wrestles with feeling called to many different vocations even though she only has one life to live in service to God. What she comes to realize, though, is that there is one vocation that all people share in common: "I understood that *Love* contains all the Vocations, that Love is all, that it embraces all time and all places . . . in a word, that it is Everlasting!"[11] This is precisely the point Aquinas has been making concerning charity, for it is the form and root of the virtues, guiding all truly good people in all that they do. Thus, there is one best way of life for everyone, for all are called to conform

11. Thérèse of Lisieux, *The Story of a Soul*, trans. Robert J. Edmonson (Brewster, MA: Paraclete, 2006), 217.

their will to God's. God wills the good of creation as a whole and, by doing so, wills my good; by lovingly conforming my will to him, I also will my own good (see *ST* I-II.19.9–10). The life of charity, then, is the best life for everyone.

While charity calls each of us to will what is best, this does not mean that the best life for me would be the best life for my neighbor. We all have our own, unique vocations or callings as priestly, religious, or lay. Just as the diversity of things found in the universe is willed by God in order to manifest his goodness, so too is the diversity of vocations, of rites in the Church, and of authentic human cultures a manifestation of God's love for us (see *ST* II-II.183.2–3).

While the gift of the Incarnation allows us to see more clearly and live more fully, we still labor in "this valley of tears," as the Salve Regina poetically puts it. We must walk by faith and put ourselves in his care, trusting that by charitably doing his will we will join him in paradise. God gives a diversity of gifts that correspond to the diversity of ways in which we are called to serve him. And, again, while some callings are higher than others, God may call me to a more humble station, and I must joyfully accept this. A wonderful example of this is found in the life of Maria von Trapp (of *Sound of Music* fame), who had every intention of joining the Benedictine nuns of Nonnberg when Baron von Trapp proposed to her. She took this matter before her reverend mother, who told her, "[God] wants you to serve Him well where He needs you most, and serve Him wholeheartedly and cheerfully"; returning to the baron, she hardly gave the most cheerful response to his proposal: "Th-they s-s-said I have to m-m-m-marry you-u!" Thus began an extraordinary life filled with music, hardship, love, and sacrifice.[12]

Aquinas takes up the issue of vocations and gifts in the last treatise of the *Secunda secundae*, "Acts Which Pertain Especially to Certain Men" (*ST* II-II.171–89). While our focus will be on Aquinas's discussion of the diverse ways and states of life, a few words are in order regarding the gifts. Not to be confused with the gifts of the Holy Spirit, these are gifts of grace bestowed upon believers for the building up of the Church; with the arguable exception of rapture, these are gratuitous graces "bestowed on a man, not to justify him, but rather that he may cooperate in the justification of another" (*ST* I-II.111.1). Aquinas discusses the gifts of knowledge (*ST* II-II.171–75), speech (176–77), and miracles (178). First, the gift of knowledge pertains to either prophecy or rapture, and an interesting point he makes is that, since God gives this unique knowledge of the prophet for the good of the Church but not necessarily for the perfection of the prophet him- or herself, one can be a

12. Maria Augusta Trapp, *The Story of the Trapp Family Singers* (New York: Doubleday, 1990), 60.

prophet without possessing charity. While "prophecy requires the mind to be raised very high in order to contemplate spiritual things, and this is hindered by strong passions, and the inordinate pursuit of external things," nonetheless the prophet does not necessarily live a good life inasmuch as he or she may be lacking in charity (*ST* II-II.172.4). This is not true of the one who is raptured, for while the prophet is like a "mirror" of God's essence who does not him- or herself see God's essence (see *ST* II-II.173.1), the raptured soul is given "the vision of the blessed, which transcends the state of the wayfarer, according to Isaiah 64:4, 'Eye hath not seen, O God, besides Thee, what things Thou hast prepared for them that love Thee'" (*ST* II-II.175.3). Whereas the prophet's knowledge is mystical, yet imperfect, the one who is raptured gains a fleeting glimpse of the beatific vision that makes him or her both wiser and more loving. Second, the gift of speech is divided into tongues and words, the latter being again divided into using words to teach, please, or sway the hearers (see *ST* II-II.177.1). Both of these gifts pertain to evangelization, tongues allowing the evangelizer to understand and use the language of the evangelized, speech allowing him or her to share the gospel. Third and finally, through the gift of working miracles the evangelizer is able to confirm the supernatural truths concerning God that he or she seeks to share with others, thus making them sharers in the supernatural virtue of faith.

Now that we have discussed the gratuitous graces God bestows upon certain individuals for the sake of building up the Church, we are ready to focus on the ways the believer can seek perfection. Thus we return to our second point—namely, the distinction between the contemplative and the active life, or the distinction between the virtues of the intellect seeking truth and the virtues of the will by which we perform right actions. While theology does not negate this distinction, it does bring the contemplative and active together in a way that reason alone could not, for theology is unique in being both a practical and a theoretical science: "Although among the philosophical sciences one is speculative and another practical, nevertheless sacred doctrine includes both; as God, by one and the same science, knows both Himself and His works" (*ST* I.1.4). That being said, Aquinas goes on to say that theology is more properly considered a theoretical science, and this speaks to the point that the contemplative life is in itself more perfect than the active life.

Aquinas's discussion of the best life is twofold, for he looks at the best way of life in general (active or contemplative) and then the states of life by which these are lived out (episcopal or priestly, religious, lay). The distinction between the active and the contemplative life and a decided judgment that the latter is best are as old as philosophy itself; we could even say that to be a philosopher *is* to make such a distinction and *to be* contemplative. For example, Thales, the first philosopher, unwittingly showed the folly of this decision by being so preoccupied with the stars that he fell down a well. Yet this supposedly foolish philosopher had the last laugh: as Aristotle reports, Thales once used his knowledge of the stars to predict a bumper olive crop, cornered the market by buying all of the olive presses, and thus showed that "it is an easy thing for philosophers to get rich if they want to, though that is not what they are serious about."[13] Pythagoras, another one of the early philosophers, was once asked what a philosopher is, and in answering "he compared life to the Great Games, where some went to compete for the prizes and others went with wares to sell, but the best as spectators; for similarly, in life, some grow up with servile natures, greedy for fame and gain, but the philosopher seeks for the truth."[14]

The active/contemplative distinction, as well as the superiority of the contemplative life, finds confirmation in the New Testament story of Martha and Mary: when Martha, "who was *distracted* with much serving," complains to Jesus that Mary does not help her serve but instead sits at Jesus's feet listening to his teaching, Jesus responds with, "Martha, Martha, you are anxious and troubled about many things; one thing is needful. Mary has chosen the good portion, which shall not be taken away from her" (Luke 10:41–42; emphasis added).

As we saw at the end of chapter 1, Aquinas's response to all of this is not to reject the philosophers' search for Wisdom but to reveal the folly of thinking that reason and nature alone can serve as guides. Reason itself knows its own limitations, and thus the contemplative life of the philosopher must give way to the active life, to the life of seeking union with God through the cultivation of some modicum of justice toward him—namely, the virtue of religion. Yet the Christian has a sure guide in faith, and thus it would seem that the philosophers were right to hold up the contemplative life as best, even if they lacked the resources to live it.[15] The contemplative life consists in knowing and loving God's beauty (see *ST* II-II.180.1), and thus the moral virtues, which pertain to the active life, are decisively lower than the theological and intellectual virtues (see *ST* II-II.180.2). As Aquinas points out, "In the future life of the blessed the occupation of external actions will cease, and if there

13. Aristotle, *Politics*, trans. Joe Sachs (Newburyport, MA: Focus Publishing, 2012), 1259a17–19.

14. Diogenes Laertius, *Lives of Eminent Philosophers*, vol. 2, book 8, trans. R. D. Hicks, Loeb Classical Library 185 (Cambridge, MA: Harvard University Press, 1925), 326–28.

15. In St. Gregory of Nyssa's *The Life of Moses*, book 2, he compares the Israelites taking the Egyptians' prized possessions to the Christians taking philosophy from the pagans. Philosophy is properly "owned" by the Church as she seeks to bring all to Christ.

be any external actions at all, these will be referred to contemplation as their end" (*ST* II-II.181.4); while moral actions are necessary in this life, they are a means to the end of the contemplative life and thus of lower standing.

This agreement with the philosophers needs to be qualified, however, for Aquinas is concerned not only with the theoretical virtue of wisdom but also with the theological virtue of charity; as we pointed out, this changes everything, for charity is love of God and neighbor in God. Even if the contemplative life is the best, it may not be the best *for me*; God may call me to serve others in a way that hinders my ability to live contemplatively: "Sometimes a man is called away from the contemplative life to the works of the active life, on account of some necessity of the present life, yet not so as to be compelled to forsake contemplation altogether" (*ST* II-II.182.1ad3). Were I to refuse this calling, I would also forfeit the contemplative life, for I cannot know and love God without doing his will. I should not despair if God calls me to the active life, for while the contemplative life is in itself better and even more meritorious, "it may happen that one man merits more by the works of the active life than another by the works of the contemplative life. For instance through excess of Divine love a man may now and then suffer separation from the sweetness of Divine contemplation for the time being, that God's will may be done and for His glory's sake" (*ST* II-II.182.2). God is calling me to what is best *for me* as a member of his Body, and so by serving in the soup kitchen I may be rewarded with a greater knowledge and love of God than will be given to a contemplative monk who imperfectly fulfills his own vocation.

As one of the preeminent twentieth-century interpreters of Aquinas, Jacques Maritain, explains in "Action and Contemplation," the Greeks were aware that contemplation is superior to action but mistakenly concluded from this "that mankind lives for the sake of a few intellectuals."[16] Christianity's innovation with regard to the Greek conception of contemplation is fourfold: (1) "love is better than intelligence";[17] (2) the transfiguration of the notion of contemplation to be oriented toward love of the one contemplated—that is, God; (3) work as a dignified activity inasmuch as it is a participation in God's creation ex nihilo; (4) contemplation, or, better, "entrance into the very states of God, of God Incarnate,"[18] is for everyone. The universality of love makes possible, even for those called to an active life, a participation in contemplative life. And, on the part of those committed to contemplation in the fullest sense, generosity will abound as they seek to share the good news.

16. Jacques Maritain, "Action and Contemplation," in *Scholasticism and Politics* (Indianapolis: Liberty Fund, 2011), 172.

17. Maritain, "Action and Contemplation," 173.

18. Maritain, "Action and Contemplation," 175 (emphasis removed).

This leads us to consider the state to which we are called: episcopal or priestly, religious, or lay. And here again we must make the important distinction between what is best in itself and what is best for me: while the celibate life of the bishop or priest, monk, or nun may be in itself better than the married life—for freeing myself from "worldly affairs" in order to more freely serve God is a mark of perfection (see *ST* II-II.184.5)—this would only be best for me if it were my calling. While the contemplative life is in itself the best, God calls certain people away from this life in order to build up his Church. First and foremost, the highest state to which one can be called is that of bishop (see *ST* II-II.184.5–7), and two points should be observed here: (1) the office of bishop is a "burden" that one should not seek; yet, if one is called to it, it can be embraced as the means to most "abundantly" love God (see *ST* II-II.184.7ad2; 185.1–2); (2) even though the bishop is called to an active life, not only should he not "forsake the contemplative" (*ST* II-II.185.2ad1), but he must even be "foremost in contemplation" (*ST* II-II.184.7ad3) in order to share the fruits of his reflections with those in his care.

Second, without going into the details of Aquinas's comparison between priests and deacons on the one hand and monastics on the other, a central point he makes is that "the pre-eminence of order excels in the point of dignity, since by holy orders a man is appointed to the most august ministry of serving Christ Himself in the sacrament of the altar" (*ST* II-II.184.8); thus, second to the bishop in perfection is the priest.

Third, even in the religious state, where one would seem most free to live a contemplative life, Aquinas ranks the purely contemplative life below the life of preaching and teaching: "For even as it is better to enlighten than merely to shine, so is it better to give to others the fruits of one's contemplation than merely to contemplate" (*ST* II-II.188.6).[19] That being said, Aquinas would agree with the warning given to monks by the great spiritual master of the East, St. John Climacus: "After our renunciation of the world, the demons suggest to us that we should envy those living in the world who give alms and console [the needy], and be sorry for ourselves as deprived of these virtues. The aim of our foes is, by false humility, either to make us return to the world, or, if we remain monks, to plunge us into despair."[20] We must not succumb to the temptation to put the active above the contemplative, even if the contemplative must give way to the active as the higher is called to serve

---

19. This passage is often associated with the Dominican Order as a whole and is the source of one of their mottos: *contemplare et contemplata aliis tradere* (to contemplate and hand over to others the fruits of contemplation).

20. St. John Climacus, *The Ladder of Divine Ascent* 2.3, ed. Community of Holy Transfiguration Monastery (Brookline, MA: Holy Transfiguration Monastery, 2012), 60.

the lower. As Thomas Merton notes, "Saint Thomas is here teaching us that the so-called mixed vocation can only be superior to the contemplative vocation if it is itself *more contemplative*."[21]

Fourth and finally, the lay state is ordered toward holy matrimony, which allows for a unique bond of friendship and the rearing of God's children. While Aquinas never took up the question of the role of contemplation in the married life, we can apply his insistence that bishops be preeminent in contemplation to husbands and wives: certainly the greatest duty of a parent is to teach and preach to their own children.

We are wayfarers upon this earth and are called in various ways to build up Christ's Body in the here and now. Still, we must not lose sight of the goal: beatific vision, or union with God, all the angels, and saints. With this in mind, we conclude our study of the best way of life with a discussion of the best life in the *patria* (the "fatherland" or "native city," Aquinas's term for heaven).

The contemplative life is best, and yet it cannot fully be lived here below. Even the best life of the bishop combines the contemplative and the active, though this will not be necessary in heaven, for preaching, teaching, and care of souls will cease. As St. John depicts in Revelation, the heavenly Jerusalem "has no need of sun or moon to shine upon it, for the glory of God is its light, and its lamp is the Lamb. . . . His servants shall worship him; they shall see his face, and his name shall be on their foreheads. And night shall be no more; they need no light of lamp or sun, for the Lord God will be their light, and they shall reign for ever and ever" (Rev. 21:23–22:5). All in heaven will be taken up in the beatific vision, a perfect act of knowing and loving God and neighbor in God.

Yet two points must be made here regarding this vision: First, this perfect act is only relatively perfect, for only God can know himself insofar as he can be known (see *ST* I.12.7), and only God can love himself "as much as He is lovable" (*ST* II-II.184.2). Second, while all in heaven know and love God in his essence, the extent to which each shares in the beatific vision differs: "He will have a fuller participation of the light of glory who has more charity; because where there is the greater charity, there is the more desire; and desire in a certain degree makes the one desiring apt and prepared to receive the object desired" (*ST* I.12.6).

We often hear it said that hell is "getting what you want," and there is something to this; however, we should recognize the deeper truth that what we truly want is to know and love God and that those who share in the beatific vision are satisfied because they receive in proportion to how ardently they

---

21. Thomas Merton, *The Seven Storey Mountain* (New York: Harcourt, Brace, 1948), 416.

desired him. Seen from this deeper perspective, those caught up in sin suffer from a *lack* of desire, for by seeking bodily pleasures, worldly power, and the like, they limit themselves to a banal finitude and ultimately end up wanting precisely because they asked for too little. By contrast, the more one grows in virtue, the more one's desires increase; by being so inflamed with longing, one opens more widely the channels of grace and is promised a greater share in the world to come.

5. Christ as Exemplar; Sacraments as Instruments of Life in Christ

Background Reading: ST III.1, 7, 9, 60–63, 69

We now have a relatively complete account of a good life and what is required in order to lead it, but we still should ask, "How can we enter into it? How do we receive the grace that infuses charity into us?" The goal of moral theory is not so much to know what is good but to become good, and so it is important to at least point to the path to perfect virtue despite knowing that actually traveling on it is another matter entirely. The *Tertia Pars* of the *Summa Theologiae*, which Aquinas unfortunately left unfinished, provides a twofold answer for entering into the life of charity: (1) Jesus Christ, who is true God and true Man; (2) the sacraments as bestowers of grace. We will focus on two points concerning Christ: first, the Person of Christ; second, Christ as Head of the Church. After discussing these points, we will address what it means for the Christian to be like Christ, being mindful of the distinction between Christ as Head and disciples as members. Finally, this chapter concludes with a brief reflection on the centrality of the sacraments in moral life.

One of the most distinctive doctrines of orthodox Christianity is the Incarnation, the belief that Jesus Christ is both true God and true Man. Attempts to remove this "stumbling block to Jews and folly to Gentiles" (1 Cor. 1:23) by denying either the divinity of Christ or his true humanity are almost as ancient as the Church itself. The first Ecumenical Council of Nicaea (325) was convened to address the Arian heresy, which rejected Christ's divinity, and to this day a central feature of Catholic worship is the profession of faith in Christ as "the Only Begotten Son of God, born of the Father before all ages. God from God, Light from Light, true God from true God, begotten, not made, consubstantial with the Father."[22]

Aquinas devotes the first twenty-six questions of the *Tertia Pars* to the Incarnation and provides a nuanced articulation of orthodox teaching con-

---

22. *Missale Romanum*, 3rd ed., English translation (Totowa, NJ: Catholic Book, 2011).

cerning the Person of Christ. For our purposes, the main points to be made are that Jesus Christ is (1) one Person subsisting in two natures; (2) in every respect a human being, sharing all things with us except sin. First, we would not want to think of Jesus Christ as first God and second a man, as if to suggest that there was a man named Jesus Christ who became God (see *ST* III.4.2–3); rather, Jesus Christ is a single person in whom is united two natures (see *ST* III.2, 16–19). Second, this means that Jesus Christ had a human soul and body and all of the faculties (intellect, will, passions) this implies (see *ST* III.5). Thus, Christ possessed the virtues, the grace that unites man with God (see *ST* III.8), a will united to God's will (*ST* III.18), and human knowledge (see *ST* III.10–12). Further, since the death of the body is a punishment for sin, and Christ is sinless, it is only because Christ willed to atone for our sins that he was subject to death, and indeed death at the hands of others (see *ST* III.14).

Let us turn now to Christ as Head of the Church. The life of Christ is unique in human history, for to him alone belonged the task of redeeming us from our sin. While there is much to be learned from Aquinas's study of Christ's life (*ST* III.27–59), our focus will be on his role as Head of the Church. It is precisely because he is Head that Christ's redemptive passion gives us new life; as Aquinas puts it, by his passion "grace was bestowed upon Christ, not only as an individual, but inasmuch as He is the Head of the Church, so that it might overflow into His members" (*ST* III.48.1). Only Christ could offer himself as a sacrifice that would be "a sufficient and a superabundant atonement for the sin and the debt of the human race" (*ST* III.48.4), for he alone as God and Man could charitably offer up a worthy life pleasing to God (see *ST* III.48.2). Christ is Head of the Church, and even of those outside the Church (see *ST* III.8.3), uniting humanity in charity, bestowing grace abundantly. Despite his unique role as Head, there is a limited sense in which members can take on the role of Christ, for while Christ alone provides "the interior influx of grace," bishops provide "exterior guidance" in particular times and places (*ST* III.8.6). Nonetheless, it is important to hold fast to the distinction between Christ as Head of the Church and the baptized as her members, for this helps us to properly understand what it means for us to be, not Christ, but Christlike.

The greatest temptation of human existence is to think of oneself as God, to worship self rather than God. This is the story of the fall, and God in his great love for us offers his only Son as our victim: we get what we want, the death of God's Holy One, and yet discover through this deicide that we are empty inside without him. In the moral life, the manifestation of this is to think that we alone *make* ourselves happy, that our cultivation of virtue is the sole cause of our happiness. This is why moral philosophy must be completed by moral theology, for we must acknowledge our lives and virtues as gifts and acknowledge our radical incompleteness before God if we are to satisfy the desire of our heart of hearts. Put differently, we must seek a mediator who can bring us before the King and plead our cause; a good life is not about raising ourselves up as if we were God, but about revering Christ as sole mediator and bestower of grace (see *ST* III.25–26).

By coming to know who Christ is and by acknowledging him as the King of Kings, we come to know who we are: we learn (1) what in us is a result of sin, (2) what our limitations are as human beings, and (3) what excellences are proper to us as adopted sons and daughters of God. First, most importantly, as we said in discussing Christ's willingness to offer himself up for us, death itself is a result of sin. Further, because Christ was without sin, he was not subject to ailments and disabilities, nor to disordered passions, and thus we learn that these are rooted in the sin of our first parents.

Second, lest we think of our limitations as human beings as being entirely due to sin, we learn about Christ that, as man, he could not comprehend God (*ST* III.10.1–2); neither in the garden of Eden nor in the beatific vision are we to be God, but rather God-like, and we must always remember this distinction. Connected with this is a point concerning Christ that might startle us: Christ did not have faith. In our state as pilgrims, even were it not for sin, we need faith in order to know the truths about God that surpass reason; as God, Christ is not subject to this limitation: "From the first moment of His conception Christ saw God's Essence fully. . . . Hence there could be no faith in Him" (*ST* III.7.3). In addition, even were it not for sin, we cannot storm the gates of heaven: our nature does not make us worthy of life with God; rather, the abundance of his goodness freely bestowed upon us does. In this respect, Aquinas speaks of divine "adoption," and Christ alone does not stand in need of such adoption (see *ST* III.23.4).

Third and finally, as we discussed in chapter 1 regarding the passions, it is proper to us as bodily creatures to feel joy, sadness, hope, fear, and all of the passions; thus, the example of Christ, who experienced not only these but also wonder (see *ST* III.15.8), reminds us that the passions are goods proper to us, not evils to be expunged.[23] Yet, although Christ was subject to the

---

23. And, it should be pointed out, strictly speaking, as spiritual beings neither God nor the angels experience passions. As Nicholas Lombardo points out, "Passions like love and joy are analogously present in God, but passions that imply some perfection, such as sadness and anger, which each imply the experience of some evil, cannot be analogously present in God" (*The Logic of Desire: Aquinas on Emotion* [Washington, DC: Catholic University of America Press, 2010], 83). Christ experiences these because he is truly human.

passions, he also teaches us the excellence we should be seeking, for in him the passions were perfectly subject to reason; Aquinas, following St. Jerome, uses the term "propassion" to indicate this perfected state of the soul: "'Lest a passion should hold sway over His soul, it is by a propassion that he is said to have "begun to grow sorrowful and to be sad"'; so that it is a perfect 'passion' when it dominates the soul, i.e. the reason; and a 'propassion' when it has its beginning in the sensitive appetite, but goes no further" (*ST* III.15.4). In addition, we learn from Christ that prayer is a perfection of our nature, that no matter how much we excel in virtue and grace, we must always seek to grow in union with God through prayer to him; as Aquinas puts it, as a man Christ had a human will, and since "prayer is the unfolding of our will to God, that He may fulfill it" (*ST* III.21.1), even Christ needed to place his human nature in God's hands. Further still, if we cultivate our relationship with God through prayer and reception of grace, we will never be disappointed in prayer, for, like Christ, we will only will what God wills for us (see *ST* III.21.4).

Let us conclude our study of moral theology with a few words on the sacraments as the means by which God bestows grace. One of the themes Aquinas constantly returns to in his reflections of the person and life of Christ is the goodness of the human body. We are not spirits, but ensouled flesh and blood; the "body is a temple of the Holy Spirit" (1 Cor. 6:19), and we receive grace and grow in it through bodily actions. Even though Christ was not in need of ritual purification, and despite the fact that such rituals could not bestow salvific grace, he submitted himself to the rites of the old law, specifically circumcision (see *ST* III.37) and the baptism of John (see *ST* III.38–39). Christ's submission to these rituals teaches us that God bestows his grace upon us by public rituals administered by the legitimate authorities of the Church, that bodily signs are the means of salvation. These are the sacraments, the sensible signs by which God makes us holy (see *ST* III.60).

The sacraments are necessary for salvation, for it is through them that God bestows his grace upon us and restores us to union with him (see *ST* III.61–62). This last point reminds us that, just as the natural virtues must be completed by the infused virtues, so must the natural desire to live for God be completed by the sacramental life. Moral philosophy must give way to moral theology and acknowledge with St. Ignatius of Antioch that salvation comes from Christ as Head of the Church through his sacraments: "Let that be deemed a proper Eucharist, which is [administered] either by the bishop, or by one to whom he has entrusted it. Wherever the bishop shall appear, there let the multitude [of the people] also be; even as, wherever Jesus Christ is, there is the Catholic Church."[24] The happiness for which we each long can only be obtained by taking up our proper role in the Body of Christ, and for this reason moral theory is completed by a study of how justice and charity are to be put in practice in economic and political life.

24. Ignatius of Antioch, *Epistle to the Smyrnaeans* 8, in *The Ante-Nicene Fathers: Translations of the Writings of the Fathers down to A.D. 325*, ed. Alexander Roberts and James Donaldson, 10 vols. (repr., Peabody, MA: Hendrickson, 1994; New York: Christian Literature, 1885–1887), 1:89–90.

Economic Theory

3

The Goods of the Earth
and the Good Life
(Economic Philosophy)

One man gives freely, yet grows all the richer;
    another withholds what he should give, and only suffers want.
A liberal man will be enriched,
    and one who waters will himself be watered.
The people curse him who holds back grain,
    but a blessing is on the head of him who sells it.
He who diligently seeks good seeks favor,
    but evil comes to him who searches for it.
He who trusts in his riches will wither,
    but the righteous will flourish like a green leaf.

                    —Proverbs 11:24–28

For what will it profit a man, if he gains the whole world and forfeits his life?
Or what shall a man give in return for his life? For the Son of man is to come
with his angels in the glory of his Father, and then he will repay every man for
what he has done.

                    —Matthew 16:26–27

1. Introduction

Since every activity, from throwing a Frisbee to running a business, must be directed to the ultimate goal of happiness, the study of economics presupposes a strong foundation in moral theory. As we will see, knowing what material goods are mine or yours and what their value is requires a proper understanding of the virtues and of how the goods of this world are to be used in the pursuit of happiness. In light of this moral foundation for economic theory, we should review the main results of our study thus far.

Moral theory is the study of how to become happy, which is to say, of how to achieve the end or purpose of human existence. We cannot achieve this end without a proper formation in the virtues, for the virtues allow us to perform those actions which make us happy. Within the limits of human nature and the study of moral philosophy, the imperfect happiness that can be achieved is the result of acquiring and practicing the four cardinal virtues (prudence, justice, fortitude, and temperance) and the virtues annexed to them. And, as perfecting of our nature as these are, the one who acquires them inevitably grows in a recognition of their ultimate imperfection, for the justice toward God that goodness demands (i.e., religion) cannot be practiced in its fullness. It is by nature, then, that one must turn to God for help, seeking his perfecting grace.

Moral theology reveals how grace perfects nature in that happiness is a result of God (1) bestowing faith, hope, and charity; (2) infusing cardinal virtues and secondary virtues; (3) granting the gifts and fruits of the Holy Spirit; and (4) leading us along the perfecting path of the Beatitudes. The happiness of this life is directed to the final, perfect happiness found in the beatific vision. Most generally, we could return to a point we made in the beginning of the first chapter: a good life consists in *being* good, not in *having* goods, for goodness and being are coextensive, and having must be oriented toward being. Economic theory is more about persons than about things, for it teaches us how to direct the material goods at our disposal to the end of the true good, human happiness. It is with this last point that we begin our study of economics.

To study economics as a science in the contemporary sense would be to focus on the acquiring, transacting, preserving, and so forth of material goods, and in such a way as to leave aside the question of the purpose of these goods. We think of sciences as "value neutral" and thus blind to the question of the purposes of things: modern economics can tell you how to make a profit, but not whether you should. Economics is indifferent to whether you are buying car parts or human body parts, selling Hondas or babies; instead, it leaves such matters to the law or to your own moral code to determine whether specific transactions are right.

This is not sufficient for economic theory as Aquinas understands it, for, to repeat: having is oriented toward being; the use of material goods must be directed to the end of human happiness. As Andrew Yuengert puts this in his insightful study on the relationship between ethics and economics, "Economics is at the service of ethics; it employs its own methods, which are worked out at a certain distance from ethics, but even its methods are ultimately judged in the light of ethics."[1] In the running of a business, for example, we must ask ourselves how our products or services are promoting our own happiness, that of our families and communities, and that of our customers. Economic philosophy studies how the good pagan—that is, the one who possesses the acquired virtues—puts them into practice in regard to material goods and in the context of his or her life as a whole.

The term "economics" is derived from two Greek words: *oikos* ("house") and *nomos* ("custom" or "law") and thus translates roughly as "the laws or rules of the household." Economic theory, then, asks, "What are the rules or guiding principles for the running of a household, for its *being* good as a place where its members can flourish?" Notice that economics is primarily about households, and secondarily about individuals. This is an important point to which we will keep returning: economics is not the study of my material well-being, but that of my community, and of myself as a member of that community. Our study of this relationship between households, persons, and material goods is divided into the following sections: (1) the ownership and use of property; (2) the acquired virtues in economic life; and (3) value.

2. The Ownership and Use of Private Property

Background Reading: ST II-II.66

Given the presuppositions we are likely to be unaware of when we try to determine what it means to own material goods, it may be helpful to begin with a standard modern approach to private property. One of the distinctive features of modern economic and political thought is the general insistence that the right to private property is absolute. John Locke, for example, who is often seen as the founder of modern liberalism, envisions a state of nature in which the earth belongs to all, and he proceeds to show how private property arises. On his account, the common possession of all things is negated as soon

1. Andrew Yuengert, *The Boundaries of Technique* (Lanham, MD: Lexington Books, 2004), 64.

as humans mix their labor with the goods of the earth. A man who tills the ground, thereby improving it, by this act makes this land his own. The reason for this is that man owns his own person, and this self-ownership extends to his work. While Locke limits the claim of the individual in this state of nature to those goods which he can use before they spoil, the presumption is that property rights cannot be overridden by competing rights such as the needs of others.[2] As a matter of fact, a central reason for leaving the state of nature and entering into political community is to protect this natural right to private property.[3] And, again, while there are limited cases in which private property may be confiscated or used without consent (e.g., the fire department may tear down someone's house to prevent a fire from spreading),[4] in general individuals are free to decide what to do with their own property. Since the bulk of private property in any developed society consists in nonperishables, there are almost no restrictions on how much one may rightfully own. And, to push this to an extreme, one has a right to neglect or destroy one's own property even if this prevents others from securing the basic goods necessary for survival.[5]

The modern liberal approach to property emphasizes the rights of the individual over and against society, and in doing so tends to minimize the social obligations that come with property ownership. By contrast, Aquinas's focus is on private property as legitimate given that it is the best means for *society* to flourish. As he explains, the goods of the earth were given to man "to use . . . for his own profit, as they were made on his account" (*ST* II-II.66.1). Yet in using them he must always bear in mind that he is not their principal owner: "The rich man is reproved for deeming external things to belong to him principally, as though he had not received them from another, namely from God" (*ST* II-II.66.1ad2). While for the sake of political life, the language of property ownership is invaluable, in the philosophical sense it would be more appropriate to speak of stewardship, for this term better conveys the responsibility to use those things in one's care for the good of the community. Just like my person, I am entrusted with material things so that I can more profitably serve God and neighbor.

Even though the goods of the earth were given in common to all, there are three reasons why the ownership of private property is legitimate: this

---

2. See John Locke, *Two Treatises of Government*, 2.5.

3. See John Locke, *Two Treatises of Government*, 2.7.

4. See John Locke, *Two Treatises of Government*, 2.14.

5. For an interesting discussion of the right to destroy, see Lior Jacob Strahilevitz, "The Right to Destroy," *Yale Law Journal* 114 (2005): 781–854; to be fair to Locke, it is not entirely clear what he thinks about such extreme cases, and he does not hold that the right to private property is without some restraints given the rights of those who are in need.

arrangement (1) ensures better care for these goods, as man is more solicitous over those things which belong to him; (2) allows for a more orderly society by establishing a clear demarcation of responsibility for such goods; (3) helps prevent quarrels over material goods. We should be chastened by this teaching, for we are made mindful of our own sinfulness, and not our dignity, as at least part of why private property is necessary. To take examples from the business world, is it not the case that our appetites are emboldened and more delicate when the company is paying for our meal? That we are less careful over our purchases and more likely to waste goods when the company credit card is involved? Would that we served one another from the common stock rather than enlarged our own share when nobody is keeping tabs.

In his treatment of private property, Aquinas distinguishes between "the power to procure and dispense" (*ST* II-II.66.2) material goods, on the one hand, and the use of them, on the other. It is beneficial to society for its members to have power over material goods, and yet those members must recognize that their use of these goods is to be guided by concern for the good of the community as a whole. Economic philosophy is not centered on abstract individuals buying and selling widgets[6] but on concrete members of a community of households and neighbors who are fathers or mothers, sons or daughters, employees or employers, and so forth. What I rightfully own and how I should use it depends on the circumstances of my life and of my community. Whereas modern economics wants to focus exclusively on whether I obtained property legitimately and leaves me free to do whatever I want with my property, Aquinas insists that I always bear in mind my social role and the fact that my property must serve my community. As Mary Hirschfeld puts this, "Assigning property rights is useful, but those rights are not ours by nature. By contrast, we tend to think that individual property rights are held by virtue of some right proper to us. . . . Our sense of ownership, then, connects our property more closely to our beings than would be the case if we had Thomas's understanding of the nature of ownership and thus exacerbates our sense that we must sacrifice if we wish to meet the needs of others."[7]

As Aquinas observed regarding the rich man, we tend to forget that we are entrusted with material goods and imagine that we have sole ownership over them to do as we please. While Aquinas would agree with Locke that we cannot let our goods spoil, this does not go far enough; we abuse our

6. In economics, "widget" is a placeholder name for any type of personal property. It is like *x* in mathematics (e.g., person A owns thirty widgets that she intends to sell).

7. Mary Hirschfeld, "Standard of Living and Economic Virtue: Forging a Link between St. Thomas Aquinas and the Twenty-First Century," *Journal of the Society of Christian Ethics* 26.1 (2006): 66.

ownership claims when we use these goods in a selfish manner: "Man ought
to possess external things, not as his own, but as common, so that, to wit,
he is ready to communicate them to others in their need" (*ST* II-II.66.2).
We must always ask ourselves whether or not we hoard our goods for some
remotely possible need, or rather hold them in waiting for those who might
need them more than we do. As St. John Chrysostom starkly puts it: "The
rich man is a kind of steward of the money which is owed for distribution
to the poor. He is directed to distribute it to his fellow servants who are in
want. So if he spends more on himself than his need requires, he will pay the
harshest penalty hereafter. For his own goods are not his own, but belong to
his fellow servants."[8]

To put this teaching on material goods more positively for those who are
financially well endowed, giving of one's wealth is the means by which one
achieves freedom from "the burden of riches."[9] Material goods bind us to
worldly cares, and the solid foundation they provide us in the valley of human
affairs can make it difficult for us to ascend the lofty peaks of the spiritual
life. On this point Aquinas stands with the Church fathers, who exhort us to
curb our desires so as to understand the true distinction between wealth and
poverty: "The rich man is not the one who has collected many possessions
but the one who needs few possessions; and the poor man is not the one who
has no possessions but the one who has many desires."[10] In this sense, one
can be rich in the eyes of the world though poor in spiritual goods, and yet
this does not preclude being wealthy in both senses: those who possess many
material goods as stewards for the poor are truly wealthy both in the valley
and on the mountain.

One final point concerning private property: Aquinas goes so far as to say
that, in times of pressing need, one can rightfully take the property of another.
Since "whatever certain people have in superabundance is due, by natural law,
to the purpose of succoring the poor," and since it sometimes happens that
a poor person's "need be so manifest and urgent, that it is evident that the

8. John Chrysostom, *On Wealth and Poverty*, trans. Catharine P. Roth (Crestwood, NY:
St. Vladimir's Seminary Press, 1984), 50.

9. As St. Basil the Great says, Christ invites us "to cast off the burden of riches by distributing to the poor." *An Ascetical Discourse and Exhortation on the Renunciation of the World
and Spiritual Reflection*, cited in *Saint Basil: Ascetical Works*, trans. M. Monica Wagner, CSC
(Washington, DC: Catholic University of America Press, 1970), 15. See *ST* II-II.32.5ad5 for
Aquinas's favorable citation of St. Basil.

10. John Chrysostom, *On Wealth and Poverty*, 40; see also *The Rule of St. Benedict in English*, trans. Timothy Fry, OSB (Collegeville, MN: Liturgical Press, 1981), 57, where St. Benedict
discusses the distribution of goods: "Whoever needs less should thank God and not be distressed,
but whoever needs more should feel humble because of his weakness."

present need must be remedied by whatever means be at hand," in such cases the needy lawfully takes what belongs to another (*ST* II-II.66.7). An example of this might be a starving man who comes upon a cornfield and takes an ear of corn. Further still, Aquinas allows for the taking of another's property in order to help someone else who is in need (see *ST* II-II.31.3ad3). While Aquinas certainly recognizes the importance of private property and views these as extreme situations, his point is to emphasize the priority of persons over things, of being over having.[11]

3. The Acquired Virtues in Economic Life

Background Reading: ST II-II.47.11, 57.1–3, 58, 61.1, 80, 106.1, 117, 141

We have just seen that private ownership and use of property must be directed to the good of one's community, and now we discuss the role of the virtues in procuring this good. Moral theory seeks to establish the good of the person, especially in his or her capacity to seek the happiness that is found in willing the good of the other. Economic theory seeks to establish the good of the household and of one's neighbors in relation to that household. Economics seeks, then, "household happiness" or, less awkwardly, domestic well-being—that is, the condition in which the material goods of daily living are secured for each member of the household and these members use them virtuously in relation to themselves, to one another, and to neighbors.

Most broadly, the acquired virtue of justice is the focus of economic philosophy. That being said, all four of the cardinal virtues, and a host of secondary virtues, must be practiced in order to secure domestic well-being. Here we take up the central, natural virtues for economic activity: (1) economic prudence; (2) justice and the secondary virtues of (3) piety, (4) gratitude, and (5) liberality; (6) magnificence, which is a secondary virtue to fortitude; and two virtues annexed to temperance: (7) abstinence and (8) sobriety.

Recall that prudence is that virtue by which practical reason determines the proper means to the right end in a particular situation. For example, the soldier does not reason out whether or not to be brave, but rather what the appropriate means are to acting bravely in this particular circumstance. Since we must bring reason to bear on every situation of our lives, every action

---

11. It is worth noting that Aquinas does not appear to sanction, even in an extreme circumstance, using violence. So, for example, while I could take corn from a farmer's field if I were starving to death, I could not attack him should he try to prevent me. Admittedly, Aquinas does not make this explicit, but from the context it would seem that such is his view.

involves prudence; there is nothing unique, then, in claiming that economic action requires prudence. However, there is a unique type of prudence necessary for economics: since the types of goods that one seeks in moral, economic, and political theory are different in light of their respective ends, "there must needs be different species of prudence corresponding to these different ends, so that one is 'prudence' simply so called, which is directed to one's own good; another, '[economic] prudence'[12] which is directed to the common good of the home; and a third, 'political prudence,' which is directed to the common good of the state or kingdom" (*ST* II-II.47.11).

That there is a kind of general prudence which allows one to act reasonably in any situation, but particular kinds of prudence for the unique goods that reason seeks, just makes good sense of our own experiences. The fact that I know how to look after my own affairs does not guarantee that I know how to run a household, much less a nation. Surely we can all think of people who fit this description: "Bob is a great guy, but I'm not surprised to hear that he's in debt up to his ears." Such people may lack the proper managerial skills that one needs to keep a house in order, may not be able to plan a meal calendar, or may find paying their taxes more confusing than metaphysics, and so forth. Economics requires a specialized knowledge that can only come from experience coupled with study, and this is what is meant by economic prudence.

The second cardinal virtue, justice, is the central virtue of economic activity, and so we will devote considerable attention to it. We will leave out some aspects of Aquinas's theory of justice that are more applicable to political theory, focusing here on (1) right (*ST* II-II.57), (2) the nature of justice itself (*ST* II-II.58), and (3) the distinction between commutative and distributive justice (*ST* II-II.61). After outlining these aspects of Aquinas's theory of justice, we will discuss the three secondary virtues to justice that are relevant to economic philosophy (piety, gratitude, and liberality). First we must discuss "right," which is not to be confused with "rights" as we use that term today, a point that we will return to in chapter 7.

Unlike rights, which are something owed to me, or which I possess, in light of my humanity, right is an objective state that I seek to know and establish between myself and others. What is unique about justice in comparison to the other virtues is that justice seeks to establish a right relationship between people. For example, whereas temperance regards my control over my own

---

12. The Latin here is *oeconomica*, and I have changed this from "domestic" to "economic." The original translation has the benefit of making it clear that economics is rooted in the family, for the word "domestic" is derived from the Latin word for "house" (*domus*). But, given that we are making it clear in our study that economics studies the common good of the household, it seemed better to use the more literal translation.

bodily desires, justice regards what I owe to another person. *Ius* (pronounced "EE-uice"), which can be translated as "right" or "the just," is the term used to indicate the object of justice, and, since justice "denotes a kind of equality" (*ST* II-II.57.1), right is the objective determination of what we owe to one another. Thus, as Romanus Cessario explains, justice has "a purely objective foundation."[13] Further, right is divided into "natural" and "positive," for some things are equal to one another by nature, and others by agreement. For example, whereas it is by nature that someone returns what he borrows, it is by agreement that he pays the owner a certain amount of money should he lose or damage the object borrowed. It is important to recognize that, whereas in some cases what is fair or equal is fixed by nature, in other cases humans must themselves decide this. We will return to this point in chapter 5 when we consider the role of human authority in establishing what is just.

Second, in chapter 1 we discussed the definition of justice—namely, "a habit whereby a man renders to each one his due by a constant and perpetual will" (*ST* II-II.58.1). Justice requires that one be willing to treat others fairly in all circumstances, thereby setting aside one's personal interest. Further, since every deed affects one's community as a whole, in one sense justice is "general" or "legal" insofar as one's object is the common good as such; thus a police officer who courageously risks his life while on duty is performing an act of justice, as is a temperate woman who does not eat more than she should at a public feast because she recognizes that there is not enough to go around. In this case the moral object one pursues is directed by the will to an end that goes beyond the particular end of the virtue in question. While the police officer's object is to protect an innocent person, his intention is to use this act of courage as a means to promoting the common good, and this makes it an act of general or legal justice. More specifically, though, one speaks of "particular justice," or the virtue whereby the members of society are related to one another as persons. Justice, then, as a particular virtue, allows us to establish relationships of equality between one another, especially in regard to material goods. Again, we will return to general justice in chapter 5, for it belongs to politics to direct our actions to the common good.

Third, particular justice is divided into two types: commutative and distributive. Commutative justice governs the exchange of goods and seeks to establish equality between them; distributive justice governs the distribution of common goods and also factors in the character or contribution of the persons involved. In the case of two persons exchanging goods, commutative

13. Romanus Cessario, OP, *The Virtues, or The Examined Life* (New York: Continuum, 2002), 129.

justice demands that the value of these goods be equal; in the case of a community such as a family or state, distributive justice requires an assessment of the contributions made by each person. For example, imagine that the mayor is your neighbor and he needs to borrow six eggs so that he can make a pound cake. The next day, he gives you three eggs and claims that this is fair because he is much more important than you are. This is clearly unjust, for in the exchange of goods the character of the persons involved is irrelevant. This injustice demands restitution, which "is an act of commutative justice, occasioned by one person having what belongs to another, either with his consent, for instance on loan or deposit, or against his will, as in robbery or theft" (*ST* II-II.62.1). On the other hand, if the town treasurer is distributing surplus goods and gives more to the mayor than to you, this allotment seems fair given his greater contribution to the town's well-being (assuming that the mayor is truly working for the common good of the town rather than his own good).

Notice that distributive justice comes into play in households, in businesses, and in any other kind of community, and so is not solely a political issue (see *ST* II-II.61.1ad3). Part of economic theory is determining how much of the common store of goods a mother should give to each of her children, or a boss to his employees, and justice cannot be met in the abstract here, but requires the economic prudence by which the right can be established.[14] Now that we have a grasp of what justice itself is, we can turn to three secondary virtues—piety, gratitude, and liberality—that are important for economic theory.

As Aquinas states in *ST* II-II.80.1, to the virtue of justice are annexed secondary virtues that "fall short of the perfection" of justice in specific relationships such as with God (religion) and parents (piety). Further, some of these secondary virtues regard what Aquinas calls the "moral due" as distinct from "legal due" and determine what one owes another in terms of "the rectitude of virtue"; here again a distinction must be made: these virtues that regard the moral due are such that either (1) rectitude cannot be maintained without them (i.e., truth, gratitude, and revenge) or (2) they contribute to a greater degree of rectitude (i.e., friendship and liberality). Quoting Cessario again, who calls these secondary virtues to justice "virtues of civility," the first type are "indispensable for common life because they regulate those exchanges that make up human *communicatio*[,] . . . [whereas the second type are those] that contribute to living a happier experience of everyday life, or that simply

---

14. I am leaving out the virtue of equity here (see *ST* II-II.120) since this virtue comes into play as a result of politics. Thus, and again, we will return to it in chap. 5.

develop more pleasant living."[15] With these general points in mind, let us start with piety.

Aquinas begins his treatment of piety by observing that humans are naturally in the condition of debtors, for their being and sustenance are received from another. First and foremost, the human person is a debtor to God and thus must cultivate the virtue of religion. Secondly, "the principles of our being and government are our parents and our country, that have given us birth and nourishment" (*ST* II-II.101.1); as Aquinas goes on to include family in this list, piety turns out to be concerned with parents, family, and country. Religion and piety are coupled, then, as virtues by which one "pays back," to the extent possible, those who are responsible for one's life. While piety is primarily about honoring and serving one's parents, it can involve financial obligations as well. If our parents become poor, the virtue of piety demands that we support them (see *ST* II-II.101.2), and this is where piety is important for economics. I owe my material goods to my parents, if and when they are in need, for this is in part how I honor them for giving me the gift of life.

Next, gratitude or thankfulness is that part of justice having to do with benefactors. If I borrow eggs from my neighbor and say, "I will pay you back tomorrow," then failing to fulfill my promise is a violation of commutative justice and demands restitution. If, on the other hand, I borrow eggs from my neighbor and she says, "Don't worry about it, you really don't need to pay me back," then I do not owe her anything in the legal sense. However, I now have a "moral debt" that must be repaid through gratitude. While this could be met by giving her some of the cake I made, it could also be done by thanking her next time I see her or by some other token of appreciation. As Kenneth L. Schmitz says, "If a gift is to reach its maturity, true to type, then it needs to be received with gratitude and not compensated for by a return gift."[16] Further still, and similar to the case of impoverished parents, should my benefactor herself be in need later in life, I am morally obligated to help her. Interestingly, Aquinas points out that, in the sense that gratitude can lead to what Schmitz calls a "fresh act of giving,"[17] this should not be done right away, and we should even consider giving our benefactor more than he or she gave us; these are both ways of avoiding the impression that this is a mere exchange (see *ST* II-II.106.4, 6). For Aquinas, life is more about gift-giving than exchanging, and for the study of economics this is an important reminder to direct material goods toward such higher goods as family and friendship.

15. Cessario, *Virtues*, 147.
16. Kenneth L. Schmitz, *The Gift: Creation* (Milwaukee: Marquette University Press, 1982), 51.
17. Schmitz, *Gift*, 53.

The third and final virtue annexed to justice that is important for economic theory is liberality.[18] A good person neither "desires . . . [money] nor loves it" (*ST* II-II.117.5ad3) and thus is ready to part with worldly goods when a neighbor is in need of them. As such, a liberal giver is kept from the vices of covetousness and, to the extent that she gives of her worldly goods under the guidance of prudence, from prodigality. While liberality is an important virtue for one's own moral formation, it is distinct from justice (as well as piety and gratitude) in the sense that one can maintain a proper, albeit imperfect, relationship toward a neighbor without practicing it, "since justice pays another what is his whereas liberality gives another what is one's own" (*ST* II-II.117.5). And at the same time, since liberality is a part of justice, in another sense one does owe it to a neighbor to be a liberal giver. As we said regarding private property, when one gives the needy one's own, one is giving what has been entrusted to oneself for the purpose of meeting the needs of others. Thus, in one sense liberality goes beyond justice in that the starving man does not have a legal claim to my corn, and yet in a more important sense liberality is a part of justice in that I have a moral obligation to give him what he needs. If this were not true, he could not rightfully take the corn in the case of extreme need without being guilty of theft. We could say, then, that liberality gives what is mine in the legal sense of what has been entrusted to me, and, in the moral sense, gives what is his: in a restricted sense of justice, liberality goes beyond it; in the broadest sense, liberality is a part of that virtue by which we give to another what is due.

The next virtue on our list is magnificence, which is a secondary virtue to fortitude. Like liberality, magnificence depends upon a proper disregard for one's own possessions; yet magnificence goes beyond liberality in two respects: magnificence (1) requires that one possess an excess of material goods[19] and (2) is concerned with doing great things (*magna* = great things; *facere* = to do or make), and for this reason magnificence is a part of fortitude rather than of justice.[20] Aquinas's examples of situations calling for magnificence are weddings, providing oneself "with a suitable dwelling," acts that bring honor to individuals or to the state, and religious observances (see *ST* II-II.134.1–3). Yet one could also think of situations such as responses to natural disasters or

18. It is worth noting that Aquinas is hesitant to consider liberality a species of justice given that it seems to go beyond justice to give to another what is one's own. Yet he includes it in his list of virtues annexed to justice and also discusses it in the *Treatise on Justice*. Further, if it is not annexed to justice, under which virtue would it fall? Fortitude, perhaps?

19. Though see *ST* II-II.134.3ad4 for a qualification of this point.

20. On this point, see *ST* II-II.134.4.

dire poverty in which a magnificent woman would use her wealth to provide resources for the destitute.

The final two virtues in our study of economic philosophy are annexed to temperance: abstinence and sobriety. It may seem odd to include in a list of "economic" virtues ones that pertain to how much I eat and drink: What does how much I eat and drink have to do with what I owe my neighbor? We will return to this question, but let us begin with an explanation of each virtue in turn. We use the term "abstinence" to refer to the complete withdrawal from an object. For example, we say of teenagers who pledge not to have sex before marriage, or of Catholics who do not eat meat on Fridays in Lent, that they are "abstinent." While Aquinas recognizes that this is one use of this term, by abstinence he means the use of reason to regulate how much and what one eats. To practice the virtue of abstinence, then, is to bring one's appetite under the control of reason, so that we eat what is appropriate for health, for the good of our character, and with due regard to the members of our society (see *ST* II-II.146).

Similarly, sobriety is not about saying no to alcohol, but about regulating how much one drinks (see *ST* II-II.149). Not only does Aquinas point out that "no meat or drink, considered in itself, is unlawful" (*ST* II-II.149.3); he also claims that "the measured use [of intoxicants] is most profitable" (*ST* II-II.149.1). As with any moral virtue, sobriety is the mean between two extremes, one of excess (drunkenness) and one of deficiency (unnamed; see *ST* II-II.150.1ad1). A sober drinker, then, is one who drinks a moderate amount of alcohol given the circumstances of his or her own bodily constitution and the occasion in question. While two drinks may be vicious for a pregnant woman, it would not be so for grandma; while even one drink may not be appropriate before class, it may not be enough at a wedding reception.

What does all of this have to do with determining my economic duties? We pointed out that one of the considerations that reason must account for when regulating how much one eats is "due regard to the members of our society"; the same would apply to drink. While Aquinas does not provide any examples or elaborate upon his meaning here, he may have in mind the biblical concern with eating meat sacrificed to idols and St. Paul's teaching that, while the mature Christian need not worry about such things, at the same time doing so may scandalize a weak brother (see 1 Cor. 8). However, I do not think that Aquinas's point is limited to such cases, but is a broader point about how much we should eat in light of the needs of others. In every act we perform or fail to perform there is the aspect of how we affect our neighbors. If there are members in my community who will go without food or drink tonight and I eat gluttonously and drink excessively, I have acted viciously not only toward myself but also toward my neighbor. In this regard Aquinas favorably quotes St. Ambrose, who puts it rather starkly: "It is the hungry man's bread that you withhold" (*ST* II-II.66.7). Again, private property is entrusted to me as the means by which I help promote the good of my society as a whole. Given the limited resources of the world, abusing my body with excessive food and drink harms the members of my community whom I have failed to serve by serving myself too much.

4. Value

Background Reading: ST II-II.77–78

One aspect of American economic life is that the vast majority of our business transactions are done without negotiating the price, bartering, or haggling. Many of the goods we purchase state in no uncertain terms what their value is, stating things like "a $20 value" or "suggested retail price $20." Even when we buy an item for less than the stated price, we are given the impression that we are getting it for less than it is worth: "This weekend only! 20% off the sticker price!" We tell ourselves that we got a deal because this brand-new Chevy is worth $30,000 but we only paid $24,000. And, what about labor? Does my labor or that of another have an objective value? Again, in American life, we would get the same impression: How often do service companies tell us that replacing our brake pads, servicing our furnaces, cleaning our teeth, is worth so many dollars, but that they are willing to do it for less?

Isn't there something odd about all of this? Do material goods or labor really have an objective value? And, if so, is it just to pay for them less than they are worth when we get a "deal" or even a "steal"? Could we not say that the value of a good or service is entirely subjective, for it is nothing other than what I am willing to pay or to be paid? It is silly to think that such claims about the objective value are anything other than a marketing tool or a claim about the most the provider of the good or service anticipates getting. The just value is whatever the parties to the transaction agree upon, and for no other reason than that they agree. The same could be said about salaries. There's just something foolish about complaining that my salary is unfair, for I agreed to it. Is it possible for my salary to be unjust if I have freely signed the contract?

Such are the questions that come under the topic of value. And, this is an area in particular where we wish Aquinas would have written a sustained treatise.[21]

---

21. There are at least two other places where Aquinas discusses economic value and usury, in *De emptione et venditione ad tempus* (On buying and selling on credit) and in his *Commentary*

What we have instead are two brief questions on cheating (*ST* II-II.77) and usury (78). These do lay out a pretty clear theory of value with regard to the exchange of goods, but they say little about services and wages. In order to get at how he understands value, we will first outline the points he makes in these two questions. After doing this, we will attempt to outline what he means by value in the context of what we have learned about the ownership and use of property as well as the virtues of economic life. And, one other point to add: given that Aquinas's focus in his discussions of transactions is on commutative justice, we will not address here questions concerning distributive justice. In particular, when it comes to assessing just wages, we must factor in how the profit or surplus goods of the company should be distributed out to the various employees based on such factors as how hard they worked, the number of years they have served the company, and their particular needs. We will return to distributive justice in chapter 7 when we discuss what the Church calls a "living wage."

Both cheating and usury are discussed as vices in relation to the virtue of justice. Question 77 is divided into four articles, and we will discuss them in order, using the sale of a used car as an example. In article 1, Aquinas speaks of the "just price" as if it were fixed and objective, for he claims that it is unjust to sell an object for more than it is worth or to buy it for less than it is worth. Since commutative justice is about establishing equality between items exchanged, demanding more money for a material good than it is worth is to demand more than the right, the object of justice.

Imagine that your neighbor is selling you his 1986 Dodge Omni and you both want to be fair to each other but do not know how much a just price would be. You could both consult a used-car value guide or take the car to a mechanic who could estimate its value; such methods could be used to establish a just price, and to pay more or less than that would be unjust. Other things being equal, let us say that a 1986 Dodge Omni is worth $1,500, and thus to pay even $1,499 or $1,501 for it would be unjust. However, Aquinas goes on to say that the seller may demand more than an object is worth *in itself* if he "will suffer if he be without it" (*ST* II-II.77.1), and thus he may ask for what it is worth *to him*. In such a case, the buyer must compensate the seller for his loss by paying him how much it is worth to him. Imagine that my neighbor is in debt and must sell his beloved Omni, his only form of transportation. In such a case, the just price would be calculated by adding the worth of the car to the loss he would suffer from not having a vehicle at

---

on Aristotle's "Nicomachean Ethics," book 5. For the reader who wants to go beyond the introduction provided here, these are well worth careful study.

all; there would be nothing wrong with him saying, "I know it's only worth $1,500, but it's worth $2,000 to me given how much I rely on it."[22]

Note that the same does not apply to the needs of the buyer: the seller acts unjustly if he demands more than the just price in light of the buyer's need, and so your neighbor could not ask you for $2,000 because you are in need, only because he is. That being said, Aquinas adds that a man who gains more from the object than its just price "may, of his own accord, pay the seller something over and above: and this pertains to his honesty" (*ST* II-II.77.1). We should note that the term he uses here is *honestas* and that this is the same term he uses in the context of "moral debt." I would argue, then, that Aquinas is suggesting that the man who does not give the seller more in light of the benefit he receives thereby acts immorally and that this would be a failure to exercise the virtue of gratitude. We would probably assume that a 1986 Dodge Omni does not have too many years left in it and that both you and your neighbor expect that you will drive it into the ground within a year or two. If you are still driving it around in five years and you have put very little additional money into it for maintenance, it would be fitting that you find some appropriate means to thank him for it.[23]

In article 2 of question 77 Aquinas makes the uncontroversial claim that a faulty object cannot justly be sold for the same price as one in good condition and that a seller who knowingly does this commits sin. Similarly, a buyer who knows the seller to be ignorant of the object's true worth acts unjustly if he buys it for a lower price. Returning to the 1986 Dodge Omni, I will add details from my own experience with the wondrous Dodge Omni: when I was in college, my friend bought an Omni for $200. Even in 1995, as we found out when the steering wheel actually fell off as we were climbing the Siskiyou Summit, $200 was about what such a Detroit product was worth. However, I have come to discover that not all 1986 Dodge Omnis are alike and that Omni GLHS Shelbys are worth today upwards of $10,000. So if you go to buy the Omni from your neighbor and he tricks you into thinking it is one of the Shelbys when it is not, he defrauds you; on the other hand, if you know that it is a Shelby and he does not, you are morally obligated to reveal its true value to him.

---

22. This may sound like distributive justice since one of the factors is the situation of the people making the exchange. However, recall that distributive justice is about surplus goods that a community holds and that it must fairly give to its members based on some sort of merit. Such is not the case here.

23. This leads to an interesting question that Aquinas does not take up: If I buy an object for less than its conventional value because the seller needs to get rid of it, do I thereby take advantage of her? If she cannot ask me for more than its value because of my need, why can I offer her less because of her need? I encourage the reader to try to apply the principles we discuss here to this case.

More revealingly for our purposes, Aquinas makes two additional claims in his replies to objections:[24] the value of an object (1) depends on "conditions of time and place" (*ST* II-II.77.2ad2) such as scarcity of the object and needs of the community and (2) is determined by its usefulness for the purpose of human living. Having a cheap, reliable car may be of more value in the country, where an automobile is a necessity, and of less value in the city, where people might be more interested in owning a car as a luxury good. Let us return to the point in chapter 1 that ethics is both subjective and objective, for the same is true of value: value is objective in that human need is fixed by what is necessary for happiness; value is subjective in that in different times and places what contributes to happiness will differ. While all humans need food and drink, in some places these are easier to obtain than in others and therefore less valuable relative to other material goods.

While the main point in article 3 (that not revealing the hidden defects of an object is unjust) is not so much relevant to the subject of value, Aquinas's reply to the objection that this would require a merchant who is selling wheat to announce that other vendors are on their way is. Aquinas makes an interesting distinction here: while it is not unjust for a seller to ask for a higher price for his wheat than he would get when the other vendors show up, failing to announce that other vendors are on their way indicates a lack of perfect virtue. Aquinas does not elaborate on this, but perhaps we could say that there is a lack of liberality here, for the seller does not give what is his (the high price) to the buyer. Whatever virtue is required here, a point we should take from this is that, again, the value of an object to some extent reflects market conditions, for wheat is worth more when it is scarce, and less when it is abundant.

Finally, article 4 provides a nice transition to the topic of *ST* II-II.78: usury. Here Aquinas is concerned with the justice of making a profit from buying and selling, as distinct from transacting with another for mutual need of the objects in question. It is one thing for my neighbor to sell his car to me because he has need of other goods, and another for him to buy a car at a low price and then try to sell it to me for a profit. While Aquinas adheres to the traditional view that it is unnatural to trade for a profit given its connection with greed, he modifies this in an important way: "Nothing prevents gain from being directed to some necessary or even virtuous end, and thus trading becomes lawful. Thus, for instance, a man may intend the moderate gain which he seeks to acquire by trading for the upkeep of his household, or

---

24. This should serve as a reminder that the replies and objections are not to be ignored. Many a reader of Aquinas makes this mistake.

for the assistance of the needy: or again, a man may take to trade for some public advantage, for instance, lest his country lack the necessaries of life, and seek gain, not as an end, but as payment for his labor" (*ST* II-II.77.4). While a businessman must still sell things for the just price—for a good end does not justify a bad means—there is nothing unjust about buying objects where they are in abundance, transporting them to a place where they are in scarce supply, and charging a higher price in exchange for one's labor and costs.[25] That being said, we must insist that this activity be directed to good ends such as supporting one's family or the poor. Money cannot be an end, and we cannot call someone "well-off" who makes a lot of money but does not use it morally.

One final point before moving to question 78: again, unfortunately Aquinas does not spend much time addressing the value of labor. We will extrapolate principles in our summary, but we should point out here that his recognition that one can charge for his labor in order to support his household or serve the poor indicates that the just price reflects the value of the object plus the value of the labor understood as the means by which one provides for one's family.

Question 78 takes up the topic of usury, and, once again, Aquinas defends the ancient philosophical as well as biblical prohibition against making money off of money: "Money . . . was invented chiefly for the purpose of exchange: and consequently the proper and principal use of money is its consumption or alienation whereby it is sunk in exchange. Hence it is by its very nature unlawful to take payment for the use of money lent, which payment is known as usury" (*ST* II-II.78.1). Aquinas's analogy could make for a memorable scene in a comedy: imagine John buys a bottle of wine for $10 on credit from Tommy; when he returns to Tommy's place the next day, Tommy asks him if he drank the wine: "Delicious. What a night last night!" exclaims John. "Well then," pronounces Tommy, "you owe me $10 for the wine, and $5 for the good time." To sell wine is to sell the use of it, and to demand that someone pay for both the ownership and the use of such things is to demand payment twice, a manifest injustice. Such is the case with money, for it was invented for the sake of use, and thus to loan money, and then charge for its use, is to demand payment twice.

While usury is always wrong, Aquinas does return to the point he made earlier regarding the just price: recall that, whereas the seller cannot charge

---

25. While Aquinas does not completely repudiate making a profit when one has in no way improved the object in question, nor transported it, etc., an interesting question is whether activities like scalping are morally acceptable. Since the scalper does not seem to do anything other than artificially make tickets scarce and hoard tickets with the aim of preventing others from buying them at the face value, I would argue that his is an immoral trade.

extra because of the buyer's need, he can charge extra for his own loss. In the case of making a loan, it is legitimate for the lender to charge "for compensation for the loss he incurs of something he ought to have" (*ST* II-II.78.2ad1). Additionally, and as stated before in regard to benefits from an object purchased, the borrower may incur a moral debt of gratitude and in such a case could give the lender additional money or some other good as a token of appreciation rather than as a contractual return.

When you go to buy your neighbor's 1986 Dodge Omni, perhaps you do not have the cash up front. Another neighbor does have the cash and is willing to loan it to you, but this means (1) he cannot buy that dirt bike he just spotted for sale across town and (2) due to inflation, his money will be worth less in six months than it is now.[26] It is perfectly just for him to ask for $2,200, or whatever the opportunity lost is worth added to inflation. Additionally, you might be morally obligated to give him something extra for the loan as a sign of gratitude, whether it be giving him rides in your Omni, buying him a gift card, or some other token of appreciation.

There is much more we could say about usury (Aquinas even wrote a separate treatise on the topic), though this is sufficient for our purposes; we can conclude by summarizing what we have learned about value in general. And, it is worth mentioning a point about the relationship between value and the virtues. In all of this it hopefully becomes clear to us why the simple desire to be just is not enough. The complex economic situations we find ourselves in require not only virtues like justice and liberality, whereby we will the good of another, but also the economic prudence by which we determine the means to this laudable end. As Ernest Bartell explains, "The true price for St. Thomas, because it accurately expresses value, should be consistent with the whole hierarchy of ends which economic goods serve: individual material needs, common or social needs, the virtuous life and ultimately the man's own supernatural end. It is this scale of values that economic prudence should bring to the market."[27]

At the end of our discussion on private property (§2 of this chapter, above) we briefly mentioned the passage in *ST* II-II.66.7 where Aquinas claims that it is lawful to take another's property in a case of need. In that context, he says,

> according to the natural order established by Divine Providence, inferior things are ordained for the purpose of succoring man's needs by their means. Wherefore the division and appropriation of things which are based on human law, do

---

26. Admittedly, inflation is not a reality that Aquinas would have had to address, but it is reasonable, based on his principles, to include it in the loss from the loan.

27. Ernest Bartell, "Value, Price, and St. Thomas," *Thomist* 25 (1962): 350.

not preclude the fact that man's needs have to be remedied by means of these very things. Hence whatever certain people have in superabundance is due, by natural law, to the purpose of succoring the poor. For this reason Ambrose says, and his words are embodied in the Decretals (Dist. xlvii, can. Sicut ii): "It is the hungry man's bread that you withhold, the naked man's cloak that you store away, the money that you bury in the earth is the price of the poor man's ransom and freedom."

This nicely summarizes Aquinas's teaching on value. Whereas we tend to treat the value of an object as entirely subjective, letting the individual desires of buyers and sellers dictate the market price, Aquinas focuses on need. The goods of the world are bought and sold for the purpose of meeting human needs, and this is to say that virtue, whereby such goods are rightly used in order to meet the needs of daily life, is the measure of value. Put differently, the value of an object must always be rooted in human nature, in a proper understanding of the end or purpose of human existence. As Mary Hirschfeld says, "Thomas repeatedly teaches that material goods are of value only insofar as they are in service of human virtue."[28]

Christopher A. Franks explains Aquinas's understanding of value by means of the distinction between exchange value and use value: whereas exchange value takes individual desires and market forces as unquestionable givens, use value is "rooted in qualities of things that are antecedent to human desires."[29] Put differently, use value reflects an object's fittingness for "the pursuit of virtue."[30] While Franks's first formulation taken out of context suggests a false dichotomy between human desire and the human good, the second formulation makes the important connection to virtue: the value of an object must always be rooted in human nature, in a proper understanding of the end of human existence. This means that an exchange of objects is not necessarily simply because the two parties agreed to the terms or because the two objects have the same market value. While both of these are important factors, commutative justice is not obtained in such a case unless either the values assigned to the objects reflect how they "satisfy the needs of life" or, if a profit is obtained by either party, the profit is directed to some good end such as "for the assistance of the needy." A similar point could be made with regard to distributive justice, liberality, and magnificence, for determining what one owes to another requires a knowledge of how the worldly goods

28. Hirschfeld, "Standard of Living and Economic Virtue," 63.
29. Christopher A. Franks, *He Became Poor: The Poverty of Christ and Aquinas's Economic Teachings* (Grand Rapids: Eerdmans, 2009), 51.
30. Franks, *He Became Poor*, 95.

at one's disposal can be used to meet the needs of others as fellow seekers of the human good, happiness. For example, if a virtuous woman discovers that a poor man has great need for an object that she herself possesses, and if she realizes that she has little need for the object in question, she readily gives it to him because she recognizes that its use value is greater for him than it is for her. Based upon these brief reflections on value and of what virtue demands regarding worldly goods, St. Basil the Great's expression "the burden of riches" makes more sense: the more one possesses, the more time and mental energy one must devote to meeting the material needs of others.

Let us conclude this chapter on economic philosophy by pointing out that, unlike the market-forces account of value, this teaching allows us to articulate what is wrong with putting a value on the use of a woman's body, on body parts, or on human beings for sale on the black market, and so forth. A perverse society will surely assign relative values to sex, human organs, and even human beings, but economics and we as economic agents must insist on a proper moral vision in the assessment of value. Nothing in this world is worth more than a human soul, and we should value material goods in such a way that we, unlike Esau, do not sell our soul for a mess of pottage.

4

The Goods of the Earth
and Perfect Happiness
(Economic Theology)

The earth is the LORD's and the fulness thereof,
  the world and those who dwell therein;
for he has founded it upon the seas,
  and established it upon the rivers.
Who shall ascend the hill of the LORD?
  And who shall stand in his holy place?
He who has clean hands and a pure heart,
  who does not lift up his soul to what is false,
  and does not swear deceitfully.

—Psalm 24:1–4

Help a poor man for the commandment's sake,
  and because of his need do not send him away empty.
Lose your silver for the sake of a brother or a friend,
  and do not let it rust under a stone and be lost.
Lay up your treasure according to the commandments
  of the Most High,
  and it will profit you more than gold.
Store up almsgiving in your treasury,
  and it will rescue you from all affliction;

more than a mighty shield and more than a heavy spear,
it will fight on your behalf against your enemy.

—Sirach 29:9–13

1. Introduction

Economic philosophy teaches us that the goods of this world are valuable only insofar as they can promote human happiness. My happiness in this world may depend upon the possession of material goods, but more importantly it depends upon their right use as determined by virtue. This humbling recognition that the goods of this world are given to me so that I may more readily serve family and neighbor is rooted in an even deeper teaching of economic theology. My very life itself and my baptism into eternal life are gifts, for to be is to be good, and the goodness that is my being is a gratuitous participation in God's own "I AM" and in the passion of his Christ. To bring these lofty metaphysical pronouncements down to earth, let us use the martyrdom of St. Maximilian Kolbe as an example of what it means to live life as a gift.

Maximilian Kolbe was a Polish priest who dedicated the end of his life to sheltering refugees, hiding as many as two thousand Jews from the Nazis. In 1941 his monastery (which he was using as a refugee camp and hiding place) was closed down, and he was sent to prison, eventually ending up in Auschwitz. Throughout the horrible ordeal of watching his fellow inmates die, and even though he himself was repeatedly beaten by the guards, he provided solace as he could, especially through prayer. As if this were not enough, Kolbe took the place of a fellow prisoner, a husband and father, who had been selected out to be starved to death in an underground bunker. Kolbe and nine other men descended into the bunker, where he led them in prayer to the end of their lives, and then he himself was killed by lethal injection. In all of this, St. Maximilian Kolbe modeled a life rooted in the understanding that both life itself and life in Christ are gifts.

Whereas acquired virtue demands on occasion that we give of what is ours to those in need, it does not ask us to sacrifice our own bodily well-being, much less our lives. But grace perfects nature. It is one thing to say that my goods are for my community, quite another to say that my life itself is for my Savior and that my happiness was made possible by his death on the cross. Jesus Christ, fully God and fully Man, is the model of a life lived well, and he shows his greatness by laying down his life for our sins, not because we are worthy but because he is Love. Hence, "of all virtuous acts martyrdom is the greatest proof of the perfection of charity" (*ST* II-II.124.3).

The martyrs are witnesses to true justice, gratitude, liberality, and so forth by being true lovers: "Greater love has no man than this, that a man lay down his life for his friends" (John 15:13). The gospel message of love is manifest in those who, upon conversion, give away all of their material goods, thus liberating themselves from worldly cares. Alternatively, there is a host of saints like Katherine Drexel and Nicholas of Cusa who put their worldly goods at the disposal of the poor, using their wealth to meet the needs of the dispossessed.

Economic theology teaches us how to live out the Beatitudes, or how to direct the acquired and infused virtues, gifts, and fruits to the proper use of material goods so that we may receive perfect happiness. In all of this, let us remember Christ's exhortation: "Lay up for yourselves treasures in heaven, where neither moth nor rust consumes and where thieves do not break in and steal" (Matt. 6:20). This chapter is outlined as follows: (1) loving God by loving neighbor as self; (2) living the Beatitudes: the infused virtues, gifts, and fruits in economic life; and (3) the theological meaning of value.

2. Loving God by Loving Neighbor as Self

Background Reading: ST II-II.25–27, 31.2–3, 32.6, 8, 9, 44.7

Economic theology, like moral as well as political theology, insists upon a proper ordering of charity: charity is first and foremost love for God. Only because of this love are we able to love our neighbor as ourselves, for only then do we love ourselves as God loves us. It is all too easy for us to get caught up in doing good things that God wants us to do but never doing them out of love: it is one thing to pursue the moral object that God commands, quite another to have love for God as our end. We must repeat to ourselves again and again the words of St. Paul: "If I give away all I have, and if I deliver my body to be burned, but have not love, I gain nothing" (1 Cor. 13:3).[1] Not only does loving God make true love for neighbor possible; it also enjoins and demands it, for we cannot love God if we do not love our neighbor.

---

1. This is even true in prayer: one can pray the Rosary, attend daily Mass, and so forth as acts of obedience and fail to couple them with love. As St. Benedict says, "We must know that God regards our purity of heart and tears of compunction, not our many words. Prayer should therefore be short and pure, unless perhaps it is prolonged under the inspiration of divine grace." *Rule of St. Benedict* 20.3–4, in *The Rule of St. Benedict in English*, trans. Timothy Fry, OSB (Collegeville, MN: Liturgical Press, 1981), 48.

On the other hand, the way that we love our neighbor in God is by rooting ourselves in communities that give shape to the manner in which we manifest God's love. We are not isolated individuals called to random acts of love; rather, we are relational beings situated in complex relationships with family, friends, parishioners, monastics, clergy, citizens, and so forth. Let us work through some key passages from Aquinas on love for neighbor in order to make all of this clearer. After doing so, we will outline a basic framework for what it means to love neighbor as self in the context of community.

First, in *ST* II-II.25 Aquinas makes it clear that we love God and neighbor by one and the same act of charity, for "what we ought to love in our neighbor is that he may be in God" (25.1). In article 4 he explains that love for God allows us to love ourselves properly, for friendship with God extends to "the things of God such as ourselves," and also to sinners (article 6), enemies (articles 8–9), angels (article 10), and even demons (article 11).[2]

Second, while love for God and neighbor belong to the same act, there is an order of love, and this is the topic of question 26. To speak of an order of love is to recognize a prioritizing or ranking of the various objects of our love. Most obviously, God is to be loved first and foremost, "for He is loved as the cause of happiness, whereas our neighbor is loved as receiving together with us a share of happiness from Him" (article 2). After love of God is love of self, and then love of neighbor.

It may seem odd to us that Christian life, despite its call to serve others and its emulation of Jesus Christ as one who laid down his life, still prioritizes self-love over love for others. But let us explain this by way of an example: imagine a close friend of yours comes to you one day and asks, "Would you do something for me?" to which you reply, "Of course, anything." "Look," he responds, "I'm in a bad way. I need you to help me steal my neighbor's 1986 Dodge Omni." How would you respond? If you refuse to serve as his accomplice, could he rightfully say that you do not love him enough?

Aquinas's point here is that true love is never compatible with sin and that, in loving ourselves more than our neighbor, we are putting our spiritual good over the good of friendship. As Jean Porter puts it, "The individual should not let anything, including concern for another's spiritual well-being, lead him or her to destroy through sin the friendship that he or she has with God."[3] Loving ourselves properly by clinging to God above all else is the condition for true friendship. True friendship demands you to say, "Friend, I love you

---

2. Love demons? Read articles 6 and 11: Aquinas's reasoning is a great example of how one applies the metaphysical principles we discussed in chap. 1 (§2).

3. Jean Porter, "*De Ordine Caritate*: Charity, Friendship, and Justice in Aquinas' *Summa Theologiae*," *Thomist* 53.2 (1989): 207.

so much that I would *never* steal for you." By putting our own good before that of others, we are actually being better friends, for friends try to outdo one another in performing virtuous acts that benefit others.

That being said, it would seem that what Maximilian Kolbe did is incompatible with the order of love: How could one lay down his life for a friend if he is supposed to love himself more than a friend? More generally, it would seem that acts of selfless giving, of liberality, charity, and the like, are incompatible with the order of love. Aquinas introduces a helpful distinction here: humans are both spiritual and bodily creatures, and to truly love ourselves is to love what is spiritual in us for its own sake and to love what is bodily as a means to the end of spiritual love (article 5). Thus, the order of love is (1) God, (2) myself as a spiritual being, (3) neighbor, (4) myself as a bodily being.

If the same friend has gotten mixed up in drug use and is running with a dangerous group of people, loving him may require you to put his spiritual welfare above your own bodily well-being. While love never demands forfeiting my salvation, it may demand forfeiting my possessions, including my earthly life itself. Again, St. Maximilian Kolbe is such a powerful witness of Christian living because he gave up not just his material goods but his very bodily existence; by loving his fellow inmates more than his own body, he simultaneously showed how much he loved himself as a child of God.

The next question we should ask in thinking through the order of love is "Who is my neighbor?" While the story of the good Samaritan helps us to understand the universal call to love all people, it also points to the fact that love of neighbor is concrete and particular: *this* Samaritan was on the road between Jerusalem and Jericho, came across *this* victim of robbers, brought him to *this* inn, and so forth. Love of neighbor is not some vague desire for the well-being of the human race, but love for the particular people whom I encounter on the journey that is my life. Notice that Christ does not command us to love "mankind" but to love "our neighbor." I can claim to love mankind and yet hate my neighbor's guts. Loving our neighbor is difficult indeed, for our neighbor has poor personal hygiene, or gets under our skin, or is even a vicious human being.[4]

As the saying goes, "charity begins at home," and it can often be easier to love a stranger than that brother who is always leaving toothpaste all over the sink, that uncle who always shoots his mouth off about politics, or that

---

4. This was one among many lessons I have learned from the marvelous novels of Fyodor Dostoevsky. I cannot recommend his works enough, especially *Crime and Punishment* and *The Brothers Karamazov*. If five-hundred-page books from Russian authors are not to your liking, the same point is made by Linus van Pelt of *Peanuts* fame: "I love mankind . . . it's people I can't stand!" (November 12, 1959).

manipulative and miserly cousin. Acknowledging that we should love the
sinner and hate the sin (see *ST* II-II.26.7ad1), love of neighbor should be
stronger for those who are nearest to us (article 6). We cannot choose our
family, and often not our neighbor, either. While we might not be surrounded
by the most virtuous people in the world, they are nearest to us and thus the
most direct objects of our love: "It follows from the very words, 'Thou shalt
love thy neighbor' that those who are nearer to us are to be loved more" (*ST*
II-II.44.8ad3). Let us pause to consider what a challenge this teaching is.

When I moved to Latrobe, Pennsylvania, in 2007, the first neighbors I met
were a young couple with a baby girl. The father (who was not married to
the mother) was on house arrest; the mother was swearing like a sailor and
smoking a cigarette with baby on hip. They were crude and untrustworthy,
and it was no surprise when they were both arrested for shoplifting six months
later. Yet I eventually reproached myself for my reaction to meeting them.
My first thought was to make them go away: "What were we thinking when
we moved here? We've got to get rid of these people!" It wasn't long before
I saw my own hypocrisy: "Look at me, fancying myself the good Christian
moving into the neighborhood, and I begin by mentally kicking those in need
of spiritual guidance out of the neighborhood; from me they did not get the
greeting of Christ but the condemnation of the Pharisee."

The call to love is a challenge when we recognize the hard truth that seeing
Christ in all people truly means *all* people, especially those whom God brings
before us as companions on the way. So, while we must love all people equally
insofar as "we wish them all one same generic good, namely everlasting happiness" (*ST* II-II.31.7ad1), as shown at the very least by praying for the salvation
of our fellow Christians and also for unbelievers (see *ST* II-II.31.2ad1), our
love is to be ordered properly, from nearest to farthest away. More particularly, after love of God (who is nearer to us than we are to ourselves) and love
of my own soul, Aquinas orders love of neighbor as follows: (1) parents,[5]
(2) spouse, (3) children, (4) other members of the family, (5) other members
of my community. That being said, it is important to recognize that loving
one person more than another does not always and everywhere mean doing
more good for that person.

Imagine that my neighbor has struck it rich and is now in a position to
give away his 1986 Dodge Omni. Though he loves me more than he loves a
stranger, it may be appropriate for him to give it away to a complete stranger
who is more in need of it than I am (see *ST* II-II.31.3). While Aquinas is in-

---

5. In article 10, Aquinas claims we should love our fathers more than our mothers. We will
take up the flawed biology he relies upon in his reasoning in chap. 7 (§2).

sistent that in such matters "it is impossible to lay down a general rule" (*ST* II-II.31.3ad3), in *ST* II-II.31.3 he briefly mentions intriguing questions (that we will not take up here) such as whether one ought to take another person's property in order to help someone in need or whether one should abandon one's parents or one's children if forced to choose between them.

The point that I should love those nearer to me more than those further from me needs to be coupled with the awareness that beneficence (*ST* II-II.31) and almsgiving (*ST* II-II.32) may require special attention upon those who are further when those who are nearer are less in need. We will return to the particular role of beneficence and almsgiving in economic life in the next section. Here let us briefly conclude with an attempt to spell out in a bit more detail the last order of love, love of other members of my community.

We must first acknowledge that we can only speak in generalities here. In specific circumstances there will be not only a different order of bestowing benefits on others but even a different order of love. For example, Aquinas points out that on the field of battle one loves a fellow soldier more than one loves parents, and more generally, "in matters where we are free to do as we choose," we love friends more than even our own family members. That being said, Aquinas insists that the stability of our relationship with those united by blood necessitates a love for them that is naturally more closely joined to our love for ourselves. Even in those cases where love for friend is greater than love for family members, "we are more beholden to [kin] in the providing of necessaries" (*ST* II-II.26.8ad1).

Following the principle we have established of prioritizing the nearer over the further insofar as we must stand ready to benefit them, the first type of "other" would be friends; second would come immediate neighbors who share a common living place with me. These are the people who, like it or not, I see daily and not as a matter of choice; they are physically nearest to me, and thus I have an obligation to act charitably toward them. Third would be those who are in some form of immediate association with me, such as fellow parishioners, clerics, religious; students, teachers, administrators; citizens of or workers for the same local government. These are the people who, while I may not know them all personally, are friends of friends, or at least sharers in the common spaces of daily life such as the church, library, park, school, post office, and municipal building. Fourth would be those who are joined together as members of the same region, from a county or diocese up to a political state. These people are followed by fellow citizens and leaders in my nation or, in the case of the Church, bishops' conference or rite. Fifth and finally comes love of all peoples, first all those joined together under the bishop of Rome (and especially the bishop of Rome himself), and then unbelievers.

Notice that in each of these categories are included two types of organization: secular/political and spiritual/religious. How are we to prioritize these? In general the spiritual bonds that unite us in the Body of Christ are more central to who we are as God's children, and so love of fellow parishioners; of members of the diocese, bishops' conference, or rite; up to love of fellow Catholics should be stronger than love of next-door neighbors, fellow townspeople, citizens of the same state or nation, and humans generally. That being said, again, it is impossible to make general rules for such matters that will meet every particular case. Further, there is the additional difficulty for Catholics who do not attend the nearest geographical parish, because they attend either a monastic liturgy, Mass at another church, the Extraordinary Form of the Mass, or liturgy in another rite. In all of this Aquinas reminds us of the need for prudence and for discerning how the Holy Spirit is calling us to make manifest the God who is Love.

3. Living the Beatitudes: The Infused Virtues, Gifts, and Fruits in Economic Life

Background Reading: ST II-II.30, 52, 87, 106, 124, 146, 147

Now that we have spelled out how the supernatural virtue of charity is to be directed to God, self, and neighbor, we need to specify the economic acts that it induces us to perform. Just as general justice does not so much perform its own actions as direct the acts of the other virtues to the common good, in one sense charity does not perform specific actions but directs acts of liberality, magnificence, and the like to the greater glory of God. As the form of the virtues, charity does not involve one in unique acts in regard to neighbor so much as it provides a deeper motive for performing them. It is one thing to give to another because she is owed this or because I do not love money, quite another because she is a child of God. In this sense, the just and liberal giver to whom charity is added performs the same actions as she did prior to receiving the supernatural virtue of charity. She pursues the same moral objects, though she wills a deeper end than does the just and liberal person.

Further, just as particular justice comes into play in situations involving certain kinds of goods, so too does charity have its own acts, and even a secondary virtue of its own, mercy, that particularize its activity.[6] We will start with the more immediate acts that charity calls for—namely, beneficence and almsgiving. After discussing these, we will turn to the infused virtues

---

6. On the distinction between general or legal and particular justice, see chap. 3 (§3).

operating under the guidance of charity—namely, (1) infused economic prudence, (2) justice, (3) religion, (4) liberality, (5) infused fortitude in the act of martyrdom, (6) magnificence, (7) temperance, and (8) abstinence. We will conclude with a discussion of the gifts pertinent to economic theology—namely, knowledge, wisdom, counsel, piety, and fortitude—and also the general role of the fruits in economic life.

Before working through these virtues, it is worth addressing a question that the attentive reader might ask: Given that, as we saw in chapter 2 (§3), charity is a virtue found only in the Christian who is free from mortal sin, can only Christians practice beneficence, mercy, and almsgiving? If so, this seems wrong: surely any person with a good heart can extend beneficence or friendship to strangers, have mercy on others, and give alms to the poor.

Yes, only Christians in the state of grace can practice these virtues, and yet that does not mean that the one who possesses the acquired virtues cannot perform the same kinds of actions that Christians would perform. The difference, though, is that such a person cannot have the requisite virtue. It is one thing to feel pity for a homeless woman, quite another to bring this passion under the guidance of God's will. Further, recall that one can perform just acts without being just, for even the unjust person will often do what is just out of fear of getting caught for doing otherwise.[7] As Aquinas says in regard to almsgiving: "Almsgiving can be materially [i.e., one can perform the moral action] without charity, but to give alms formally, i.e. for God's sake, with delight and readiness, and altogether as one ought, is not possible without charity" (*ST* II-II.32.1ad1). Again, Aquinas is using the distinction between moral object and end here, for one need not have the virtue of charity to have the object of beneficent action, though one cannot perform beneficent actions virtuously without having as one's end love of God and neighbor as self. As Stephen Pope comments, "Love for the poor involves not simply the donation of money or material goods but also and more importantly the love of friendship—the deeper giving of self that involves affective union and communication as well as benevolence."[8] With this distinction in mind, let us turn now to charity itself.

First, charity performs two kinds of unique acts in economic life—namely, acts of beneficence and almsgiving. Beneficence is an external act of charity whereby one gives out of friendship to another in view of "the general aspect of good" rather than simply giving what is owed or giving out of consideration

---

7. See chap. 1 (§5) on the difference between *doing* the good and *being* good.

8. Stephen Pope, "Aquinas on Almsgiving, Justice and Charity: An Interpretation and Reassessment," *Heythrop Journal* 32.2 (1991): 168.

of one's own detachment from worldly goods (*ST* II-II.31.1). Whereas justice looks to repay debt, beneficence looks to bring about good for others simply because they are friends. While we could redescribe this as repaying the debt one owes to God, it would be better to think of acts of beneficence as rooted in one's desire to be like God, the bestower of gifts.

Imagine that you are in Philadelphia on vacation, taking in the great sites where our nation was born. As you go to buy your lunch from a street vendor, a homeless man approaches you and asks for money. Recognizing that money might do this man more harm than good (for he might spend it on drugs), you buy him a meal instead. As a Christian, you could explain to him that you are doing this because of your debt to God: "God has done so much for me, and so I am giving him back what was really not mine to begin with." This is fine as far as it goes, though it does not go far enough. First, what would you say if the man says, "Well, thanks for nothing, then. You are just using me to pay back God." Notice that your debt-based understanding does not personalize your act; you did not seem to care about this man and his suffering, but rather about your own salvation. This should remind us of imperfect contrition, when we feel sorry for what we have done not because it was wrong but because God sees everything. Second, such a motive does not connect us with the God who is Love, the God who gave himself as gift and sacrificial offering for us, out of love for each one of us individually. Beneficence is about befriending others as God has befriended us, seeking the good of another simply because he or she is a fellow human being.

In all of this, though, we must recall the order of love: we cannot help all people, and so we must show beneficence to others within our means. If you were to buy this homeless man his lunch, and then come home penniless to your starving wife and children, this would be unjust and uncharitable. Again, either human reason or the Divine rule must guide every action, and it is contrary to both to meet the need of the stranger in the marketplace while failing to meet the needs of those under one's own roof. That being said, our formation in the virtues and gifts of the Holy Spirit will allow us to recognize those unique circumstances in which our greater love for God necessitates prioritizing beneficence toward strangers. As Aquinas puts it, "We ought to be most beneficent towards those who are most closely connected with us. . . . [And] yet this may vary according to the various requirements of time, place, or matter in hand: because in certain cases one ought, for instance, to succor a stranger, in extreme necessity, rather than one's own father, if he is not in such urgent need" (*ST* II-II.31.3).

While beneficence is a direct act of charity, almsgiving is an act of mercy, and so we must discuss the virtue of mercy before discussing almsgiving.

Charity is unique among the three supernatural virtues in that it has a secondary virtue annexed to it, mercy. Mercy, which is the subject of question 30, is not so much about what actions one performs as it is about an interior state, a feeling of pity for the distress of another. This may sound to us like sympathy, and it is hard to see why it would be a virtue: Is not feeling pity at the distress of another an involuntary reaction?

The whole art of storytelling, be it in comic books, high literature, or movies, depends upon our ability to connect ourselves with the good or bad fortune of the characters. The storyteller can assume that if she can make her characters relatable to us, we will emotionally share in their triumphs and failures. Further, feeling such pity seems to be nothing more than self-interest: we feel for these people because we imagine such tragedies befalling ourselves. Why do we cringe when we watch the latest video of a skateboarder's mishap, a texter walking into a pole, or an innocent bystander being hit in the head by an errant Frisbee? We "feel their pain" as if it happened to us; it is not them we feel bad for, but ourselves as imagined sufferers of such pains. What is virtuous in all of this?

It is one thing to have an emotional response, quite another to bring that passion under the guidance of reason. Recall that passions in themselves are neither morally good nor bad (chap. 1, §4). Mercy is not simply feeling pity, but "a movement of the intellective appetite [or will], inasmuch as one person's evil is displeasing to another" (ST II-II.30.3), a movement that, in turn, regulates the passion. When we have charity in our hearts, compelling us to love all people as ourselves, we have formed in our faculty of will the habit of grieving with those in distress and wanting for them the good that we want for ourselves. Mercy is this virtue by which the Christian is united in will with all of God's children. Aquinas even goes so far as to say that, while charity is the greatest human virtue insofar as it unites us to God, "the sum total of the Christian religion consists in mercy, as regards external works" (ST II-II.30.4ad2).[9] It seems odd for Aquinas to call mercy an "external work," for thus far it seems that mercy is about the internal state of charity-directed pity. Yet it is one thing to pity another and leave it at that, quite another "to succor him if we can" (ST II-II.30.1). Mercy is not simply the charitable feeling of pity but also the desire to ameliorate the suffering of others. Thus, mercy directs the external act of almsgiving as the means by which charity is shown to neighbor.

Works of mercy are of two kinds, corporal and spiritual. The traditional works of corporal mercy, with the exception of burying the dead (which can

9. Further still, mercy, and not charity, is actually the greatest virtue in itself: God, who is above all, most shows his greatness by his mercy (see ST II-II.30.4).

be found in the book of Tobit), are listed explicitly by Christ in Matthew 25:34–40 as imperatives for those who shall enter the kingdom of heaven. The spiritual works of mercy are not directly found in any one biblical source but may be inferred from various passages. Given the centrality of the works of mercy to the Christian life, it may surprise the reader that Aquinas does not discuss them in the question on mercy. Again, for Aquinas mercy is first and foremost an interior disposition, and in *ST* II-II.32 we discover that the merciful's desire to help those who are suffering gives rise to a specific external act, almsgiving: "Almsgiving is an act of charity through the medium of mercy" (*ST* II-II.32.1).

Given that our focus is on economic actions, let us list the corporal acts of mercy: (1) feeding the poor, (2) giving drink to the thirsty, (3) clothing the naked, (4) harboring the harborless, (5) visiting the sick, (6) ransoming the captive, (7) burying the dead. And notice that these are not optional (see article 5). Aquinas goes so far as to argue that "in a case of extreme necessity, . . . it would be lawful . . . to commit a theft in order to give an alms" (*ST* II-II.32.8ad1).[10] Outside of such extreme cases, and following the prudential teaching we outlined in the last section regarding the order of love, we must recognize that we cannot help all people all the time and that we must help those under our care before we help the stranger (see articles 6 and 9). And yet, even when we meet these basic needs, surely many of us will have surplus left over. As in the case of the widow in Luke 21, this surplus may be very small, and we must bear in mind the lesson of that story: "The widow who gave less in quantity, gave more in proportion; and thus we gather that the fervor of her charity, whence corporal almsdeeds derive their spiritual efficacy, was greater" (*ST* II-II.32.4ad3).[11] We must overcome a natural selfishness that we probably find within ourselves on those rare occasions when we have more money than we need: rather than ask ourselves, "Who needs this money?" we instead ask, "What can I buy?" Our first thought in regard to our surplus is how to pamper ourselves rather than how to help those who go without even the necessities of life. And we may excuse ourselves by saying that we cannot give of our surplus, for we may need it in the future: "I can't give away any of the 10 pairs of shoes in my closet, for I might need them all one day."[12] Yet we must remember Christ's command "not [to] be anxious about

10. The patient reader may still be thinking about the promise in chapter 1 to discuss Robin Hood, which we will do in chap. 5.

11. I have changed the translation of *eleemosyna* from "almsdeeds" to "almsgiving" given that this is the more common contemporary term.

12. And, yes, I reproach myself here. A further issue is how one should look at contemporary practices such as saving for retirement. Does this go against Christ's command? I leave

tomorrow" (Matt. 6:34), for this attitude usually stems from a desire to rely upon ourselves rather than God, to trust in our own prudence rather than in his providence. Almsgiving combats this tendency to hoard up our earthly goods rather than merit those spiritual goods waiting for the lover of God and neighbor in heaven.

Now that we have discussed the direct economic actions flowing from charity, we turn to the infused cardinal and secondary virtues of economic life. Recall that the cardinal and secondary infused virtues, under the guidance of charity, allow us to direct our actions by "the Divine rule" and thus to our supernatural end of life with God, and that Aquinas uses the example of temperance to explain this. Whereas acquired temperance regulates how much one should eat in terms of bodily health and the right use of human reason, infused temperance regulates how much one should eat with an eye toward spiritual growth and union with God, thus commanding things like fasting and abstinence from meat on proscribed days (see chap. 2, §3). Further, to the extent that charity directs every virtuous action, all of the moral objects one pursues have as their end love of God and neighbor. In economic life, we could say that the infused cardinal and secondary virtues are the means by which charity is manifested toward God and neighbor, so that we take up Christ's teachings regarding the poor and especially the Beatitudes. While we must bear in mind that all of the cardinal virtues will call for different actions in their infused forms, we will focus here on just a few: infused economic prudence, justice, religion, liberality, infused fortitude in the act of martyrdom, magnificence, temperance, and abstinence. Additionally, we are in the unfortunate situation of having to piece together various aspects of Aquinas's teaching that he himself does not clarify: Aquinas does not clearly tell us when he is discussing the infused virtue and when the acquired. With all of this in mind, we will follow the general principles we have established regarding the order of love and the actions enjoined by charity.

Following on our comments regarding almsgiving, acquired economic prudence would not demand that one so disregard his own bodily welfare as to give away all his surplus goods. Would not this seem imprudent from a worldly perspective? Yet this is precisely what infused economic prudence demands, for its job is to determine the appropriate circumstances for giving away our earthly possessions, keeping in mind the order of love and the needs of those under one's care. Infused prudence knows when to give to the beggar on the street, or, in the extreme case, when to give away one's kidney,

---

the reader to think this through, but I offer an initial distinction between saving for a frugal retirement and saving for a luxurious one.

and when not to. Again, this is not random acts of kindness: the poor father with an impoverished family at home does not randomly give away his last loaf of bread to the beggar on the street. The charitable, prudent giver bears in mind the order of love and reasons out how to meet his obligations in the concrete circumstances of his life, and all with an eye toward the supernatural and perfect end of eternal life. As Aquinas puts this: "[This] is both true and perfect [prudence], for it takes counsel, judges and commands aright in respect of the good end of man's whole life" (*ST* II-II.47.13).

Similarly, infused justice looks beyond the natural order to the supernatural. Since God's justice goes beyond earthly justice—for he is Justice Itself, and he is the merciful giver who is a debtor to no man—infused justice must be rooted in the charity without which one cannot be truly just. As Kevin A. McMahon says in reflecting upon the role of the bishops in guiding economic life, "Knowledge of revelation is an aid to establishing peace and justice in the community at large because of the insight into the good for man that the Gospel offers."[13] Aquinas even goes so far as to favorably quote St. Augustine in a way that equates justice to charity: "Justice is the love of God and our neighbor which pervades the other virtues" (*ST* II-II.58.8ad2). Let us just make one point concerning how infused justice goes beyond acquired justice: whereas one can in a sense maintain acquired justice with a neighbor even though one falls short of the moral due, the same cannot be said of infused justice. Infused justice acts under the guidance of charity as the means by which we show love to God and neighbor in situations involving giving what is due. And, as we cannot give God what is due without loving our neighbor as ourselves (see 1 John 4:20), infused justice demands giving the fullness of moral due, even when this goes beyond the legal due. As Aquinas puts this, while human law allows for many transactions that deviate from the just price, "the Divine law leaves nothing unpunished that is contrary to virtue. Hence, according to the Divine law, it is reckoned unlawful if the equality of justice be not observed in buying and selling" (*ST* II-II.77.1ad1). Infused justice gives others their due in light of the charity God works into our hearts, which we did not earn. God's merciful gift of salvation provides the true foundation for assessing what we owe to others.

Under the virtue of infused justice are two virtues that are important for economic theology, religion and liberality. While religion is concerned first and foremost with interior acts by which the will renders to God what is fitting (e.g., adoration and prayer), it also extends to such external acts as bodily

---

13. Kevin A. McMahon, "Economics, Wisdom and the Teaching of the Bishops in the Theology of Thomas Aquinas," *Thomist* 53.1 (1989): 92.

reverence and sacrifices. Further still, religion, under the guidance of charity, is concerned with assisting our neighbor in order to give God what is due. Let us quote Aquinas in full here:

> [Religion] has other acts, which it produces through the medium of the virtues which it commands, directing them to the honor of God, because the virtue which is concerned with the end, commands the virtues which are concerned with the means. Accordingly "to visit the fatherless and widows in their tribulation" is an act of religion as commanding, and an act of mercy as eliciting; and "to keep oneself unspotted from this world" is an act of religion as commanding, but of temperance or of some similar virtue as eliciting. (*ST* II-II.81.1ad1)

This language of "eliciting" versus "commanding" should remind us of the relationship between acquired justice and the other acquired virtues: temperance elicits the virtuous man to eat moderately, and justice commands him to do this because, for example, there is not enough food for everybody in the community.

Initially, then, it would seem that these external acts of religion are ones that the other virtues such as mercy would already enjoin, but Aquinas points out that tithing is an act of religion (*ST* II-II.87). The reason for this is clear when we realize that tithing was instituted by God as the means by which the Levites were given their pay for priestly ministry. God established tithing so that his ministers would be justly "compensated." While the precepts concerning tithing as laid out in the Old Testament are not binding, the Church has the legitimate authority to obligate the laity to pay tithes to support their priests. And whereas in the Old Testament one type of tithing was to the ministers and a second to the poor, the Church has established one tithe given to the ministers, out of which they serve the poor. Thus, religion establishes the economic justice of supporting the clergy, and also of assisting them in helping the poor. We can see the wisdom in all of this: any decent person who has visited a city and been approached by a variety of beggars has surely asked himself how he can truly help them given that he does not know their characters or circumstances. The answer to this is to seek out the nearest parish, for churches, at their best, are places where the needy in the community are known and helped as unique persons with differing needs, talents, and failings.

The other virtue under justice is infused liberality. Infused liberality could be defined as an ordinate attachment to money that allows its possessor to freely give away his or her surplus goods out of love for God (see *ST* II-II.117.6). Whereas acquired liberality is compatible with the desire to free oneself from attachment to money for one's own sake or with the desire to build up the common good, infused liberality directs this desire, through charity, to the Divine good. In addition, while infused liberality shares in common with beneficence and almsgiving that it is motivated by love of God, it is more mediately placed under justice because it regards the use of external things rather than affection toward those to whom one gives.

There is one act of infused fortitude that we must briefly mention—namely, martyrdom—and also one secondary virtue to infused fortitude, magnificence. Martyrdom is an act of infused fortitude to which there is no acquired analogue, for it belongs only to those who offer up their lives for Christ. While the most obvious examples of martyrdom come from those who are killed because they profess their faith, Aquinas's definition is broader: "Martyrdom consists essentially in standing firmly to truth and justice against the assaults of persecution" (ST II-II.124.1). He goes on to say (using John the Baptist as his example) that anyone who dies as a result of performing virtuous deeds out of love for God is a martyr. Serving the poor does not always make one popular, and might even involve one in situations in which one's life is in danger. The humble servant of the poor who is trying to show the world the truth about God's love and also establish Divine justice for the least among us may be the victim of a tyrannical leader or of a stray bullet in a drug shooting. To live out economic theology is to put oneself in God's hands, and sometimes into the clutches of wicked people.

Briefly, infused magnificence allows those who have extraordinary surplus to perform great deeds of love for neighbor. Returning to St. Katherine Drexel, upon her father's death she inherited the equivalent in today's currency of over $100 million and devoted the rest of her life to using this vast wealth in service to the poor. Few of us will have an opportunity to practice this kind of magnificence, and yet, as Aquinas points out, if we cultivate the habits of being merciful and liberal to others, we obtain at least the disposition for magnificence should God ever "burden" us with such wealth (see ST II-II.134.1ad1).

The last two infused virtues are temperance and abstinence. We have already discussed Aquinas's example of infused temperance, which goes beyond acquired temperance in that it looks to bring the body under subjection so as to grow closer to God. Infused abstinence has a specific act unique to it: fasting. While fasting is primarily concerned with one's own spiritual good, and Aquinas does not discuss how fasting contributes to the economic good of neighbor, we can include it here as a virtue that beneficence, almsgiving, liberality, and so forth can direct toward the good of our neighbor. If I deny myself food for spiritual growth, I can give what now becomes surplus to support the need of others. When we hear that forty-eight million people in the US alone will go to bed hungry tonight, let us imagine what the seventy million Catholics could do to bring down this number significantly if, for example, they observed the equivalent of the Ash Wednesday and Good Friday fasts on every Friday of the year. And let us think for ourselves how small changes in our own habits can help us love God more fully and serve Christ in the poorest among us.

The last topic in our discussion of how one lives out economic theology is the role of the Holy Spirit in guiding our actions. In particular, we will briefly discuss the gifts of knowledge, wisdom, counsel, piety, and fortitude, and also the role of the fruits in general. First, recall that the gifts are "perfections of man, whereby he is disposed so as to be amenable to the promptings of God" (*ST* I-II.68.2), and that the gifts do not direct us to different actions than those that the infused virtues enjoin. Rather, each gift provides us with a habit that makes us more docile and receptive to God's guidance (see *ST* I-II.68.3). The gifts of knowledge and wisdom, which are coupled with the third and seventh beatitudes (mourning and peacemaking), respectively, provide us with the practical insight by which our faith more easily gives rise to charitable actions (*ST* II-II.9, 45).

The fruits are interior acts by which we delight in the performance of virtuous acts. While all virtue requires the appropriate interior disposition, when we reflect on how much the infused virtues demand of us, from giving away our surplus goods to undergoing martyrdom, it is no wonder that the Holy Spirit would need to work with our hearts in this unique way. Think of the expression "give until it hurts." Such is the Christian vocation, if we couple it with another one, "love hurts." The fruits work upon our heart, opening it to the ever-greater depths of charity and giving it entrance into the mystery of God's interior life of knowledge and love, where our heart can find rest. And, to conclude, in all of this we should recall that the Beatitudes outline the path to perfection, calling us to love even poverty itself as the fullness of economic life.

4. The Theological Meaning of Value

Background Reading: ST III.40.2–3

Let us begin our discussion of theological value by recalling what we said about value in chapter 3 (§4). While value does reflect market conditions and what people are willing to pay for goods, more importantly, it is rooted in the needs of human nature. The value of an object is a measure of how it contributes to virtuous living—which is to say, happiness. In our example of buying a 1986 Dodge Omni from a neighbor, we pointed out the variety of factors that each party to the deal must consider in order to assess how justice can be met and how exercising the virtue of gratitude complements the transaction.

Just as perfect happiness goes beyond imperfect happiness, infused virtue coupled with the gifts and fruits goes beyond acquired virtue; as grace perfects nature, theological value adds to an economic assessment of how goods can contribute to storing up wealth in heaven. It is one thing to assess how the goods I own or seek to own contribute to justice, another how they contribute to charity. How could this economic transaction with my neighbor bring grace to us both? Better, how can God use this Omni as an instrument of his grace? Even in such daily actions, I must ask myself how to connect the moral object of paying a fair price to the end of building up the kingdom of God. Everything at my disposal and everything I seek to obtain is a means by which I seek eternal life for myself and for my neighbor. As Kenneth L. Schmitz comments, "The Lord is the donor who institutes the order within which the thing has its value, within which the giver gives, and within which the recipient receives. 'O God, you give that I may give.'"[14]

Concretely, recall that your neighbor had to sell his Omni even though he needed a car. How can you bring Christ to your neighbor in this situation? Could you connect him with your pastor, who may know of someone who is giving away a car? Could you put him in touch with a Christian employer you know who can help him get a better job, and in a workplace in which theological value is understood? Theological value must bring love for God and neighbor as self into every economic transaction. Again, recall the example of St. Maximilian Kolbe, who gave up everything of earthly value, even his life, out of a recognition of the immeasurable value of the beatific vision. Assessing theological value requires a fundamental recognition that life and the fullness of life are both gifts given freely, that they cannot be repaid, and that the best way of life is one of offering up to God the gifts of our time and talents as members of the Body of Christ. More particularly, theological value is assessed in reference to our universal vocation of love and our particular vocation as priestly, religious, or lay. We will discuss these points in the following order: (1) Christ as the role model for measuring theological value, (2) theological value assessed generally in terms of the vocation of love and (3) specifically in terms of our unique vocations or orders of love.

14. Kenneth L. Schmitz, *The Gift: Creation* (Milwaukee: Marquette University Press, 1982), 63.

The Incarnation is a testimony to the value of human life itself, to the fact that God wills man for his own sake. A discussion of theological value must begin with Jesus Christ's sacrificial atonement for our sin and with his call to follow him even "unto death, even death on a cross" (Phil. 2:8). Think of how often Jesus uses economic language when discussing salvation, such as in the parable of the talents (Matt. 25:14–30) or of the pearl of great price (Matt. 13:45–46). Jesus concludes with economic language in this central teaching on the meaning of discipleship: "Then Jesus told his disciples, 'If any man would come after me, let him deny himself and take up his cross and follow me. For whoever would save his life will lose it, and whoever loses his life for my sake will find it. For what will it profit a man, if he gains the whole world and forfeits his life? Or what shall a man give in return for his life?'" (Matt. 16:24–26). Theological value begins with the God-Man and orients our goods and very lives toward his.

Aquinas most directly speaks of this participation in the life, death, and resurrection of Christ in the context of the sacraments, for it is by participation in liturgical life that we live most fully. As St. Paul puts it, "We were buried therefore with him by baptism into death, so that as Christ was raised from the dead by the glory of the Father, we too might walk in newness of life" (Rom. 6:4). And, as Jesus says, "Truly, truly, I say to you, unless you eat the flesh of the Son of man and drink his blood, you have no life in you; he who eats my flesh and drinks my blood has eternal life, and I will raise him up at the last day" (John 6:53–54).

In terms of living in the world, Aquinas sees the martyr as the one who most perfectly embodies the teachings of Christ concerning the value of human life: "Martyrs are so called as being witnesses, because by suffering in body unto death they bear witness to the truth . . . made known to us by Christ" (ST II-II.24.5). Through martyrdom, St. Maximilian Kolbe united himself fully to Christ and provided a witness to us of how to rank the relative value of worldly goods.

To bring this fundamental teaching about theological value to the particular subject of how to use wealth, let us first recognize that Jesus Christ shows how infused temperance is compatible both with a life of fasting and with a life of feasting: "Both these lives are lawful and praiseworthy—namely, that a man withdraw from the society of other men and observe abstinence; and that he associate with other men and live like them" (ST II-II.40.2). We are called "to become all things to all men" (1 Cor. 9:22), to fast with those who fast, feast with those who feast, and yet in both only eat or drink as is befitting for our salvation as well as that of our neighbor. Further, Christ voluntarily took on poverty, because this is fitting for a preacher and for revealing to the world his godly nature and mission (see *ST* II-II.40.3). Thus, both in his temperance and in his poverty, we see that there is not one way of Christian life but a variety of ways based on our respective characters, cultures, and callings. That being said, since we all share in the vocation of love, we are all called to practice charity, beneficence, merciful almsgiving, justice, liberality, and so forth under the guidance of the Holy Spirit. We do not want to think of these as optional or only for priests, monks, and nuns. As Aquinas points out, we are all called to the perfection of love, even if only some of us are called to certain counsels of Christ through which we live out this love (see *ST* II-II.184.1–4).

The concrete manner in which we live out this vocation of love is as priestly, religious, or lay, and our economic actions must be rooted in this. While we have already discussed the order of love for the laity in their families, we could conclude by briefly mentioning two things. First, the priestly life, especially for a parish priest, involves ordering one's love to those who are under one's care. The priest is a spiritual father and has a special obligation to care physically and spiritually for his children in the Body of Christ. To some extent this means assessing the relative value of material goods donated to the parish in terms of the needs and merits of the members of the whole community, yet more importantly it means practicing justice, beneficence, liberality, and so forth in the distribution of the sacraments.[15] And the priest must be a liberal giver in this regard, for he does not own them, but is entrusted with their care so that he may serve as an instrument of God's grace: "For a minister is of the nature of an instrument, since the action of both is applied to something extrinsic, while the interior effect is produced through the power of the principal agent, which is God" (*ST* III.64.1).

Second, the religious life involves a similar obligation to the members of one's monastery, convent, or the like, and also usually requires a vow of poverty. While poverty is a counsel and not a command for those who seek perfection, when a monk or nun takes it up, a special connection to Christ, who became poor so that we might become rich (see 2 Cor. 8:9), is established: "The religious state is an exercise and a school for attaining to the perfection of charity. For this it is necessary that a man wholly withdraw his affections from worldly things" (*ST* II-II.186.3). That being said, religious, in taking up the counsel of poverty, will clearly have few surplus goods at their disposal. It might seem, then, that their participation in the deeds enjoined by economic

---

15. Note also that distributive justice comes into play here, for the priest is the head of a community entrusted with the task of distributing its good, material and spiritual, to the members within it.

theology would be minimal, and yet this is not so. Not only does the self-sufficiency for which monastic communities strive provide a living witness to others of the joy of stripping oneself of worldly cares for material goods,[16] but, more deeply, they have a unique role to play in the economy of salvation. What they show us is that all of these corporal works that the virtues enjoin must be rooted in prayer, for the greatest gift we can give to those in need is our prayer that they open up their hearts to the God who gives bountifully.

Let us conclude this chapter by pointing to Luke 12:35–48. Jesus has just admonished his disciples not to worry about earthly goods and to set aside all worldly cares. In addition, he has just given the commandment that we have tacitly referenced throughout our discussion of economic theology: "Sell your possessions, and give alms; provide yourselves with purses that do not grow old, with a treasure in the heavens that does not fail, where no thief approaches and no moth destroys. For where your treasure is, there will your heart be also" (Luke 12:33–34). In this context, Jesus tells a parable about a master who has left his servants in charge of his belongings while he is away. Upon his return, the master finds some of them awake and others asleep. After questioning from Peter regarding the meaning of this parable, Jesus speaks of a sinful servant who beat his fellow servants and ate and drank to excess out of the common store. The master, who, like a thief, comes when no one is expecting, "will punish him, and put him with the unfaithful" (Luke 12:46). Now the disciples understand, and hopefully so do we: God is this master, and we are his servants. All things that we own are merely loaned to us, and much hangs on whether we use them well or ill. Let us not be "put with the unfaithful" for failing to use our lives and goods well, for perhaps even doing many good things, but not doing them out of love for God and neighbor as self.

---

16. One of the principal "tourist attractions" in Pennsylvania is the Amish country. How many visitors go because they are curious, and leave asking themselves if they could live more simply?

PART 3

Political Theory

5

The Common Good
in the Earthly City
(Political Philosophy)

When Gentiles who have not the law do by nature what the law requires, they are a law to themselves, even though they do not have the law. They show that what the law requires is written on their hearts, while their conscience also bears witness and their conflicting thoughts accuse or perhaps excuse them on that day when, according to my gospel, God judges the secrets of men by Christ Jesus.

—Romans 2:14–16

Let every person be subject to the governing authorities. For there is no authority except from God, and those that exist have been instituted by God. Therefore he who resists the authorities resists what God has appointed, and those who resist will incur judgment. For rulers are not a terror to good conduct, but to bad. Would you have no fear of him who is in authority? Then do what is good, and you will receive his approval, for he is God's servant for your good. But if you do wrong, be afraid, for he does not bear the sword in vain; he is the servant of God to execute his wrath on the wrongdoer. Therefore one must be subject, not only to avoid God's wrath but also for the sake of conscience. For the same reason you also pay taxes, for the authorities are ministers of God, attending to this very thing. Pay all of them their dues, taxes to whom taxes are due, revenue to whom revenue is due, respect to whom respect is due, honor to whom honor is due.

—Romans 13:1–7

1. Introduction

In chapter 1 we showed the inadequacy of the contemporary perception that ethics (1) is about rule following, (2) must be either objective or subjective, and (3) is limited to one aspect of our lives—namely, situations in which one must do one's duty or what one ought to do as opposed to what one wants to do. As Aquinas understood it, moral philosophy is about character formation; is both objective and subjective insofar as it tells us how humans in general, and each one of us in particular, ought to live; and is about our lives as a whole since its task is to teach us the path to happiness. One of the extended examples we used was of a young Frisbee player, and we showed how even this recreational activity involves moral components. As we discussed, every action we perform must be situated within the context of our lives as a whole, and of the lives of those whose paths cross ours: in one situation she is playing with her friend who is low in spirits, in another she is neglecting to do her homework. In each case the action is the same in the physical sense, but morally speaking we can praise her for an act of friendship or blame her for neglect of her studies. While we must know what is right and wrong in the abstract, more precisely we must know what to do here and now. Happiness is not the reward for following the rules; it is the fruit of joyfully embracing a life of giving others their due. In a word, moral philosophy teaches us to follow the path of justice and provides a fleeting glimpse of this path's heavenly destination.

In chapter 3 we applied this general moral framework to care for material goods. And, again, we saw that economic philosophy cannot be studied in isolation from moral philosophy, nor by treating humans as abstractions who buy and sell widgets. As we put it there, one cannot be good at economics but bad at ethics. Determining a fair price requires a solid understanding of the human desire for happiness, and thus how material goods can be put in the service of the virtues that are truly valuable. Economic philosophy cannot deal in widgets, but must deal in goods that are more or less valuable in the concrete lives of those who buy and sell them. Further, my property is mine only in the qualified sense that this is the best arrangement for promoting the good of the community as a whole. The goods entrusted to me and to you have their value to the extent that they can be used in acts of justice, liberality, and the like. An extended example we used in part 2 was of buying a neighbor's 1986 Dodge Omni, and we saw how many objective and subjective factors must be weighed in the balance in order to be just toward him.

What does all of this have to do with political philosophy? How could playing Frisbee or buying a 1986 Dodge Omni be a matter of concern to the politician, the soldier, or the voter? Are not morals the private concern of citizens, rather than the public concern of politicians? Is not economics supposed to be free from political interference, for a market is a place where free citizens voluntarily enter into agreements, not a court of law where the government determines the rules and issues the verdicts?

Hopefully our study of Aquinas's moral and economic philosophy has allowed us to anticipate how he would respond: If moral philosophy teaches us that the best life is the life of justice, and economic philosophy studies what it means to be just in the use and exchange of material goods, then political philosophy, which studies how to establish and promote justice in a community, must be integrally related to ethics and economics. Once we acknowledge that our moral and economic actions are concerned with questions of justice, and that justice is the immediate object of politics, we must recognize the legitimacy of a government that is concerned with the moral and economic actions of its citizens. Put more strongly, a government cannot be called "good" unless it promotes just moral and economic relationships between its citizens. While this does not necessarily mean that Uncle Sam should oversee the Frisbee player's game or tell you how much you have to pay for the Omni, it does mean that he wants to assist us in connecting our own desire for happiness with the desires of our fellow citizens. What it means for me to practice the virtue of justice is, at least in part, a matter of obeying the laws of my country and the legitimate decisions of political authorities. It is one thing for me to pursue my own happiness in concert with the happiness of the members of my family and immediate neighbors, quite another to look out for the happiness of the whole community. To use a musical analogy, trying to sing a song is hard enough, singing with a few friends is harder still, and harmonizing a choir is nothing short of masterful. As Aquinas puts this in his *Commentary on Aristotle's "Politics"*: "The city includes all the other societies, for households and villages are both comprised under the city; and so political society itself is the highest society. Therefore, it seeks the highest among all human goods, for it aims at the common good, which is better and more divine than the good of one individual" (*CAP* 1.1.11). Politics is entrusted with the difficult task of helping the citizenry freely embrace lives of justice.

In light of these points, we can see again how Aquinas's philosophy is "both/and": what is right to do as a member of a community is in some sense universal and objective, but in another sense it is subjective and a matter of living in accordance with the good customs and laws of my country. Political philosophy is the study of how rulers and ruled can cooperate in the pursuit of the common good, which good is understood as nothing other than the imperfect happiness of the members of *this* particular community. Our discussion of this third and final, yet first and foundational, branch of the practical study of human affairs is divided as follows: (1) politics as organic and concerned with the common good; (2) natural and human law; (3) the best form of government *in itself*, *in practice*, and *for us*; (4) the virtues of political life in relation to the forms of government and law; and (5) just war and the limits of obedience.

Before working through these points, it is worth mentioning that we will often find it necessary to rely on two texts other than the *Summa*—namely, Aquinas's *Commentary on Aristotle's "Politics"* (CAP) and *De regno* (DR). The reason for this is that these two texts, neither of which Aquinas completed, contain important aspects of his political theory that are not made explicit in the *Summa*. While we will rely upon the *Summa* wherever possible and will cross-reference important points from these other two texts with the *Summa*, at times we will structure our presentation around these two works. This is especially true in our opening section's discussion of the origins of politics.

2. Politics as Organic and Concerned with the Common Good

Background Reading: DR 1.1

Modern political philosophy tends to structure its understanding of government around an agreement between self-interested individuals that originates in what is called "the state of nature." On this account, we are asked to imagine human beings in a primitive, natural condition and recognize that they would inevitably end up in conflict with one another. The dearth of resources, competition for the same goods, and so forth would make this state of nature a state of unending war. Eventually, human beings would come up with a way to end this violence and learn how to work together, or at least not against one another. This arrangement would come about via a contract stipulating common rules as well as a means by which to create and enforce them. Thus politics is born, and humans are freed from the state of nature. Politics, then, is an artificial means by which to escape from nature via what is called a "social contract." Humans are born free, and the coercive power of governments is legitimate because humans freely gave up their own self-rule in exchange for the peace and security afforded by life in political community. Finally, we should note, it is hard not to read the history of the US through the lens of modern political philosophy, both because the original colonies and US government were founded through contracts and because the founders themselves were influenced by this social contract theory.

While Aquinas would not deny that humans originally lived outside of political communities, nor that some measure of coercion is necessary to keep humans from harming one another, his understanding of the origin of politics is decidedly different. First of all, Aquinas would reject the claim that political community is formed in reaction to a warlike state of nature. Undoubtedly this is a possibility in certain circumstances, but in general politics is a response to the natural desire for happiness. While it is true that human beings need material goods and a peaceful condition in which to enjoy them, more importantly they need virtue and friendship, both of which can be developed to their fullest in a community governed by law: "There is in all men a certain natural impulse toward the city, as also toward the virtues" (*CAP* 1.1.40). Not only is a community necessary for the attainment of happiness (for we need the guidance of family, friends, and law in order to acquire the virtues that allow for happiness), but even when we possess the virtues we need friends in order to be happy. As Aquinas says, the good man needs friends "that he may do good to them; that he may delight in seeing them do good; and again that he may be helped by them in his good work" (*ST* I-II.4.8). And, since what holds families, friends, and neighbors together is a common rule of law, politics is necessary for happiness.

Secondly, the social contract approach to politics is rooted in a false dichotomy between nature and art or artifice. Recall our discussion in chapter 1 (§2) of the term "nature." We often think of nature as an original state, or as "what happens." In this sense, the natural state of the human being is the primitive condition, prior to culture and political community. However, Aquinas holds a richer understanding of nature as the goal or end sought, or as "what ought to happen." In this sense, the natural state of humans is life in political community, for in it they can develop the virtues that allow them to live most fully: "The man who founded the city kept men from being most evil and brought them to a state of excellence in accordance with justice and the virtues" (*CAP* 1.1.41). Virtue is "second nature" in that the presence of virtue completes the natural potential for actions in conformity with goodness, beauty, and truth. Thus, life in a political community is actually more natural than life in a cave, for only in the former can one achieve the true goods that the caveman by nature seeks. Aquinas uses the classic "ship of state" metaphor to indicate the purposive nature of politics: "A ship, for example, which moves in different directions, according to the impulse of the changing winds, would never reach its destination were it not brought to port by the skill of the pilot" (*DR* 1.1.3). The city is most natural because in it humans most fully assist one another in achieving the happiness for which we were made.

What I mean by the expression "politics as organic" in the heading to this section is that political community is the natural result of the human pursuit of happiness. Wherever we find a group of human beings, we will find, either now or in the future, law and government. Today we often want to resist this conclusion, and this is understandable given how much evil has been brought into the world by governments in just the last hundred or so years. In addition, the impersonal nature of modern governments, which rule upwards of a hundred million people and are centered thousands of miles from the citizens they supposedly represent, makes us think that there must be some alternative. And so we fantasize about utopias in which people freely rule themselves, societies without coercion and nonetheless with perfect cooperation. Yet we do not have to read *Animal Farm* or *Lord of the Flies* to realize that utopias truly are "no place" (*u-topia*).

Imagine yourself as one of the original European settlers in the New World. You set off on your own in the wilderness and finally come across a natural spring surrounded by fertile lands, an ideal location for making your home and building a life. As it turns out, eleven others stumble across the same place; finding them to be agreeable companions, you decide to establish a community together. Leaving aside the difficulty of determining what property (if any) will be private, what (if any) public, and how legitimate claims to ownership would arise, imagine that your free and equal, lawless and peaceful community finds it necessary to guard the community from marauders who occasionally raid at night. To whom will you entrust this task? How about taking turns? Perhaps each person can take one of the twelve months of the year. But who will be stuck with the winter months? The nights are longer and colder. Do you draw straws? What would you do if one of your members gets the short end and then cries out, "It's not fair!"?

As Aquinas saw it, the very fact that we have the ability to communicate verbally is an indication that what binds us together as humans is our common pursuit of justice: "Human speech signifies useful and harmful things, and so just and unjust things, since justice and injustice consist of persons being treated justly or unjustly regarding useful and harmful things" (*CAP* 1.1.21). Your little community of twelve must be bound together by justice, for unless each of the members is treated fairly, discord will arise. And as soon as a conflict arises, it is inevitable that the members will seek to resolve disagreements via some form of rudimentary government. Agreements, rules, enforcement, and the like are necessary features of communal life, and, with an important exception, this little thought experiment conveys Aquinas's understanding of politics as the organic fulfillment of such a natural process.

The important exception is that communities are not formed by rational, self-interested adults entering into contracts, but by husbands and wives with sons and daughters, families and neighbors with friends and enemies. Humans are not like mushrooms springing forth overnight fully formed out of the earth, but sons and daughters who slowly mature into rational and relational beings. For humans, to be is to be relational: we become who we are, and come to know who we are, as members of communities that we did not choose but were born into. And this is the story that Aquinas tells, starting with the domestic community of husband and wife and ending with the political community of rulers and ruled.

Following Aristotle's presentation on the origin of politics, Aquinas sees the political community, or "city," as the last stage in a development that starts with male and female. Male and female by nature seek out one another and begin families. Families themselves provide many of the basic goods necessary for daily life, and yet they will find it necessary to enter into relationship with other families, thereby forming a village. And even here, while the material needs of human life may be met, the needs of life as a whole still remain unmet. The city is that self-sufficient community that has everything humans need, not just materially but morally and intellectually as well: "And since there are indeed different grades and orders of these associations, the ultimate association is the political community directed to things self-sufficient for human life. And so the political community is the most perfect human association" (*CAP* prologue). It is by participating in ruling and being ruled, by following settled laws that provide a "school" in virtuous living, that humans develop into the prudent, just, courageous, and temperate beings that their natural desire for happiness induces them to be. As Aquinas says, "The political community's existence results in human beings living, and living well insofar as the laws of the political community direct the life of human beings to virtue" (*CAP* 1.1.17).

Finally, the fact that humans find their fulfillment in political community means that situating their own good within the good of the community as a whole is central to happiness. A community has a "common good," and this good is not juxtaposed with my own good, but with the evil of harming another for the supposed benefit this would bring to myself. In everything we do, we seek the good of our own happiness. But, as becomes especially evident when we come to realize that the highest acquired virtue is justice, or willing the good of another, it turns out that our own good is interwoven with the good of another. On this point Aquinas takes up Aristotle's lead in saying that humans seek their good as members of communities and that this seeking finds its perfection in willing the good of the political community sharing the common pursuit of happiness. The common good, then, is the happiness of the community understood as a union of persons who are, through participation in this community, made happy.[1] I cannot achieve my own good unless I will the good of the community, placing my own actions at the service of the common good. This is why politics is so important, for it "considers the ultimate and complete good regarding human affairs" (*CAP* prologue).

This very notion of a common good, though, might strike us as problematic to the extent that the citizens are seen as "parts" of the "whole" that is the political community. Human beings exist for themselves, and the very language of wholes and parts suggests that the citizens can be used as means to the good of the city. Yet and again, Aquinas insists that we think of the common good in terms of an organic unity in which securing the good of the whole is simultaneously securing the good of the parts. Just as I am happy if and only if all the parts of my soul and body are "happy," so too is the city only "happy" if its members are. Contrariwise, "any good or evil, done to the member of a society, redounds on the whole society: thus, who hurts the hand, hurts the man" (*ST* I-II.21.3).

Even in the extreme case of the death penalty, in which Aquinas allows the community to "cut off" one of its members in order to protect itself, two things stand out: first, it is never permissible to kill an innocent person in order to promote the common good (see *ST* II-II.64.6). This would be an injustice, and the community can never act immorally toward one of its members in order to promote its own good. Second, even in such a case the good of the accused is looked after, both in the sense that it is good for a wicked man to face justice and in the sense that the community seeks to give him the opportunity for repentance (see *ST* II-II.64.3). While the common good of a particular community may require punishing its members, this is not to harm them but to help the convicted find the happiness that can only come through a just life or death.[2]

1. There is much dispute over whether or not the common good is "limited/instrumental" in that its purpose is to serve the good of families and individuals, or if this good promotes a sort of transcendent "communal happiness." We will return to this issue in chap. 7 in our discussion of how to apply Aquinas's political theory to contemporary political realities.

2. Jacques Maritain makes a helpful distinction between individuals and persons: as individuals we are subordinate to the city, yet as a person with a supernatural end each one of us is a whole that transcends the city. See "The Human Person and Society," in *Scholasticism and Politics* (Indianapolis: Liberty Fund, 2011), 73–76.

3. Natural and Human Law

Background Reading: ST I-II.90–91.3, 92, 93.3, 95–97

As we saw in the case of our imaginary community of twelve members, it is inevitable that humans will join together to form governments that can provide laws by which the common good can be promoted. And yet what should these laws be? Are they simply the product of the human will, of whoever is in power imposing them on us? How do we go about determining if laws are good or bad?

Law often seems to us to be arbitrary, and we may feel that we are its slaves rather than its beneficiaries. Imagine that you are taking your first spin in that new-to-you 1986 Dodge Omni, driving down a wide country road on a sunny day, not a pedestrian in sight. Despite these perfect conditions, the speed limit is only 35 mph, and this seems unreasonable. "Why can't I drive a little faster on this road? It's perfectly safe," you find yourself thinking as you struggle to keep your foot from giving it more gas. You begin a steep descent, and despite your attempt to keep it at 35 miles per hour, you hit 45 by the time the hill tapers off. Enter the police siren. . . . When the officer pulls you over and insultingly asks, "Can't you read?" you try to explain that you were riding the brake and that 35 seems unnecessarily slow. Rather than sympathize with you, he points to his badge and angrily says, "When you get one of these you can decide how fast to drive. Here's your ticket; I'm sure the judge will agree that you should be able to go as fast as you feel like driving." As he drives off, you can't help but mockingly laugh at the sign on the side of his car that says, "To Serve and Protect."

Such is our experience with the law in many aspects of our lives. Law appears to us to be an arbitrary command that we must obey simply because those in power say so. We know that those in power are put there by our votes, but they do not appear to take note of this fact. If only these man-made laws were like the laws of physics or of economics, for these are objective and intelligible. In the natural world, the law is not arbitrarily imposed nor is it in the interest of the powerful. Rather, it is an impersonal guide to action, and by willingly following its "decrees," we are given the power to move about the world and use our knowledge to good effect. Why can't the laws be *for us*, and assist us in making our lives better?

Aquinas's understanding of law fits exactly with our recognition that human laws should not be arbitrary but rather should be framed for the benefit of the governed. As he tells us in *ST* I-II.90.4, law "is nothing else than an ordinance of reason for the common good, made by him who has care of the community, and promulgated." Law comes not from the arbitrary decision of some authority's will but from reason. Think of how differently you would have reacted had the officer explained that at the bottom of the hill is a playground, and people have to cross the street to get to the parking lot. Suddenly you go from judge to judged, for you recognize that you were driving at an unreasonable speed. Secondly, law is framed for the common good, trying to promote the happiness of all, not just the happiness of the Omni driver. Thirdly, it is because those in authority are in a position to assess the various factors and uses of the road that they can care for the community as a whole. Whereas you saw only your side of things, the lawgiver saw the whole. Finally, to "promulgate" the law means to "make it known," and it is reasonable that you receive a ticket for driving over the clearly posted speed limit.

And, as a corollary to all of this, notice two things: First, the definition of "law" does not include the use of force. It is not part of the definition of law that a punishment is meted out to those who do not obey it. While this is implied since the one with care of the community differs from private citizens in that he or she can punish those who do not obey (see *ST* I-II.90.3ad2), Aquinas is emphasizing that law is not bald power, but authority wielded on behalf of the common good. Second, and consequently, this means that a political authority who commands or prevents actions for his or her own benefit does not, properly speaking, make a law. Quoting St. Augustine, Aquinas emphasizes that "that which is not just seems to be no law at all" (*ST* I-II.95.2). Human laws derive their authority not so much from the decision of the lawmaker, nor even from the consent of the governed, but from their justice and the objective determination of the right (*ius*). This is made clear from Aquinas's division between kinds of law in *ST* I-II.91.

In *ST* I-II.91.1, Aquinas explains that the most fundamental kind of law is eternal law, or that law by which God governs the community of creation as a whole. God is Supreme Reason itself, and his providence looks to the common good of even "the birds of the air" (Matt. 6:26). This law is promulgated to the irrational animals by their instincts, for they are like arrows shot out of a bow, naturally pursuing their own good. We, too, follow this eternal law, though we do so under the guidance of reason as creatures who are willed for their own sake.

This unique way of participating in eternal law is called natural law: "The rational creature is subject to Divine providence in the most excellent way, in so far as it partakes of a share of providence, by being provident both for itself and for others. Wherefore it has a share of the Eternal Reason, whereby it has a natural inclination to its proper act and end: and this participation of the eternal law in the rational creature is called the natural law" (*ST* I-II.91.2). Like irrational animals, we have a natural instinct that directs us to our own good. Unlike the irrational animals, we need to be directed by more than this instinct, for we must use reason in assessing the various goods to which instinct propels us and must reject apparent goods that instinct would blindly pursue to our ruin. Reason allows us to be provident for ourselves and also to look out for the good of others. This "other-regarding" aspect of natural law makes possible the human laws that governments justly enact. But before we get to these, we must specify the content of the natural law somewhat, and also show why natural law alone is not a sufficient guide to our own happiness.[3]

First, all of natural law is rooted in the fundamental apprehension of our practical reason that good is to be sought, and evil avoided. As Aquinas puts this, "This is the first precept of law. . . . All other precepts of the natural law are based upon this: so that whatever the practical reason naturally apprehends as man's good (or evil) belongs to the precepts of the natural law as something to be done or avoided" (*ST* I-II.94.2). In its reflection on our natural instincts, reason discovers three other basic precepts regarding what is good for us: (1) like all substances, we ought to preserve our bodily existence; (2) like all animals, we ought to propagate our species; and (3) unique as rational animals, we ought to live harmoniously in society and seek "to know the truth about God" (94.2).[4]

3. Our introduction to natural law opens us up to a host of issues debated by scholars today. Most directly, a school of thought known as "new natural law theory" (e.g., Germain Grisez, John Finnis, and Joseph Boyle), while not necessarily articulated as an interpretation of Aquinas, has been criticized by a variety of Thomistic scholars (e.g., Ralph McInerny, Benedict Ashley, Sean Coyle, and Jean Porter). Again, in keeping with our introductory purpose, we will try to lay out the starting points upon which there is general agreement. Those interested in deeper study of natural law should read the works of the forenamed scholars (see bibliography to part 3), and also Martin Rhonheimer's *Natural Law and Practical Reason: A Thomist View of Moral Autonomy*, trans. Gerald Malsbary (New York: Fordham University Press, 2000), which, while friendly to new natural law theory, places more emphasis on the virtues than they are wont to do.

4. The interpretation of what these precepts are, how they are connected, and their relationship to virtue is a good example of how new natural law theorists disagree with their critics. In John Goyette, Mark S. Latkovic, and Richard S. Myers, eds., *St. Thomas Aquinas and the Natural Law Tradition: Contemporary Perspectives* (Washington, DC: Catholic University of America Press, 2004), which contains essays by leading scholars from various camps, Benedict Ashley claims that "these three basic needs form a hierarchy" in that at times it will prove necessary to sacrifice bodily needs for the good of our family, or leave our families for the highest good, friendship with God (Ashley, "The Anthropological Foundations of the Natural Law," 13). According to Ralph McInerny the three precepts are simply an unfolding of the first: the law to do good and avoid evil can be stated more precisely as follows: "The perfection, the completion, the good in the sense of the ultimate end, is to be pursued and whatever is incompatible with that end is to be avoided" (McInerny, "The Principles of Natural Law," as cited in William E. May, "Contemporary Perspectives on Thomistic Natural Law," in Goyette, Latkovic, and Myers, *St. Thomas Aquinas and the Natural Law Tradition*, 133). For a new natural law

Natural law provides us with a basic framework for our actions, but clearly these general laws are not enough for the specifics of our lives: Is killing another person in self-defense sanctioned by the first precept? Does the second precept allow for polygamy? Would the third precept rule out violent sports such as boxing and football? More generally, how does one account for actions in which one forgoes the first or second precept for the sake of the third (e.g., martyrdom or celibacy for the kingdom)? As Aquinas goes on to point out in articles 4 and 5, while all people grasp the fundamental precept of the natural law (do good and avoid evil), and while the three primary principles are also known by all, the particular circumstances of human life require a host of secondary principles, and this is where humans so easily err.

Let us return to one of our central examples: private property. As we discussed in part 2, God gave the material goods of the earth to all in common, and yet human reason rightfully allows for private property. We can see now that this is rooted in the third primary principle of the natural law insofar as its concern is with the harmonious living of the members of society. Since reason discovers the practical advantages to the community of private property, it formulates secondary principles such as "do not steal" or "only take from the common store of goods what is necessary for your own good." Since the needs of various members of the community, and of communities in different times and places, are variable, these secondary principles must be adapted to changing circumstances; put differently, due to the variability of circumstances, the secondary principles (unlike the primary) do not bind us always and everywhere. Remember the example of the starving man in the cornfield. If he takes the corn, he violates a secondary principle of the natural law. And, if he does not, he violates the first primary principle. Aquinas himself uses the classic example from Plato's *Republic*: while it is generally true that one should return what one borrows, it would be wrong to do so if the owner intended to use the object in question for some evil purpose (see *ST* I-II.94.4). More formally, the point is that the primary principles of natural law are universal and without exception, whereas the secondary principles "[may fail] the greater the number of conditions added" (*ST* I-II.94.4). Again, natural law contains what is objectively true everywhere and always, as well as what is subjectively true here and now.

Not only is it the case that the secondary principles will not apply in certain circumstances; further, "in some [people] . . . reason is perverted by passion, or evil habit, or an evil disposition of nature" (*ST* I-II.94.4), and thus they will

---

theory response to such claims, see May's thorough analysis and criticism of the positions of, among others, both Ashley and McInerny (113–56).

not have knowledge of certain secondary principles. While all people know the primary principles of natural law (even if vice prevents them from applying them; see *ST* I-II.94.6), the fallen condition of human existence means that not all have the virtue to reason out the conclusions that follow from them. All of this points to the need for some public guide, some more obvious form of law that can help direct and educate the members of the community in their pursuit of the common good, and this is the task of human law.

Human law is derived from natural law in much the same way that a farmer applies the general principles of the natural sciences to his trade and to the particular circumstances of his farm. As Aquinas puts it, "It is from the precepts of the natural law, as from general and indemonstrable principles, that the human reason needs to proceed to the more particular determination of certain matters. These particular determinations, devised by human reason, are called human laws" (*ST* I-II.91.3). Thus, whereas the chemist can determine the properties of various soils, and the biologist the laws of growth and reproduction, the farmer takes these general principles and applies them to the particularities of the various plants humans have adapted to their own use. Similarly, the lawmaker takes the general principles of natural law and applies them to the families, villages, institutions, and so forth under his or her care.

Further, since the "certain matters" with which human law is concerned include changing variables such as time and place, customs and cultures, human laws must be devised differently in accordance with the common good of the community. Just as the farmer must decide which type of crops to grow, when to plant them, what soil amendments to add, and so forth, based on the conditions of his or her farm, the lawmaker frames laws with an eye toward the common good of a specific people who have habits, customs, and a culture of their own. For Aquinas, making human law is not the result of abstract theorizing about the best laws but of prudentially guiding an imperfect community toward an ever greater fulfillment of the natural law and thus to a way of life that is in accordance with nature. The goal of human law is to make the members of the community good (see *ST* I-II.92.1), but it must work gradually with the imperfect material of humans who collectively possess a variety of virtues and vices.[5] Additionally, Aquinas recognized the powerful force that custom exerts on the lives of the people, even to the point of saying that "custom has the force of a law, abolishes law, and is the interpreter of law" (*ST* I-II.97.3). Since citizens obey the law largely out of custom, laws should be rarely changed, and only when the "harm" brought about by changing the law is compensated for by a palpable good (see *ST* I-II.97.2). Is

---

5. See *ST* I-II.96.2ad2 and Aquinas's visceral example of a man blowing his nose too forcibly.

not our own cynicism today about law partly a result of how often it changes? Even if the new law is framed with a good intention, it is so easy to say of lawmakers what we say of doctors in our worst of moods: "First butter was good for you, then it was bad for you, and now it's good for you again. Why listen to them?"

Since law must work so gradually and must work with the good, the bad, and the ugly, its proximate goal is somewhat modest. Even if its ultimate goal is human happiness, it must be content with accomplishing a small but important task: keeping the wicked from harming others with the hopes that by obeying the law out of fear they eventually form habits conducive to virtue. In utopias people willingly do what is good and thus have no need for laws, but in our world "some are found to be depraved, and prone to vice, and not easily amenable to words, [and thus] it was necessary for such to be restrained from evil by force and fear, in order that, at least, they might desist from evil-doing, and leave others in peace, and that they themselves, by being habituated in this way, might be brought to do willingly what hitherto they did from fear, and thus become virtuous" (ST I-II.95.1). The law is a harsh teacher, and advice is usually better than coercion; still, governmental oversight is better than the alternative of living in a community where the wicked act with impunity. In general, given that communities include such wicked people, human law always has an eye toward what is possible for all people to obey. As a bare minimum, then, it attempts to prevent "chiefly those [vices] that are to the hurt of others, without the prohibition of which human society could not be maintained: thus human law prohibits murder, theft and such like" (ST I-II.96.2). Beyond that, the lawgiver must act like a prudent farmer who might like to plant grape vines but will settle for potatoes if that is all his or her soil can bear. We might like to live in communities in which the laws are in perfect harmony with human happiness, but we should count our blessings if we live in ones in which the discords of vice do not prevent the freedom to practice virtue.

Finally, human law can be divided into two fundamental types: the law of nations and civil law. This corresponds to the two different aspects of farming: applying general principles of the natural sciences to growing crops, and determining what crops to grow and when in this particular farm. The law of nations is derived from natural law "as a conclusion from premises," the civil law "by way of determination of certain generalities" (ST I-II.95.4). Let us explain this distinction more fully by returning to the important example of private property.

Whereas natural law does not specify if property can be possessed and, if so, how, human reason, discovering the benefits of private property, properly concludes that respecting private property, not stealing, paying back what one borrowed, and the like are laws for all people. What we previously called secondary principles *of the natural law* now appear to be part *of human law*. These "laws of nations" straddle the line between natural and human law: in one sense we can call these secondary principles part of the natural law given that they are conclusions regarding how all humans at all times should live given our common human nature; in another sense, they are the foundational human laws of society given that they are discovered by human reason when it reflects upon how humans should live in relation to one another as members of a political community.[6] Thus, the law of nations is that law that people of every country should follow in pursuit of human happiness. Since private property is in this sense derived from natural law, its relative value is similarly a reflection on its fittingness for serving the needs of human law. We could speak, thus, of a "natural value" that a material good has prior to the determinations of free markets or the decrees of lawmakers.

While the law of nations, building on the natural law, concludes that there should be general rules for private-property ownership, it does not reach to the particulars of different cultural practices, just or unjust transfer of property, and so forth. This belongs to the civil law framed for a particular community and is a matter of determination rather than of conclusion: whereas the law of nations is formulated in the way that the scientist deduces the principles of agriculture from chemistry or biology, civil law is determined in the way that the prudent farmer determines which crops to grow given the particulars of climate, soil condition, available markets, and so forth.

A further point about civil law is that, unlike the law of nations, it has "no other force than that of human law" (*ST* I-II.95.2). The classic example of this is determining which side of the road to drive on. Nature does not settle this, and, once the law does, a driver who disregards the law and thereby harms his or her fellow citizens acts unjustly. In the case of property law, while civil law cannot justly prevent the citizenry from owning private property, it can justly determine that certain common resources such as large bodies of water cannot

---

6. Aquinas provides another example of a feature of living in society that straddles the natural/human law line: "We might say that for man to be naked is of the natural law, because nature did not give him clothes, but art invented them" (*ST* I-II.94.5ad3). When I was in college, a student at UC Berkeley by the name of Andrew Martinez went to school naked, insisting that this was "natural." In one sense, "the naked guy" was obviously right: the only clothing nature gives us is our birthday suit; in another sense, he relied upon a false understanding of nature: we are rational *by nature* and, upon recognition that our birthday suit is not the best attire for riding a bicycle, controlling sexual desires, going out in snow storms, or taking trips to the moon, we devise human laws regarding what we should wear and when. Put differently, it is part of natural law to add to it what is necessary for our own flourishing.

be owned. For example, the two neighboring states of Washington and Oregon differ on precisely this point, for in Washington one can own ocean beaches, but in Oregon one cannot. Why is it unjust in Oregon to prevent others from visiting the beach in front of your property? Because the State of Oregon determined that this was important for the common good.[7] Somebody must decide such questions, and communities are governed by authorities precisely so that this can be done. Consider the complexities involved in determining who owns a particular property in the following cases.

Imagine a British citizen is going through old family records and discovers that three hundred years ago her ancestors owned a piece of land in what was then the colony of Pennsylvania. This land was incorporated into an American family's farm when her loyalist ancestors fled the New World over two hundred years ago. Would this be a case of theft? Consider a different scenario: imagine a Jew who fled to America prior to World War II and returns to Poland twenty years later only to discover that a gentile family took over his property and lives there now. Would *this* be a case of theft? Finally, imagine a woman in Florida who inherits a house in Iowa but does not take possession of it for twenty-five years. When she finally heads up north she discovers that a homeless man has been living in the home and maintaining it (e.g., paying utilities, making necessary repairs) for the past twenty years. Would *this* be a case of theft? While I personally would consider only the second case theft, others might claim that the third one is as well, and still others would think that all three are. How would we settle such disputes? Aquinas's point is that neither the natural law nor the law of nations could settle such claims, and it is up to civil law to interpret how the admonition against theft is to be applied in the concrete. While this does not mean that human governments are infallible in such cases, it does mean that part of what it means to be just is to submit to the reasonable decisions of human authority.

Before concluding this section, it is worth pointing out that determining the value of material goods seems to straddle the line between the law of nations and civil law. On the one hand, since value is a measure of human need, and this is the same for all regardless of nation, we can speak of natural value. On the other hand, since value is relative to times and places, customs and cultures, value is a reflection of how a particular community meets the needs of its members. We could call this "conventional value." As Aquinas says in regard to an analogous distinction between natural and positive right, "The

---

7. This does not prevent us from arguing that Oregon was wrong in this determination (or, conversely, Washington). The point is that nature does not settle what is just here, and it belongs to the competent authority to decide how the community will confront this issue.

human will can, by common agreement, make a thing to be just provided it be not, of itself, contrary to natural justice, and it is in such matters that positive right has its place. . . . If, however, a thing is, of itself, contrary to natural right, the human will cannot make it just, for instance by decreeing that it is lawful to steal or to commit adultery" (*ST* II-II.57.2ad2). Taking advantage of a poor man by giving him pennies on the dollar for his goods is a form of theft and cannot be made just simply because the law says it is. However, determining that a thief must pay so many dollars as restitution for the damage inflicted upon a victim is just because the judge has decided it to be so based upon the facts of the case, the relevant laws, and precedent. Even if there is a natural value for material goods in general, in the particulars of times and places, conventional value is usually the concern of the lawmaker or judge.

Recall that Aquinas thinks it is just for material goods to cost more in one place than in another and to charge a different price based on one's own needs. In light of this, civil law can assess whether or not a just price has been paid for an item based on conventional value as dictated by the circumstances of the transaction and the general needs of the community. Yet in other cases, civil law can attempt to decree that certain goods be sold at the natural price, especially those that are vital for human needs such as clean water and food staples. That being said, this is dangerous territory, for the complexities of markets are so great that it is difficult to determine the natural value of one object (e.g., clean water) in relation to another (e.g., money). We could conclude with another example of the humble and limited role of human law, for Aquinas recognized that "if without employing deceit the seller disposes of his goods for more than their worth, or the buyer obtain them for less than their worth, the law looks upon this as licit, and provides no punishment for so doing, unless the excess be too great" (*ST* II-II.77.1ad1). Lawmakers are not micromanagers charged with the task of determining how I can be happy; rather, their task is to provide a general framework for the community, giving me the freedom to put my property and exchanges in the service of my neighbor and thereby secure the happiness that he or she, the lawmakers, and I seek in common.

4. The Best Form of Government *in Itself, in Practice,* and *for Us*

Background Reading: ST I.103.1, 3, 6; I-II.105, 106.3; II-II.50.1; DR 1.2–4, 1.7, 2.1

One of the most important questions of traditional political philosophy, if not the most important, is "What is the best form of government?" Today we think of the answer to this as settled, for democracy is the only form of government that we even recognize as legitimate. Government is either of the people or tyrannical, and thus the question for us is not about which form of government is best but whether or not a particular nation has a legitimate government. That being said, we do acknowledge that there are many forms of democracy and that democracy will mean one thing in the US and another in Japan. In this sense, we recognize the traditional distinction between the best form of government *in practice* and the best form *for us*. Further, to the extent that we still think about our lives in Christian terms, we recognize that God is the King of Kings, and thus that heavenly decrees are not a result of popular vote. And this is to acknowledge that there is a best form of government *in itself*.

When reflecting on the best form of government *in itself*, Aquinas has as his starting point God's governance over creation. As we have already observed, eternal law is the means by which God governs the universe, directing it toward its end of glorifying God. Thus, government is not an artificial or accidental feature of human life, but a feature of creaturely existence itself. Nature is purposive, and God loves creation into existence and into its perfection: "It is not fitting that the supreme goodness of God should produce things without giving them their perfection. Now a thing's ultimate perfection consists in the attainment of its end. Therefore it belongs to the Divine goodness, as it brought things into existence, so to lead them to their end: and this is to govern" (*ST* I.103.1). Further, since goodness itself is unitary—for God is One—it is fitting that government be monarchical. As Aquinas points out, "What is one in itself is a more apt and a better cause of unity than several things united. Therefore a multitude is better governed by one than by several. From this it follows that the government of the world, being the best form of government, must be by one" (*ST* I.103.3). Finally, while God rules as a King, he is not a dictator but a benevolent Lord who gives his creatures the power to participate in this kingship via their causal powers: "God so governs things that He makes some of them to be causes of others in government; as a master, who not only imparts knowledge to his pupils, but gives also the faculty of teaching others" (*ST* I.103.6). God is a choirmaster, not a puppet master, providing the music, the vocal skills, and the direction. In the case of humans, this arrangement allows for the freedom to follow or refuse his lead, and thus part of his providence is to weave our individual performances into the work as a whole. Human governments at their best are like the divine, and yet at their worst like Lucifer, the angel of light who would not serve, foolishly trying to place themselves above their Creator.

In a general sense, then, there are really only two forms of government: those that serve and those that are served. Good or just government promotes the common good of the people as a whole; bad or unjust government promotes its own good and uses the people as the means to its own ends: "If . . . a community of free men is ordered by a ruler in such a way as to secure the common good, such rule will be right and just inasmuch as it is suitable to free men. If, however, the government is directed not towards the common good but towards the private good of the ruler, rule of this kind will be unjust and perverted" (DR 1.2). Justice is "the good of another," and thus governments cannot be just unless they serve those who are ruled.

After this fundamental distinction, governments can be divided in terms of how many rule: one, few, or many. Depending on whether the government is just or unjust, these forms of government are either monarchy or tyranny; aristocracy or oligarchy; polity or democracy (see DR 1.2). It is surprising enough for us to read that monarchy and aristocracy are good forms of government given that these are generally bad words in our political vocabulary, but it is downright shocking to discover that Aquinas considered democracy to be a form of unjust government. While we use this term positively today, even for the American founders "democracy" could be used as a synonym for "mob rule" or, as Aquinas puts it, "the common people oppress[ing] the rich by force of numbers" (DR 1.2).[8] This could simply be a difference of terminology, for (1) as we will see, Aquinas does in at least one instance use the word "democracy" in a positive sense; and (2) "polity" is hardly a household word, but it would signify something like what we mean by rule of the people: polity is that form of government by which the majority rule for the sake of the common good. Yet even here we must recognize that Aquinas saw political matters differently, for, returning to the model of divine government, he did not think that polity was the best form of government.

In no uncertain terms, and on multiple occasions, Aquinas states that "a kingdom is the best of all governments" (ST II-II.50.1ad2; see also DR 1.3). Returning to what he says regarding divine government, since the end of government is to make a people one in the sense of sharing a single, common good, this is best done by what is already one. And since an assembly, group of elders, and so forth is not itself one, but only a king is, monarchy is the best form of government. Almost immediately upon stating this, though, Aquinas points out a significant problem with this arrangement: while kingship may be the best form of government, tyranny is the worst. And since "both

---

8. See, for example, *Federalist* 10, where James Madison contrasts a "pure democracy" with a republic.

the best and the worst can occur in a monarchy—that is, under government by one—the evil of tyranny has rendered the dignity of kingship odious to many" (*DR* 2.5; see also *ST* I-II.105.1ad2). The danger of tyranny is so great that kingship may be better left to God. Even if an earthly king is truly just, and even if he does not let his power destroy his integrity, will his son be so wise and just? Only one King is immortal, and all the rest can be replaced by tyrants.

In light of this danger that kingly rule presents, Aquinas discusses another kind of best government, not the best *in itself* but the best *in practice*: the "mixed" regime. Not only does kingship suffer from the danger of turning tyrannical, but it also tends to be unstable. As Aquinas, following Aristotle, points out: "All should take some share in the government: for this form of constitution ensures peace among the people, commends itself to all, and is most enduring" (*ST* I-II.105.1). Thus, *in practice*, the best form of government is mixed in the sense that it has a share in all three good forms of rule, "being partly kingdom, since there is one at the head of all; partly aristocracy, in so far as a number of persons are set in authority; partly democracy, i.e. govern- ment by the people,[9] in so far as the rulers can be chosen from the people, and [to the people pertains the election of their rulers]" (*ST* I-II.105.1).[10] *In practice*, then, the best form of government has a democratic base and yet is under the guidance of a king to whom is entrusted the care of the people. And while there are important differences between this understanding of the mixed regime and that of the American founders such that, as Richard J. Regan points out, it would be more appropriate to call Aquinas's best regime *in practice* a "constitutional monarchy," hopefully we recognize that we are not a democracy as Aquinas understood that term.[11] Rather, the US is a mixed regime in which the elected officials are popular (House of Representatives), aristocratic (Senate), and kingly (president).

Finally, this awareness of the distinction between best *in itself* and best *in practice* points us toward the third and final kind of best government: the best *for us*. Just as civil law will be framed differently in the various political com- munities throughout time and place, so too will the best form of government differ in these communities. Human law takes into account the particularities

---

9. While Aquinas uses the term "democracy" here, which seems to contradict his point that democracy is the unjust form of rule by the many, in this context he uses this term in the generic sense of "rule by the people."

10. I have modified the translation to better follow the Latin. The original translation has "the people have the right . . . ," which is misleading given that Aquinas does not think in terms of rights in the modern sense of the term. Again, we will take up the issue of rights in chap. 7.

11. See Richard J. Regan, "Aquinas on Political Obedience and Disobedience," *Thought* 56.1 (1981): 79–80.

of the community and the relative virtues and vices found therein. Since the goal of law is to educate the people in virtue, and since education must be based on what these citizens can reasonably learn given their native abilities and cultures, human law is variable. Similarly, when we discuss "democracy building" today, we acknowledge that those people who have lived under absolutist regimes, having no experience of being consulted in the framing of laws, lack the basic habits and skills necessary for successful democracy. They must be educated in democratic processes and in how political institutions that are accountable to the people function. As Aquinas pointed out in response to the question "Why did God wait so long before sending the Messiah and teaching the New Law of love?" even God must work with what is given to him: "A thing is not brought to perfection at once from the outset, but through an orderly succession of time; thus one is at first a boy, and then a man" (*ST* I-II.106.3). In some countries there are plenty of boys but few or even no men. If the people think the best way of life is having as many toys as possible and seeking the pleasures of the moment, they are not fit to choose their rulers, and perhaps are hardly capable of being ruled. And all of this reminds us of the centrality of virtue for living well, both for those who are burdened with rule and for those who are called to obey rulers who may be serving themselves rather than the common good.

5. The Virtues of Political Life in Relation to the Forms of Government and Law[12]

Background Reading: ST I-II.96.6; II-II.50; DR 1.9, 13–16

The fullest expression of natural, moral life is intrinsically directed toward citizenship and political authority. This can be seen when one reflects on the relationship between the moral virtues, for general justice ranks supreme among them insofar as it directs the acts of the other moral virtues toward the common good. Thus, the virtues in political life look to the common good and are directed thereby via the virtue of justice. Here we will discuss justice and its annexed virtues as practiced in political life, concluding with a reflection on the role of prudence.

Before analyzing the role of the virtues in political life, it is worth pausing to point out how different Aquinas's understanding of citizenship and political authority is from our own. Americans are reared on the doctrine

---

12. This section adapts some material from Michael P. Krom, "Civic Virtue: Aquinas on Piety, Observance, and Religion," *Proceedings of the American Catholic Philosophical Association* 88 (2015): 145–53.

of rights and as a consequence have little trouble recognizing the obligation of the state to render services to its citizens. Our nation could even be said to have been founded on this understanding spelled out in the Declaration of Independence, that we have rights and institute governments in order to protect and promote them. Consequently, we often have a difficult time recognizing any obligation we as citizens might have toward our government. It is true enough that when Kennedy famously exhorted us to ask what we can do for our country, we did not disagree with him. And yet we have a hard time articulating what this might mean, for we know how to speak in terms of our rights but not so much in terms of our duties. As we have intimated elsewhere, this emphasis on rights is distinctly modern, for a more ancient tradition of political discourse spoke primarily of duties or commandments as the proper language of social and political life.

Today we tend to think of ourselves not as members of families and communities into which we were born but as autonomous (i.e., self-ruled) individuals bound to one another only as a result of previous choices. This radical "individualism" leads us to look upon words like "obedience," "conformity," and "submission" with scorn. As Michael Sandel puts this when describing what he calls the "unencumbered self," the modern vision is one that rejects our social nature: "Freed from the dictates of nature and the sanction of social roles, the human subject is installed as sovereign, cast as the author of the only moral meanings there are."[13] Yet, returning to the moral theory we outlined in part 1, a good life is not so much about deciding who we are but about discovering who we are, not so much about self-willing as about self-knowing. Happiness is found by living in accordance with our nature and, with the virtues as our guides, placing our will in the service of those who have authority over us, from parents to rulers to God. In contrast to our "Don't tread on me" attitude, Aquinas thinks in terms of what Leonard Ferry aptly calls "a framework of deference."[14] Justice leads us to acknowledge our debts to others and to render our fellow citizens and leaders their due through acts of deferential self-giving.

Insofar as justice is a general virtue, it directs the acts of the other moral virtues toward the common good. So, for example, while it belongs to temperance to regulate the concupiscible passions when one is at table, justice directs the acts that temperance enjoins to the good of others. This could be accomplished by serving others first, making sure that there is enough food for

13. Michael J. Sandel, "The Procedural Republic and the Unencumbered Self," *Political Theory* 12.1 (1984): 87.

14. Leonard Ferry, "The Framework of Deference: Obedience as a Political Virtue," *Maritain Studies / Études Maritainiennes* 26 (2010): 5.

all, and so on. Further, general justice is called "legal justice" in that it takes its rule from the law governing the political community (see *ST* II-II.58.5). As Michael Pakaluk explains, "General justice . . . is simply doing what is right and required according to the principles or laws regulating the behavior of members of an association, as members."[15] As we mentioned in the case of civil law, driving on the right side of the road in the US is just because the government has established this as such. One promotes the common good of the community by following this law, and thus gives others their due of safe driving conditions.

Thus, legal justice frames one's actions in the context of the common good. While to modern ears the adjective "legal" here may suggest "conventional" or even connote a contrast with "moral" (e.g., the manipulative lawyer defends an immoral man by showing that his actions were, technically speaking, legal), this is far from Aquinas's meaning. Justice is called "legal" insofar as it is regulated by both natural and human law. As Aquinas argues, "Since it belongs to the law to direct to the common good, . . . it follows that the justice which is in this way styled general, is called 'legal justice,' because thereby man is in harmony with the law which directs the acts of all the virtues to the common good" (*ST* II-II.58.5). Natural law commands us to render others their due, and yet human law is required to establish with more precision, and in particular circumstances, what is due to each. Thus legal justice is that virtue by which, given the nature of the political community, citizens maintain proper relationships with one another.

One note here to make on general justice: given that civil law does not try to promote every act of virtue, we must distinguish between being a good citizen and being a good person. In one sense, anyone who obeys the laws of his country is just, but in another sense, only the one who goes beyond the minimal demands of civil law is just. Recall the 1986 Dodge Omni example: imagine that your neighbor's Omni is the GLHS Shelby model and you do not reveal this to him. While civil law permits you to buy the car for much less than it is worth, you have still treated your neighbor unjustly. Only if we could live in the best city *in itself* would being a good citizen be identical to being a good person.[16]

In chapters 1 and 3 we focused on the particular virtue of justice. Whereas general justice looks to the common good, particular justice looks to the

15. Michael Pakaluk, "Is the Common Good of Political Society Limited and Instrumental?," *Review of Metaphysics* 55 (2001): 66.

16. This was the dream of Socrates, to live in the "city laid up in the heavens." As the reader can surely anticipate, Christianity promises that this dream can come true: in the heavenly Jerusalem God's perfect law of love is the law that all freely obey.

good of one's relations with other individuals (see *ST* II-II.58.7). We already discussed commutative justice, but said little about distributive justice. While any individual placed over a community must practice distributive justice, from the father or mother up to the king, our concern here is with the political ruler's practice of this virtue. In general, distributive justice comes into play anytime the government has a surplus of goods that should be given back to the citizens. Yet this is not specific enough, for how is one to determine the basis of this distribution? As is his wont, Aquinas tells us that it depends on the situation: "In distributive justice a person receives all the more of the common goods, according as he holds a more prominent position in the community. This prominence in an aristocratic community is gauged according to virtue, in an oligarchy according to wealth, in a democracy according to liberty, and in various ways according to various forms of community" (*ST* II-II.61.2). Thus, the ruler who practices distributive justice must do so in accordance with the type of community he or she is ruling over. Finally, there is a sense in which the citizens themselves practice the virtue of distributive justice "in so far as they are contented by a just distribution" (*ST* II-II.61.1ad3). If they live in an aristocracy, they must recognize that more will go to those who have performed virtuous actions that benefited the community; if they live in a democracy, they must recognize that the goal is to maximize liberty, even if this means not giving as much to those who have done more for the community.

Of the secondary virtues annexed to justice, observance and obedience are most central to political life, though we will add a few words concerning truth, vengeance, and friendliness. First, observance concerns itself with establishing equality in the public sphere. Just as a special virtue is assigned to acts toward God (religion), and another for parents (piety), so there is a special virtue for acts toward "a person who, in some way, exercises providence" (*ST* II-II.102.1). Strictly speaking, such a person must have authority over us, and thus observance is directed toward rulers; it is only in a derivative way that observance extends to "those who excel in [knowledge] and virtue" (*ST* II-II.102.1ad2).[17]

Observance demands that we acknowledge the superiority of those placed over us in a position of governance. In light of this superiority, one honors a political authority (see *ST* II-II.103); in light of this governance, one "render[s] him service, by obeying his commands, and by repaying him, according to

---

17. The Latin here is *scientia*, and I have changed this from "science" to "knowledge." *Scientia* is not limited to the objects of the empirical sciences, but more broadly includes any object that can be known theoretically (e.g., mathematical objects or spiritual beings).

one's faculty, for the benefits we received from him" (*ST* II-II.102.2). There are three kinds of acts to consider here: first, to the extent that observance demands obeying superiors, it calls upon the virtue of obedience; second, repaying for benefits would include paying taxes; third, Aquinas refers back to the virtue of piety when discussing the added consideration of paying back superiors by serving the common good.[18] An example of this third kind of act is "serv[ing] them in the administration of the affairs of the state" (*ST* II-II.102.3); this is more properly an act of piety than of observance and in modern terminology could be called "patriotism."

While observance and obedience are concerned with obligations toward authorities, truth, vengeance, and friendliness are directed toward fellow citizens. And while we might not think of these as regarding the duties of citizenship, they clearly have a bearing on civic life in that they promote harmonious relationships between members of the political community, primarily in terms of moral rather than legal debt. Truth is a part of justice in that one has a moral debt to make the truth known to another. This is an important aspect of citizenship because "it would be impossible for men to live together, unless they believed one another, as declaring the truth one to another" (*ST* II-II.109.3ad1). Vengeance is the avenging of harm against oneself or another "with the intention, not of harming, but of removing the harm done" (*ST* II-II.108.2). Finally, friendliness has to do with establishing right relationships between people, for it regards the general love that one ought to have toward all humans as manifested by affable behavior toward them. We could call this "decency" and recognize that we owe it to others whether we are walking down the street, driving our car, or gathering in a public place.[19]

Equity is that part of justice which comes into play in cases where following the letter of the law would "frustrate the equality of justice and be injurious to the common good" (*ST* II-II.120.1). If, for example, you are driving a mother who is in labor to the hospital in the middle of the night, speeding and running red lights can actually be just, assuming that you do not thereby unnecessarily endanger the mother and child, yourself, and others. Equity is an acknowledgment of the limits of human law and of the fact that the virtue of justice goes beyond mere obedience to the laws of one's political community. And yet when the law does not provide a sufficient guide for justice, how does one determine what is owed to another?

---

18. It is also worth mentioning that, in one respect, obedience seems to be unique in that it is a "tertiary" virtue, being placed under religion, piety, or observance. In another respect, though, it is a special virtue that can even in a sense be included in all acts of virtue. See *ST* II-II.104.2–3.

19. And, yes, politicians owe this to one another as well, even though it is so rarely practiced.

Recall that prudence is that virtue by which we determine the means to bring about the good ends of the other virtues, and this is our final virtue for political life. In chapter 3 (§3) we mentioned that prudence can be divided into three types, personal (ethics); economic (economics); and political (politics). Aquinas further specifies that political prudence in the fullest sense is called "regnative" and is found in the virtuous ruler, "who has to govern not only himself but also the perfect community of a city or kingdom" (*ST* II-II.50.1). In order to look out for the common good, the ruler must be both just and prudent, crafting law, policies, and decisions as the best means to bring about justice in the community. Political prudence in its generic sense belongs to the good citizen who is entrusted with the task of obeying the law as a means toward justice. This might entail acting against the letter of the law in cases where the law will not work to the common good. As Aquinas warns, this is only to be done in the extreme case. For "if the observance of the law according to the letter does not involve any sudden risk needing instant remedy, it is not competent for everyone to expound what is useful and what is not useful to the state: those alone can do this who are in authority" (*ST* I-II.96.6).

The good citizen is one who always acts justly toward fellow citizens and toward those placed in authority. For Aquinas, this covers a broad range of activity, from caring for one's parents to honoring political authorities, from telling the truth to punishing evildoers. In general, justice in this sense demands that citizens, as Josef Pieper puts it, "give . . . conscious consent to the just and equitable decrees of a political authority acting in the interest of the common good." As Pieper goes on to point out, this stance of ruled toward ruler does not imply complacence toward or acquiescence to injustice and tyranny, but it "oppose[s] a biased, negative attitude, illoyal from the very start,"[20] which one tends to find among those who are always concerned with their rights and rarely if ever with their duties.

We can conclude this section by admitting that we have made this all too easy, for not every citizen lives in a nation in which the rulers truly look out for the common good. What does the virtuous citizen do when living in a tyranny? Should he or she resist and establish true justice in the tyrant's stead, or submit, possibly even cooperating with the unjust rule? The last section of this chapter on political philosophy takes up such questions and connects the possibility of revolution to just war theory, and in this context we will finally take a look at our favorite archer, Robin Hood.

---

20. Josef Pieper, *The Four Cardinal Virtues*, trans. Richard Winston, Clara Winston, Lawrence E. Lynch, and Daniel F. Coogan (Notre Dame, IN: University of Notre Dame Press, 1966), 95.

6. Just War and the Limits of Obedience

Background Reading: ST II-II.40

Robin Hood is famous for "stealing from the rich and giving to the poor," and generations of children are taught to admire his wit and fighting skills used in defense of this noble mission. Still, surely it has occurred to the adults who recount Hood's exploits to wonder if what he did was really just, and if idolizing him is good for children. Do we really want our children, or adults for that matter, to think that they can take the law into their own hands, imposing their own understanding of distributive justice on the community? Such a notion threatens the very existence of law and order, making each person his own king.

And yet we love Robin Hood. Fortunately, we do not have to abandon him to the wicked men who would like to wring his neck. At least since the Victorian Era, the story of Robin Hood has been told as taking place in unique circumstances: the political situation in England is that the legitimate king, Richard the Lionheart, has left the country to fight in the Crusades. In his absence, his wicked brother, John, is acting the tyrant and assisting the wealthy to prey upon the poor. Thus, what out of context appear to be acts of vigilante justice turn out to be acts of obedient service to the true king and the common good.[21]

What do we do if the government is tyrannical? What are the limits of obedience? In this last section we take up this question and push it to the extreme possibility of engaging in revolution. Since this involves the use of violence in support of justice, we also discuss Aquinas's just war theory. While we touched upon the virtue of obedience in the previous section, we should elaborate on the nature of this virtue in order to understand its limits.

Aquinas begins his treatment of obedience in *ST* II-II.104 by asking whether or not "one man is bound to obey another." Without denying a certain natural equality between humans, Aquinas sees it as part of divine providence that society be hierarchically structured. Our parents are our superiors by virtue of giving birth to and rearing us; so too our political authorities are our superiors by virtue of their directing us to the common good. As Aquinas puts it: "The higher must move the lower by their will in virtue of a divinely established authority. Now to move by reason and will is to command. Wherefore just as in virtue of the divinely established natural order the lower natural things

---

21. For an introduction to the history of the Robin Hood story, see A. J. Pollard, *Imagining Robin Hood: The Late-Medieval Stories in Historical Context* (New York: Routledge, 2004).

need to be subject to the movement of the higher, so too in human affairs, in virtue of the order of natural and Divine law, inferiors are bound to obey their superiors" (*ST* II-II.104.1). Obeying the commands of our superiors is an indirect service to God, for it is he who establishes authority.

While disobedience is a vice, we must bear in mind that the generic virtue of obedience ordered under observance has to be compatible with religion and piety. Obedience is always a good, and yet sometimes this necessitates—and here I am carefully following Aquinas, who seems hesitant to provide a positive use of the term "disobedience"—*not* obeying political authority. There are two different reasons why a subject does not have to obey a political authority: "First on account of the command of a higher power. . . . Secondly, . . . if the [superior] command him to do something wherein he is not subject to him" (*ST* II-II.104.5).

In the first instance, and within the limits of philosophy as distinct from theology, two different scenarios are possible, for the higher power can be a human law (or authority) or natural law. The first scenario would arise in a regime with higher and lower political authorities—for example, if the mayor issues a command that goes against state law, or if a state passes a law that violates federal law. What comes to mind here in recent political events is the situation of a law-enforcement officer in a state that has legalized marijuana despite the fact that this violates federal law. The second scenario reminds us of the point that Aquinas made regarding unjust laws when he defined law itself. Since we are always bound to obey natural law as the law dictated by reason reflecting on the goods of nature, and since human law must be built upon and thus compatible with natural law, a human law that goes against natural law is no law at all. For example, if a political authority commands a subject to take his own life, this would violate natural law and thus is not to be obeyed.

Notice that in both of these scenarios the refusal to obey a political authority is still easily categorized as an act of obedience: in each case one is obeying a higher law, whether it be human or natural. The second reason for not obeying—namely, when a command is outside the authority's jurisdiction—does not present such a conflict between obeying two different laws. For example, if a political authority commands a subject to marry a certain, willing woman, obedience is not required. We can draw a distinction between the first and second reasons for not obeying in terms of obligation and freedom: if an authority issues a command that goes against a higher law, one cannot (rightfully) obey; if an authority issues a command that is outside of his or her jurisdiction, the subject has the freedom (other things being equal) of deciding whether or not to obey. In the case of an unmarried man being commanded to marry a specific woman who is herself willing to marry him,[22] he can choose to marry her out of respect for those in authority. One thing to consider here, though, is that obeying such commands runs the risk of enabling tyranny inasmuch as it allows a political authority to act outside of his jurisdiction and possibly amass unwarranted power.

It is important to make one last note on the limits of obedience before turning to the possibility of revolution. In the scenario of not obeying a political authority when a human law goes against natural law, it would be easy to overstate how common this might be. Human law is entrusted with the task of taking the broad, universal precepts of the natural law and applying them to particular situations. In some instances, this requires a prudential judgment as to how the common good can be promoted in less-than-ideal circumstances. For example, a human law can permit recreational drug use if it is deemed that criminalization will do more harm than good. In this case, a law-enforcement officer would have to obey the human law even though he recognizes that natural law does not allow for such drug use. On the other hand, human law may limit the actions of citizens, and even may harm them in doing so, and yet in most cases they must obey. For example, a government regulation may harm a certain industry, economic activities in general, or the education of the youth, and often one must obey it given the fragility of political stability and the grave danger of giving rise to mob rule. Natural law does not dictate the particulars of how businesses should be run, the economy regulated, or even schools funded, and so subjects are bound to obey the legitimate precepts of authority even when such a law will hinder the flourishing of the political body.

Not only can we say that bad laws should be obeyed in certain circumstances; we can strengthen this by adding that even unjust laws can demand obedience. It is worth quoting Aquinas at length on this point:

> Laws may be unjust . . . by being contrary to human good, . . . either in respect of the end, as when an authority imposes on his subjects burdensome laws, conducive, not to the common good, but rather to his own cupidity or vainglory—or in respect of the author, as when a man makes a law that goes beyond the power committed to him—or in respect of the form, as when burdens are imposed unequally on the community, although with a view to the common

22. To be clear, if she is not willing, such a marriage would not be valid anyway. The Arthurian romances contain a wonderful example of an obligatory wedding: Sir Gawain, out of obedience and loyalty to King Arthur, agrees to marry a most ugly lady, Dame Ragnelle. Dame Ragnelle, who had forced the whole predicament on the king, turns out to be a quite beautiful woman. This reality is only brought to light when Sir Gawain, in good Thomistic fashion, pays her the marital debt on the night of their wedding.

good. . . . Wherefore such laws do not bind in conscience, *except perhaps in order to avoid scandal or disturbance, for which cause a man should even yield his right*, according to Matthew 5:40–41: "If a man . . . take away thy coat, let go thy cloak also unto him; and whosoever will force thee one mile, go with him another two." (*ST* II-II.96.4; emphasis added)

Political authority is to be obeyed even when a command is unjust if not obeying would harm the common good. Notice that one can do this without being unjust oneself. For example, if a subject is commanded to pay a disproportionate tax, she suffers injustice, and yet she does not act unjustly. As a matter of fact, obedience to an unjust law, as odd as this may sound, is actually the just thing to do in this circumstance, for doing so places the common good above one's own good. In this difficult situation of being forced to obey a law that seeks the ruler's own good rather than the common good, it is still for the common good to live under a government that occasionally plays the tyrant rather than a government that is tyrannical through and through. As Aquinas relates, in the time of Dionysius the tyrant of Syracuse there was an old woman who hoped that he would continue his rule. When Dionysius discovered this, and asked her why she wished for his safety, she exemplified the harsh reasoning of one who knows that there are tyrants, and then there are tyrants: "When I was a girl, we suffered the oppression of a tyrant, and I longed for his death. Then he was slain, but his successor was even harsher, and I thought it a great thing when his rule came to an end. But then we began to have a third ruler who was even more savage: you. And if you were to be taken from us, someone still worse would come instead" (*DR* 1.6). Like the man freed of the unclean spirit, and subsequently inhabited by even more wicked ones (Matt. 12:43–45), one must not be too quick to throw off the tyrant who may be better than his advisors.

Since Aquinas is hesitant to use the term "disobedience" positively, in speaking about the extreme situation in which it becomes necessary to obey the natural law rather than the civil law, we will call this "obedient revolution." Obedient revolution could be defined as "the rightful attempt to overthrow a political authority who has issued commands that violate natural law." As quoted above, Aquinas is unequivocal in stating that unjust laws do not necessarily bind in conscience, and yet he stipulates two restrictions on this: even an unjust law must be obeyed in order to avoid either (1) scandal or (2) disturbance.

Aquinas follows St. Jerome in defining scandal as "something less rightly done or said, that occasions another's spiritual downfall" (*ST* II-II.43.1). He goes on to distinguish between direct and accidental scandal, depending upon whether or not one's action is itself sinful or merely appears to be so. For our purposes, accidental scandal is relevant: an unjust law ought not to be broken when doing so would lead others into vice. In general, the fact that one is not obeying a law would likely appear to others as an endorsement of disobedience rather than a type of obedience to a higher law. Thus, not obeying an unjust law must be done in such a manner that it is clear in the mind of others that the law is unjust and that this is the reason why not obeying is proper.

It is less certain what Aquinas has in mind when he mentions disturbance as necessitating obedience to an unjust law, for disturbance is not listed as a vice. I would submit that the opposite of disturbance is civil peace and that Aquinas is referring to the danger of promoting disobedience in the populace. This is plausible given his awareness of the fragility of political order. As we observed above, in his discussion of changes to the law (*ST* I-II.97), while he notes that changes in circumstances can necessitate changes in law, he is also aware that "the mere change of law is of itself prejudicial to the common good: because custom avails much for the observance of laws. . . . Wherefore human law should never be changed, unless, in some way or other, the common weal be compensated according to the extent of the harm done in this respect." He goes on to say that there must be either "some very great and evident benefit conferred by the new enactment" or an "extreme urgency of the case, due to the fact that either the existing law is clearly unjust, or its observance extremely harmful" (*ST* I-II.97.2), in order to justify the change in the law. Given this conservatism, Aquinas's restriction on not obeying appears to be rooted in his awareness that political order is not easily obtained and, once lost, is even harder to recover. Thus, in turning to the possibility of obedient revolution, one must always remember that this would be a last resort.

The key passage that opens up the possibility of obedient revolution is found in a reply to the argument that sedition is sometimes justified. Aquinas's response is as follows: "There is no sedition in disturbing a [tyrannical] government. . . , unless indeed the tyrant's rule be disturbed so inordinately, that his subjects suffer greater harm from the consequent disturbance than from the tyrant's government" (*ST* II-II.42.2ad3). Admittedly, one would not want to begin a revolution on such slim textual evidence. First, what does Aquinas mean by "disturb" (*perturbatio*) here? Given the context, a good case can be made that Aquinas has in mind at the very least a public, large-scale act of interfering with the government. The argument for this interpretation would be that he goes on to say that such disturbance is justified if and only if it does not lead to greater harm than would result from obeying the tyrannical rule; presumably this would not be a concern unless an organized group of citizens acted in concert. It is interesting to note that *perturbatio* is grammatically related to *turba*, which refers either to a commotion or to a crowd, mob, or multitude. "Disturbance," then, could be interpreted as referring to an act that temporarily turns the people into a multitude, thus undermining civic peace. This is always dangerous, for, as noted above, order lost is difficult to restore. And, further, it should be mentioned that this is the only case in the *Summa* in which disturbance has even a slightly positive connotation, for it typically refers to some bodily passion that interferes with the agent's ability to reason.[23]

Second, what does "inordinately" mean? Following the point about disturbance, an inordinate (dis-ordered, or not ordered) disturbance would be one that does not admit readily of a return to order. This would be the result of a failure to map out in advance the return to civic peace, and thus such a disturbance would be unjustified.

Third and finally, does a disturbance amount to a revolution? In the passage in question Aquinas says nothing about overthrowing the tyrannical government. Yet this is implied, for the reply he is making is to a concern about the dissension that arises when a tyrannical regime is overthrown. "Disturbance" can cover a range of actions, from forcing the government to desist from an unjust action, to overthrowing the leaders and setting up others in their place, to changing the very form of government to one more favorable to justice.

Does all of this amount to a defense of obedient revolution? While, again, the evidence is slim, I think it does. Here would be the conditions for such a revolution: (1) if the government's rule is so tyrannical that the only form of disturbance sufficient to rectify the situation is an overthrow of the government; (2) if a group of actors, preferably themselves public officials rather than private citizens, can organize themselves into a unit capable of both executing a plan and forming a stable government after the revolution; (3) if this plan has a reasonable chance of success; (4) if this plan does not involve them in unjustified acts of violence; and (5) if the benefit to the common good outweighs the suffering inflicted upon the subjects by the disturbance, then and only then is an obedient revolution justified.

Finally, we conclude this discussion of revolution, and this chapter as a whole, with a brief summary of just war theory. While obedient revolution does not neatly fall under this theory, understanding the condition for a just war helps us to recognize what is necessary to engage in violent acts, and what the limits of this violence are. Thus, we must distinguish between the

23. See, e.g., *ST* I-II.10.3, 24.2.

just conditions for going to war and what it means to give another his or her due when engaged in warfare.

In order for war to be just, three conditions must obtain: it must be (1) declared by the legitimate authority, (2) a response to "a fault" inflicted by another political community or its people, and (3) conducted with "a rightful intention, . . . the advancement of good, or the avoidance of evil" (*ST* II-II.40.1). It is hard to see how the first condition could be met in a revolution, save in the instance of one part of the government warring against another part. In general, the supreme political authority must declare war for it to be just. The second condition, just cause, would seem to prevent things like "preemptive strikes," and yet we could challenge even this: Is not another government that announces its intention of harming one's own community guilty of a fault? We can only wish that Aquinas had elaborated on this point, for he does not specify what a sufficiently grave fault is that would constitute a just cause. Finally, the third condition, rightful intention, guards against using the just cause as an excuse for an invasion or for wishing evil upon one's enemies. As one of my professors once joked, "It would be wrong to wish that Canada would commit some fault so that we could have an excuse to turn it into our vacation property." A just war cannot be waged unless all three conditions are met, and we must admit that they set a high bar.

It is hard to see how one man can fire a deadly weapon at another man and simultaneously have a rightful intention. Is it really possible to wish good for a man at whom you are firing a deadly weapon? In chapter 1 (§4) we discussed the example of killing a man in self-defense, and in that same passage where Aquinas discusses this, he makes an important qualification on the prohibition against killing: "It is not lawful for a man to intend killing a man in self-defense, *except for such as have public authority*, who while intending to kill a man in self-defense, refer this to the public good, as in the case of a soldier fighting against the foe, and in the minister of the judge struggling with robbers, although even these sin if they be moved by private animosity" (*ST* II-II.64.7; emphasis added). Thus violence can be used in defense of the common good, though here too we must observe moral norms (see, e.g., *ST* II-II.40.3). As hard as it may be, fighting must be conducted virtuously, so that soldiers who have taken human lives may return home without having lost their own humanity.

The goal of war is peace, and we could say that in some sense this is the goal of government in general. The common good can only be secured when there is harmony between the members of society, and yet this harmony must be rooted in the prior friendship of the members of a household. Further still, there is the harmony of the virtuous soul, in which reason, will, and the passions are in order. But all of this points to the need for a political theology, for, as Aquinas points out, "peace is the 'work of justice' indirectly, in so far as justice removes the obstacles to peace: but it is the work of charity directly, since charity, according to its very nature, causes peace. For love is 'a unitive force' . . . and peace is the union of the appetite's inclinations" (*ST* II-II.29.3). Human justice can open the door to peace, but only God's love for us can lay the foundation. In this fullest sense of what it means to be political, the earthly city must acknowledge its subordination to the heavenly city, both as embodied imperfectly in the pilgrim Church on earth and in that perfect, new Jerusalem in which there will be no cause for war.

6

The Twofold Citizenship
of the Christian Wayfarer
(Political Theology)

Then the Pharisees went and took counsel how to entangle him in his talk. And they sent their disciples to him, along with the Herodians, saying, "Teacher, we know that you are true, and teach the way of God truthfully, and care for no man; for you do not regard the position of men. Tell us, then, what you think. Is it lawful to pay taxes to Caesar, or not?" But Jesus, aware of their malice, said, "Why put me to the test, you hypocrites? Show me the money for the tax." And they brought him a coin. And Jesus said to them, "Whose likeness and inscription is this?" They said, "Caesar's." Then he said to them, "Render therefore to Caesar the things that are Caesar's, and to God the things that are God's." When they heard it, they marveled; and they left him and went away.

—Matthew 22:15–22

For he is our peace, who has made us both one, and has broken down the dividing wall of hostility [between Jews and Gentiles], by abolishing in his flesh the law of commandments and ordinances, that he might create in himself one new man in place of the two, so making peace, and might reconcile us both to God in one body through the cross, thereby bringing the hostility to an end. And he came and preached peace to you who were far off and peace to those who were near; for through him we both have access in one Spirit to the Father. So then you are no longer strangers and sojourners, but you are

fellow citizens with the saints and members of the household of God, built
upon the foundation of the apostles and prophets, Christ Jesus himself being
the cornerstone, in whom the whole structure is joined together and grows
into a holy temple in the Lord; in whom you also are built into it for a dwelling
place of God in the Spirit.

—Ephesians 2:14–22

1. Introduction

In chapter 2 we discussed how moral philosophy is completed by moral
theology, bringing this important dictum that grace perfects nature to bear
on the question of happiness and on what it means to "be perfect, as your
heavenly Father is perfect" (Matt. 5:48). Moral philosophy in particular, and
philosophy in general, cannot satisfy the human desire for Truth and for the
Perfect Good. As Aquinas argues, "If . . . the human intellect . . . knows no
more of God than 'that He is'; the perfection of that intellect does not yet
reach simply the First Cause, but there remains in it the natural desire to seek
the cause. Wherefore it is not yet perfectly happy" (*ST* I-II.3.8). Even those
exceedingly rare people who cultivate the acquired virtues achieve at best a
happiness that *they themselves* recognize to be imperfect. Thus, the infusion
of virtues, gifts, and fruits allows us to pass through this valley of tears with
the charity that casts out fears and to look forward with hope to the perfect
happiness of the beatific vision. This infusion of friendship with God and
neighbor as self allows us to go beyond human justice and to recognize that
what is due to others is not a calculation of what is mine and what is yours,
but friendship. In a word, a good life is practicing charity, or love of God and
of neighbor in the God who is Love.

In chapter 4 we applied these insights into how grace perfects nature to
economics. While charity does not negate the important distinction between
mine and yours, it deepens our awareness of how flimsy human claims to ownership are. God owns all things, and yet he is a generous giver of gifts. When
we recognize that he gave us the gift of both life and eternal life, and when we
take St. Paul's words to heart—"You are not your own; you were bought with
a price" (1 Cor. 6:19–20)—we recognize that our goods are gifts to be shared
with our neighbor. And the question "Who is my neighbor?" (Luke 10:29)
is best answered not in the abstract but in a life of love under the tutelage of
the Holy Spirit. The practice of charity begins in the home and works its way
outward to include the whole human family. The goods entrusted to me and
to you have their value to the extent that they can be used in acts of brotherly

love, piety toward our parents, and mercy toward the elderly widower down the street or the homeless child halfway across the globe.

Political theology perfects the natural desire for justice in community, for life under human laws in service to the common good, and (by pointing to the charity that holds together the perfect community of the heavenly Jerusalem) for peace between neighbors. It does this by directing these to Divine law in service to the Body of Christ; and to the peace of Christ, which alone can be the basis of friendship between neighbors. And yet political theology is not just an otherworldly teaching about what awaits us in the life to come but also a this-worldly teaching about how to put into practice Christ's command to "render to Caesar the things that are Caesar's, and to God the things that are God's" (Mark 12:17). Our study will be divided into the following sections: (1) the need for and nature of Divine law; (2) the relationship between the City of God and City of Man; (3) infused virtues, gifts, and fruits; and (4) Christians as the leaven of the political community.

2. The Need for and Nature of Divine Law

Background Reading: ST I-II.91, 98–99, 108

As we explained in chapter 5, our ability to reason and freely guide our own actions means that our participation in eternal law is different from that of other earthly creatures. This providence that the human being has over his or her own actions is worthy of a different name, natural law, to indicate this unique relationship to God as made in his image and likeness. Further, this natural law is built up by human reason so as to perfect a community of people. This human law is directed to the common good, and thus to the happiness of all of those bound by it. Yet we have seen how inadequate this human law is as a teacher in the virtues, for it is limited in scope to the prevention of those vices from which even the wicked can refrain, and thus leaves those who seek after perfect virtue to their own devices. Just as natural virtue seeks its perfection in infused virtue, human law is in need of a higher law to truly bring about a just community.

This higher, "Divine law" brings to completion our pursuit of the good life, allowing us to obey more perfectly the eternal law (see *ST* I-II.19.4ad3) and placing our desire for happiness under the guidance of revealed truths regarding how we should live. Now faith and reason can cooperate in perfecting our nature via the grace that alone can direct us to our supernatural end, the beatific vision. In his response to the question as to whether Divine law is necessary (*ST* I-II.91.4), Aquinas highlights four reasons why God had to reveal to us a law that goes beyond both human and natural law. We have already discussed the first reason—namely, that the human end goes beyond nature and thus requires revelation for its achievement—and we will devote space to the other three as a way of revisiting various points made in chapter 5 about natural and human law.

The second reason why Divine law is necessary is "the uncertainty of human judgment." Given that our judgment is fallible, and especially so in regard to the dizzying number of particular situations of moral life, we find that even well-intentioned interpreters of the natural law will reach conflicting conclusions. As Aquinas said in regard to those few wise men who reasoned to the existence of God, the knowledge of natural law as applied to the particulars of our lives "would only be known by a few, and that after a long time, and with the admixture of many errors" (ST I.1.1). This is not good enough for a God who is Love, for he wants all to be saved. God wants every person to "know without any doubt what he ought to do and what he ought to avoid" (ST I-II.91.4), and thus Divine law is necessary. Further still, think of how hard it is to avoid making mistakes in math, even when we know the right formulae and how to apply them. In matters of law, we add to this the fact that we have an interest in applying the law with a bias toward ourselves, and thus only those with perfect virtue would be able to avoid listening to passion rather than to reason. Who has not said when behind the wheel, "What a jerk, why didn't she let me into her lane?" only to find himself playing the jerk to another driver? Divine law is the necessary means to the gifted end of life with God.

The third reason why Divine law is necessary speaks to the limits of human authority. Even if we imagine ourselves in the perfect natural community in which all do what virtue demands, we cannot peer into one another's hearts. At most, human law can command virtuous deeds, but not virtuous intentions. The law can command me to drive at a safe speed or give to the needy, but it cannot command me to desire the right things or to will the good of the other. Since happiness is not simply doing the right thing, but doing it with an ordered soul in which prudence, justice, fortitude, and temperance are found, human law alone cannot make us happy. As Aquinas concludes, "Human law could not sufficiently curb and direct interior acts; and it was necessary for this purpose that a Divine law should supervene" (ST I-II.91.4).

The fourth reason returns us to the point concerning the limits of human law in the naturally unnatural communities that exist in our fallen world. On the one hand, all humans desire to know and love God; on the other hand, our vices keep us from pursuing him as our end, and even from knowing that he alone is what we desire. If human law were to attempt to bring about a society in which no bad deed went unpunished and no vice, no matter how private, went uncorrected, such law would thereby "hinder the advance of the common good" (*ST* I-II.91.4). While Aquinas does not elaborate on this point, we could connect this claim with three other points: (1) recall that Aquinas generally thinks that laws, even when less than ideal, should not be changed given how powerful custom is in guiding behavior (chap. 5, §3); (2) Aquinas points out that bad people, "being unable to bear such precepts [commanding every act of virtue]" (*ST* I-II.96.2ad2), will have "contempt" for the law; and (3) as we pointed out in our discussion of revolution, even unjust laws should be obeyed if possible given how fragile political order is (chap. 5, §6). In another context, Aquinas even favorably quotes St. Augustine on the need for human law in some situations to allow for prostitution in order to avoid the greater danger of a world "convulsed with lust" (*ST* II-II.10.11). In this respect, we could say that human law's so-called common good is really the "common lesser of two evils." More positively, this fourth reason why Divine law is necessary is a reminder that God made us free, for he wanted us to do what only a free creature could do, love him. This means that even God tolerates evils and brings greater goods out of them. How much more true must this be of human governments, for they must acknowledge their limited goal of preventing public acts of wickedness, thus acknowledging the need for a higher, more perfect guide to human action.

The human desire for justice could never be satisfied were there not a Divine law guiding interior life. Notice that this is a practical correlate to the theoretical awareness of the limits of human reason: just as human, theoretical reason discovers a cause into which its gaze cannot penetrate, so too does human, practical reason discover a need for justice in the human heart, a place inaccessible to the lawgiver. And this also points to the need for a court of law in which justice will prevail, pointing in another way to the need for a divine presence in the human world. Under the guidance of faith, reason sees that only a final judgment will satisfy our desire for good deeds to be rewarded and bad deeds punished. And yet even God had to gradually teach this lesson, for the Divine law itself has changed over time, as is appropriate for a God who can say, "My yoke is easy, and my burden is light" (Matt. 11:30).

One of Aquinas's favorite words for heaven is *patria*, or "fatherland." While Divine law is unchanging in the sense that its ultimate goal is to direct us to the fatherland, a loving father knows that he must rule his children in one way when they are young and another when they have grown older (see *ST* I-II.91.5). The Divine law contained in the Old Testament (old law) was appropriate for the time of youth, relying upon fear and the desire for earthly goods as motivators; the new law of the gospel, since it is given to grown men and women, induces via love and the desire for spiritual goods. In this final age of human existence, the fullness of revelation has been given so that we may enter into our Father's home and its "many rooms" (John 14:2).

While we will not work through Aquinas's astute observations concerning the old law, the new law, and the relationship between them, we should briefly mention that this mutability of Divine law points to an important distinction that is analogous to the two kinds of human law. Recall that human law contains both the law of nations and civil law and that, whereas the law of nations contains precepts regarding what is by nature just, the civil law can command actions that are just or unjust because human authority has established them to be so. We explained this using various property law examples such as the private ownership of beaches, squatting, and determining the fair price for an object (see chap. 5, §3). The very fact that God could change the Divine law indicates that this same type of distinction must obtain here. In the old law, this is the distinction between the moral and judicial precepts, on the one hand, and the ceremonial, on the other: whereas the moral and judicial precepts revealed "that which is just in itself," the ceremonial precepts established "that which is just, not in itself, but by being a determination of the Divine law" (*ST* I-II.100.12). Let us quote Aquinas in full on this point in his discussion of right: "The Divine right is that which is promulgated by God. Such things are partly those that are naturally just, yet their justice is hidden to man, and partly are made just by God's decree. Hence also Divine right may be divided in respect of these two things, even as human right is. For the Divine law commands certain things because they are good, and forbids others, because they are evil, while others are good because they are prescribed, and others evil because they are forbidden" (*ST* II-II.57.2ad3). Aquinas does not provide examples here, but in *ST* I-II.108.1 he mentions confessing one's faith as prescribed by the new law, and denying it as forbidden. This would seem to fall in the first category, for it is just to acknowledge God as one's Creator, and unjust to renounce him. On the other hand, the sacraments would fall into the second category, for God chose baptism, Eucharist, and the like as the means to bring us closer to him, but there is nothing in the external acts themselves that makes them just. Rather, God instituted these as necessary for human perfection because he, knowing the human heart, saw bestowing his grace through them as the most appropriate way to bring us to him. In the case of the Eucharist, since the bread and wine become his body and blood, it is a grave injustice to receive unworthily. While Aquinas does not develop a terminological distinction between these two types of law, for our purpose we will refer to them as "Divine law proper" and "ecclesiastical law."

Ecclesiastical law is that part of Divine law by which God governs his people in accordance with their needs in various times and places. Though God establishes the general framework of ecclesiastical law through revelation, he also leaves it to those humans he places in charge of his people to add precepts to this law that are appropriate for the more particular circumstance of the religious community. Whereas in the old law he left little to the discretion of his people, Aquinas follows St. James in calling the new law the "law of liberty" (James 1:25; see *ST* I-II.108.1) in that it leaves it up to the freedom of believers to discern how God is calling them to manifest the charity in their hearts. That being said, Aquinas points out that there are still ruler and ruled within the Church, and thus that superiors can determine "what [those under their care] must do or avoid" (108.1). Further, when Aquinas speaks of the precepts of the new law, he usually gives the impression that he means only what is set down in the New Testament, but in *ST* I-II.107.4 he says explicitly that "some [precepts] were added [to the new law], through being instituted by the holy Fathers." Thus, as members of the Body of Christ, we must recognize the central role played by the clergy in helping the laity stay on the path of Christ, who is "the way, and the truth, and the life" (John 14:6). And, contrariwise, the clergy have a grave responsibility to guide the flock, looking both at Divine law proper and at how strong the laity are in their faith in order to determine how much should be left to discretion and how much determined by law.[1] This is no easy task, and it is compounded by the fact that the members of this universal society must also take their orders from secular governments, some of which support, and others of which undermine, her divine mission.

3. The Relationship between the City of God and City of Man

Background Reading: ST I.96.3–4, 101; I-II.21.3–4; II-II.10.7–12, 11.3–4, 12, 39.4, 40.2, 4

We have already mentioned the central saying of Jesus on rendering to Caesar what is Caesar's and to God what is God's. For Christians, religion and politics, while related, have distinct roles to play in the lives of the faithful. The fact that the new law is a law of liberty means that Christians are

---

1. Examples from our own age are regulations on fasting and abstinence. Not only has the Church considerably relaxed fasting regulations prior to receiving Communion or during Lent, but now bishops in some places have permitted the faithful to replace the Friday abstinence from meat with another sacrificial act. Has relaxing the law and emphasizing the law of liberty strengthened the faithful or not? A difficult question, indeed.

free to live in a broad variety of political communities, each of which has its own types of laws and customs. Life under a monarchy, aristocracy, polity, or mixed regime is acceptable to the Christian so long as the law does not compel actions contrary to the demands of virtue.

St. Augustine, in his *City of God*, developed the terminology of "City of Man" versus "City of God" to describe the dual citizenship that Christians have. While Aquinas does not use this terminology directly, and even though he has a more positive view of the possibilities for justice in the earthly city than did Augustine, we will use these terms as helpful ways of speaking about political theology's understanding of how Christians should direct their actions as citizens of a secular nation and of the pilgrim Church on earth. The City of Man, or the secular political community, is a satisfactory place for wayfarers to rest their weary heads so long as they do not forget that their true home is elsewhere.

While Christianity does leave the believer the freedom to live *in* the world, it insists that he or she be not *of* the world. In order to help the faithful avoid worldliness, the Body of Christ has its own form of governance; obedience to the decrees of the successors to the apostles is of central importance for virtuous living. In theory, Divine law is perfectly compatible with the laws of the City of Man, for grace perfects nature. As Aquinas puts it, "Since man is ordained to an end of eternal happiness which is inproportionate to man's natural faculty. . . , therefore it was necessary that, besides the natural and the human law, man should be directed to his end by a law given by God" (*ST* I-II.91.4). If the Church commands her children to practice infused temperance out of charity, this would go beyond, not against, the legitimate decrees of the secular government in its attempt to direct acts of temperance to earthly justice. Yet the City of God also has authority over the City of Man, and secular rulers are wont to deny this. Conflicts, should they arise (and they inevitably will), place Christians in the difficult position of having to choose between the heavenly and the earthly, perhaps even between martyrdom and apostasy. In this section we discuss the relationship we would hope for, in which the City of Man cooperates with the City of God in their respective desires to make good citizens fit for this life and the next. After discussing the virtues of political theology in the next section, we will return to the problematic situation of conflict between the two cities in the last section of the chapter.

A first, though ultimately incomplete, attempt to show how the two cities are compatible would be to think of them as acting in two autonomous spheres, the natural and the supernatural. Secular politics aims at promoting the formation of the acquired virtues with the goal of the happiness of this life. And, so this position would go, since the acquired virtues pursue an end (the common good of the city) that can be directed to the final end (life with God), the City of Man need not pay any attention to the City of God. Human justice is real justice, and if the secular authorities look to securing this, they can be confident that they will never be in conflict with the ecclesiastical authorities.

In one sense, this "autonomous spheres" interpretation seems right, for we could recall here the distinction between the best form of government in itself and in practice: were it not for the fall, humans would have lived under the best government *in itself*, one that promoted the full range of virtuous living (see *ST* I.96.3–4; 101). Yet Aquinas is insistent that in our fallen world the human law *in practice* concerns itself with promoting a common good that we might want to call a "common decency." So long as the citizens do not commit serious offenses against one another, human law is content to leave them alone. And to the extent that it must settle disputes over property, fair prices, restitution, and so forth, it demands only that its citizens make a reasonable attempt to give each other what is due. If the citizens are unjust toward one another (even in terms of acquired justice), this "freedom to sin" can be corrected by the Church and its insistence that perfect justice be met. If I pay less than the fair price, the City of Man may turn a blind eye to my injustice, but the City of God will not, and the imperfection of human law leaves plenty of room for the perfection of Divine law.

In further defense of this interpretation, to the extent that the City of Man can approximate the best government in itself and establish true, though imperfect, justice (acquired justice), the City of God can use this for the glory of God. Again, on this account it would seem that human law does not need to take note of Divine law, for the true but imperfect end it pursues is all the same *true*. If the political authorities demand that I pay you back for defrauding you of the fair price, the ecclesiastical authorities can applaud this and ask me to recognize God's justice in all of this. The acquired virtues I form by obeying the human law never conflict with the infused virtues and, further, can be willed out of charity so as to have salvific value. If I pay you back because doing so meets the demands of acquired justice, I pursue a real good; if I pay you back because acts of acquired justice are willed by God, I pursue a Perfect Good. Whether the City of Man merely prevents serious injustices or pursues the fullness of acquired justice, on the autonomous spheres interpretation it can operate separately from the City of God, for the Perfect is not the enemy of the good. In promoting the common good that is the imperfect happiness of its citizens, human law leaves open a space for the Church to promote the supernatural, common good that is the perfect happiness of her citizens.

While there is much that is right with the autonomous spheres account of the relationship between the two cities, it is incomplete. First of all, it risks falling into the error of thinking that there are two ends to human existence, the earthly and the heavenly. Yet there is only one end, the beatific vision. Nature is inherently incomplete; the attempt to pursue happiness within the limits of nature leaves us dissatisfied. As we said at the end of chapter 1 (§6), the best that acquired intellectual virtue can do is point to a God that the intellect cannot know, thus leaving our desires unfulfilled; and the best that acquired moral virtue can do is acknowledge the need for some kind of justice with God but without any way to practice the virtue of religion. In this respect, the City of Man must point beyond itself to the one, true end of human existence. As James M. Jacobs warns, a state that rejects or is indifferent to the transcendent good of communion with God easily slides into totalitarianism: "The highest good becomes, in the absence of anything transcendent, the political order itself; in essence, as Eric Voegelin has demonstrated, politics itself becomes a religion."[2] While Aquinas is less concerned with totalizing political authority than we are today, he insists upon the need to subordinate politics to religion. Aquinas favorably cites St. Isidore of Seville in laying down that one of the conditions of human law is "that it 'foster religion,' inasmuch as it is proportionate to the Divine law" (*ST* I-II.95.3).

But what does it mean to be "proportionate" here? The defender of the autonomous spheres interpretation could point to the maxim that grace perfects nature: to be proportionate is to be just in accordance with human reason and nature, leaving charity in accordance with the Divine rule and revelation to the City of God. On this view, fostering religion might mean nothing more than not hindering its freedom to teach Divine law.[3] Yet we must now recognize the second problem with this interpretation—namely, that it conflicts with some points Aquinas makes that even many disciples of Aquinas today find troubling.

In his discussion of the supernatural virtue of faith, Aquinas discusses the vices of unbelief, heresy, and apostasy. While we today think of these as irrelevant issues from the perspective of secular politics, Aquinas thought differently. It is true that in the US even today we generally insist upon at least a veneer of religiosity from our elected officials, though we no longer make

2. James M. Jacobs, "The Practice of Religion in Post-Secular Society," *International Philosophical Quarterly* 54.1 (2014): 21.

3. This is a good place to point out the value of learning Latin: Aquinas says that human law "*religioni congruat*," and this could be translated as "agree/be consistent/harmonize with religion." Depending on how one translates this, the relationship between human and Divine law can appear to be weaker or stronger.

belief a criterion of legitimate political authority.[4] Given the intimate relation between the heavenly and the earthly, Aquinas holds that it is not enough for human law to be compatible with Divine law; it must also be subservient to it. This is true in at least three respects.

First, the Church has the authority to make pronouncements on the spiritual state of those subject to her. This power "to bind and loose" that Jesus gave to the apostles and to Peter as their leader (see Matt. 16:18–19) gives them and their successors the authority to excommunicate those who betray the true faith by falsifying (heresy) or renouncing it (apostasy). Yet the Church lacks the coercive power of soldiers and corporal punishment conducive to bringing her decisions to full effect. As Aquinas says, "If forgers of money and other evil-doers are forthwith condemned to death by the secular authority, much more reason is there for heretics, as soon as they are convicted of heresy, to be not only excommunicated but even put to death" (ST II-II.11.3). But the Church is merciful and is zealous for the conversion of the "forger" of faith. Only as a last resort, "if he is yet stubborn, the Church no longer hoping for his conversion, looks to the salvation of others, by excommunicating him and separating him from the Church, and furthermore delivers him to the secular tribunal to be exterminated thereby from the world by death" (ST II-II.11.3). Thus, human law must enforce ecclesiastical decrees so as to protect the faithful from the heretic's poisonous teachings.

Second, Aquinas does not advance a robust principle of religious liberty. The concern of secular politics is to educate the citizenry in virtue. And since holding falsities to be truths is vicious, as much as possible human law aims to promote knowledge and wisdom, as well as to root out false beliefs and ignorance. Thus, for example, human law would try to prevent things like fraudulent business claims and unsound teachings about scientific matters, as well as promote an informed citizenry and scientific inquiry. Now, while it is true that the teachings of faith exceed the competency of secular politics, nonetheless the City of Man has an obligation to assist the City of God in its mission to make the Truth, the Person of Christ, known. The Church's Divine mission is thwarted by heretics, and also by unbelievers. While those who are competent in matters of faith should dispute the false claims of unbelievers, in general "the simple people" who have never been exposed to

---

4. It is worth mentioning that, at the state level, until *Torcaso v. Watkins* (1961) it was relatively common for states to require that elected officials pass a religious test. Some states still have such laws on the books. For example, the Declaration of Rights, article 37, of Maryland's constitution states "that no religious test ought ever to be required as a qualification for any office of profit or trust in this State, *other than a declaration of belief in the existence of God*" (emphasis added).

such falsehoods should be kept from unbelievers lest they be infected by unbelievers' poisonous teachings (see *ST* II-II.10.7, 9). Now this does not mean that unbelievers should be compelled to enter the Church (see *ST* II-II.10.8), for religion is a matter of free consent. We could say, then, that Aquinas does accept a limited sense of religious liberty in that non-Christians are not to be compelled to enter the Church. That being said, he does not think that they should be left free to corrupt the faithful any more than a foreigner should be free to introduce counterfeit money into the community. It is bad enough to corrupt the economy, let alone the souls of God's children.

Third and finally, human law is subservient to Divine law in that secular authorities should themselves be members of the Body of Christ. Citizens should obey, honor, and revere their secular authorities, and this can prove harmful to citizens if the people they look up to are not models of righteous living. While non-Catholics can in principle hold authority over the faithful, (1) the Church has the authority to remove them from office and should exercise it where doing so would work to the good of the faith; (2) non-Catholics who are already in positions of authority should be tolerated when necessary, but newly appointed secular leaders should be Catholics (see *ST* II-II.10.10). Further, while unbelievers are subject to the Church's authority only in the generic sense that human law is subordinate to Divine law, Catholics who renounce their faith are subject to the Church's jurisdiction over them as members of the Body of Christ. Thus, an apostate, by the very act of renouncing his faith and his subsequent excommunication, is absolved of his political authority (see *ST* II-II.12.2).

One point we should mention here before concluding this section with a discussion of the heavenly Jerusalem is that the City of God must exercise prudence in all of this. In *ST* II-II.10.11, Aquinas discusses the religious practices, or rites, of unbelievers. Reinforcing his point regarding the safeguarding of truth, he states that the religious practices of unbelievers should only be tolerated to the extent that some good can be brought from this evil. In the case of Jews, since their rites point to the need for the Messiah, and in them "our faith is represented in a figure," toleration can be a good. However, "the rites of other unbelievers, which are neither truthful nor profitable are by no means to be tolerated, except perchance in order to avoid an evil, e.g. the scandal or disturbance that might ensue, or some hindrance to the salvation of those who if they were unmolested might gradually be converted to the faith." This qualification regarding scandal or disturbance is rather important, for it establishes that the Church should not demand her Divine right to command secular authority wherever doing so would be harmful to the faith. As Aquinas goes on to state, "The Church, at times, has tolerated the rites even of heretics and pagans, when unbelievers were very numerous." In short, while Aquinas does not adopt a theory of separation of Church and state, he does acknowledge the difference between living under Christendom, on the one hand, and under the Roman Empire, on the other. When Catholics are in the minority, they must be content with praying "for the liberty and exaltation of the Holy Mother the Church."[5]

The City of God, as it travels on its pilgrim journey here on earth, will always have a tendentious relationship with the City of Man.[6] At times those who have ruled her have become corrupted by the worldly goods that secular governments can promise, and at other times she has been forced underground, hiding in the catacombs and sending out her missionaries to try to open up a path for non-Christians to live out the law of liberty. In between these two extremes, the Church has at times found the strength to fight back against human laws that tried to prevent her liberty and exaltation. Only at the end of time, in the heavenly Jerusalem, will the City of God be revealed in all its glory, and its true citizens be fully known. In the meantime, those who seek entrance into the kingdom must stay strong in the virtues, gifts, and fruits, following the path of the Beatitudes. As St. Peter admonishes us, "Be sober, be watchful. Your adversary the devil prowls around like a roaring lion, seeking some one to devour. Resist him, firm in your faith, knowing that the same experience of suffering is required of your brotherhood throughout the world" (1 Pet. 5:8–9).

4. Infused Virtues, Gifts, and Fruits

Background Reading: ST I-II.100; II-II.39, 77.1, 101.4; III.89

The good citizen is one who always acts justly toward fellow citizens and toward those placed in authority. As we have seen, this covers a broad range of activity, from caring for one's parents to honoring the president, from telling the truth to punishing evildoers. In general, justice in this sense demands that citizens obey the laws of the land. The good Christian is called upon to obey these laws, but also to obey Divine law. This does not negate the secular obligation, but actually heightens it: since infused virtue calls us to obey the legitimate decrees of the City of Man out of charity, a failure to do so is both

5. From the Leonine Prayers still recited after the Mass celebrated in the extraordinary form of the Roman Rite.

6. For a thorough study of the relationship between Church and state in Aquinas's political theory, see part 4 of Mary M. Keys's *Aquinas, Aristotle, and the Promise of the Common Good* (New York: Cambridge University Press, 2006).

unjust and unloving. In the last section of this chapter we will also consider the case in which virtue requires one to choose God over man; here we look at the ideal circumstance in which earthly and Divine justice coincide.

Recall that infused virtue acts under the guidance of the Divine rule (chap. 2, §3), and here we could specify this as Divine law. Our concern here, then, is with what it means to be a good Christian, taking one's guidance in life from the Church as the true political community. This does not negate the necessity of obeying natural law as interpreted by human law, but this is the concern of acquired, not infused, virtue. Again, acts of acquired virtue, and particularly just acts for the common good of one's earthly city, are commanded by charity, but elicited by the acquired virtue appropriate to the action in question (see chap. 4, §3). We have already discussed which acquired virtues are necessary for good citizenship in the City of Man, and here our concern is with the infused virtues placed under the guidance of the Church. And, admittedly, we are working with scant materials here, for Aquinas does not provide an extended discussion of how the infused virtues function in the life of the Church. With this in mind, let us begin with charity and then work our way through the infused cardinal virtues and infused secondary virtues.

In chapter 4 (§2) we explained that charity establishes an order of love: (1) God, (2) myself as a spiritual being, (3) neighbor, (4) myself as a bodily being. Love of neighbor is further divided into love of (a) parents, (b) spouse, (c) children, (d) other members of the family, and (e) other members of my community. Finally, love of other members of my community works its way outward from those in my immediate neighborhood to the "neighborhood" that includes the whole human community. Yet while I should love those closest to me more than those furthest away, I may be called upon to perform acts of charity such as beneficence and almsgiving for those who are more in need despite being halfway across the globe. How do I determine to whom I should perform such acts? Since this is a question of serving the Body of Christ as a whole, charity must command the other infused cardinal and secondary virtues to elicit the appropriate acts.

Infused political prudence determines the means to the end of giving glory to God by building up his Church. As a lay member of the Church, one must look to the precepts and counsels given by ecclesiastical authority to the Church as a whole, to the dioceses within one's bishops' conference, to the parishes within one's diocese, to fellow parishioners within a parish, and to oneself through a spiritual director. A similar point could be made for a monastic under a vow of obedience and also to a priest or bishop insofar as they are subject to a higher authority within the Church. This infused prudence allows the members of the Church to serve one another in all charity so as to maintain the unity of Christ's body (see *ST* II-II.183.2ad1). For example, when Pope Francis declared 2016 as the Year of Mercy, this gave focus to the activities of the Church as a whole, and some dioceses then enacted specific "days of mercy" whereby they encouraged parishioners to join together for corporal or spiritual acts of mercy. Infused political prudence allows those under a superior within the Church to determine how God is calling them to meet these ecclesiastical precepts or counsels. To provide a more general example, given that most bishops have allowed the faithful to substitute the Friday abstinence from meat with a comparable sacrifice, infused political prudence takes this general precept and applies it to the particulars of one's own life. And, finally, the perfection of this virtue, infused regnative prudence, would belong to those who hold positions of authority in the Church, especially the pope as the Vicar of Christ. In addition to formulating ecclesiastical laws that promote the common good of the Church militant, infused regnative prudence allows a prelate to determine how and when to apply fraternal correction, charitably reproving the sinner for his own spiritual good and justly punishing him for the good of the Church as a whole (see *ST* II-II.33.3).

Infused general justice allows one to will the common good of the Church as a whole and commands the acts of the other infused virtues for this end. And, again, here we wish Aquinas would have had more to say. Whereas in *ST* I-II.61.5 he tells us that justice in the life of the Christian "giv[es] a whole-hearted consent to follow the way thus proposed," in his extended discussion of justice he gives the impression that justice looks after the common good of the secular community, whereas charity looks after "the Divine good" (*ST* II-II.58.6). What I propose to add here is a concern between these two: infused general justice looks to the common good of the Body of Christ, acting under the guidance of Divine law. It is one thing to give glory to God by loving him and neighbor in him, another to build up his Church out of love for him.[7] Further, we can see why the distinction between acquired general justice and infused general justice makes sense of our experience of life under secular and ecclesiastical authority: God infuses in the believer the grace necessary for serving him in his Church, but, for example, one can be a good Christian and still be a bad American citizen by failing to meet the specific requirements of good US citizenship (e.g., think of a pious recent immigrant from a nondemocratic nation).

7. There is some evidence for my claim in Aquinas's discussion of the moral precepts of the old law, for there he speaks of general justice in connection with obedience to Divine law (see *ST* I-II.100.12). I encourage the reader to patiently read the whole of that question for a deeper understanding of the relationship between natural and Divine law and that between acquired and infused virtue.

Infused particular justice, insofar as it falls under the guidance of ecclesiastical authority, establishes justice between the members of the Church. In matters of commutative justice, Christians must look to the teachings of the Church in determining whether their transactions with others are just according to the standard of divine justice. While the human law may allow for deviations from the fair price, "the Divine law leaves nothing unpunished that is contrary to virtue" (*ST* II-II.77.1ad1). This does not mean that the Church should issue a decree on the numerical value of the various material goods of the community, but it does mean that the guide to justice in transactions is not the human law or the freedom of contract it allows but rather the God who commands us to love our neighbor as self. Similarly, distributive justice calls upon those who hold authority in the Church to distribute goods according to the measure of the Divine rule. Recall that secular authority distributes according to its form of regime (e.g., aristocracies look to virtue, democracies to liberty). The Church is subject to a Monarch, and he provides a model of distributing his gifts by "empt[ying] himself, taking the form of a servant" (Phil. 2:7). Christ came to serve the lowly of this world, and thus distributive justice in the Church is directed toward helping the poor.

While all of the secondary virtues annexed to infused justice have a role to play in the life of the Christian, we will focus on the one of particular importance: religion. The infused virtue of religion is the highest part of infused justice in that, despite its inability to render what is due, it is concerned with the debt owed to the source of our being, God (see *ST* II-II.81.6). All of the acts of the infused virtues in service to the Church are also to be performed as a service to God. Whether one is tithing (infused observance), performing a service for the Church (infused piety), or giving away one's goods to the poor (infused liberality), these ought to look toward the end of making a fitting sacrifice of one's time, talents, and very life itself. Thus infused religion and charity work together to direct everything to God as the end of our being and to unite us to him in love.

Infused fortitude allows one to engage in spiritual warfare against sin and the demons who provide myriad temptations. While in this sense fortitude is primarily about the internal battle within one's soul, it also can require risking one's bodily life out of obedience to Divine law. As we discussed in chapter 4 (§3), Aquinas defines martyrdom broadly enough to include things like dying out of service to the poor among us. In addition to St. Maximilian Kolbe, one could think of St. Damien of Molokai, who died of leprosy, a disease he contracted while serving the dispossessed of this world. As Aquinas says, "Of all virtuous acts martyrdom is the greatest proof of the perfection of charity" (*ST* II-II.124.3). Thus, while charity is the greatest virtue strictly speaking, martyrdom is the greatest sign of love for God and neighbor.

Acts of infused temperance can be commanded by ecclesiastical law to help build up the Church, as is especially seen in commanded acts of fasting (see *ST* II-II.147). Fasting is not only a means to build up the virtue of the faithful and thus strengthen their union with God but also a way to help support the poor. Something similar can be said of the secondary virtues annexed to temperance. In the case of infused chastity, a vow of virginity not only allows a woman to give herself more fully to God, but she also is a witness to others who may suffer from sexual vices. Similarly, the man who practices infused sobriety in its most abstinent form of only partaking of the Eucharist draws himself closer to the heavenly banquet and also shows the alcoholic a higher form of intoxication. As Aquinas says, "Speaking figuratively, the consideration of wisdom is said to be an inebriating draught, because it allures the mind by its delight" (*ST* II-II.149.1ad1). This is the fullness of temperance, to be wedded to Christ as spouse and drunk only on the wine of his truth.

Finally, we mention briefly here the role of the gifts and fruits of the Holy Spirit. The gifts allow one to discern more fully how the Holy Spirit is guiding the barque of Peter to the heavenly shores. Since Christianity is a religion of truth, not of law, the freedom that it gives the believer to determine what should be done here and now requires special graces. It is usually not difficult to know what the law is, but to discern God's will in the particular instances of our lives is a real challenge. God calls each of us to play a role in building up the Church and gives us the gifts of the Holy Spirit so that we may serve him in our own, unique way: "Just as in the natural body the various members are held together in unity by the power of the quickening spirit . . . so too in the Church's body the peace of the various members is preserved by the power of the Holy Spirit, Who quickens the body of the Church, as stated in John 6:64" (*ST* II-II.183.2ad3). The fruits provide the interior joy that we should experience as members of the Body. There is no task so humble in the Church that it cannot give glory to God, but our human sense of what service means may prevent us from being the joyful giver that is pleasing to the Lord. As St. Benedict has this, there are twelve steps of humility, each more challenging than the previous, and yet at the end the one who practices them will perform good actions "without effort, as though naturally, from habit, no longer out of fear of hell, but out of love for Christ, good habit and delight in virtue."[8]

---

8. *Rule of St. Benedict* 7.68–69, in *The Rule of St. Benedict in English*, trans. Timothy Fry, OSB (Collegeville, MN: Liturgical Press, 1981), 38.

5. Christians as the Leaven of the Political Community

Background Reading: ST I-II.96.4; II-II.29, 33, 124

In Aquinas's political theory, good citizenship covers a much broader range of actions than we would normally discuss today: from care for parents to respect for authority, from patriotism to divine worship; on this account, then, the virtues necessary for politics are not simply about a kind of generic participation in political life through actions like voting but about service to family, nation, and God. Further, as this concluding section will explain, Aquinas would not think that we can construct a just nation on purely secular principles, for a partial commitment to virtue would ultimately lead to vicious behavior. Human law can do very little in establishing a virtuous citizenry, and the role of the Church is to be this leaven that builds up both the natural common good of the City of Man and the supernatural common good of the City of God. While Aquinas's political theory does not necessarily call for a Catholic nation, it does view this as the ideal. At the very least, secular authority must acknowledge the distinction between rendering to Caesar what is Caesar's and rendering to God what is God's. While this minimalist requirement for the City of Man may seem satisfactory for securing the common good, Aquinas would point out that vice is destructive of communities and that even from the natural standpoint the supernatural gift of grace is necessary for human flourishing.

Christianity demands that one strike a delicate balance between honoring earthly authority and honoring heavenly authority through acts of piety and obedience (to the earthly) and religion (to the heavenly). And since the virtues are co-related and since religion is the infused moral virtue responsible for guiding the entirety of the moral life, a failure to exercise the virtue of religion will make acts of piety and obedience imperfect at best and vicious at worst. As Gerard Joubert puts it, "A sane patriotism can be constructed only upon a reasonable religion."[9] There are two extremes into which one could fall who attempts the role of the good citizen without the virtue of religion: state worship and theocracy.

Opposed to religion as a deficiency is the vice of irreligion, or failure to render worship to God (see ST II-II.97–100). Given that someone who seeks to pay his or her debts can only do so in the proper spirit by ordering them properly (God, parents, authorities, benefactors), a lack of reverence for God will disrupt this order and lead to an improper reverence toward the other

---

9. Gerard Joubert, *Qualities of Citizenship in St. Thomas* (Washington, DC: Catholic University of America Press, 1942), 135.

members in this hierarchy. State worship is what results when an irreligious citizen directs the worship due to God to the state. This could manifest itself in such things as (1) excessive patriotism whereby one sees the purpose of one's existence in terms of serving the nation, a fault commonly known today as "nationalism"; (2) a centralism that views the highest level of government as the proper channel for addressing all social issues, a direct violation of the organic understanding of politics; (3) state-messianism, or a belief in the government as savior that results when one fails to distinguish between justice and charity; (4) active persecution of religion, feeding the tendency of government to act as "jealous god" that cannot tolerate any competing claims to authority.

Opposed to religion as excess is superstition, which "offers divine worship either to whom it ought not, or in a manner it ought not" (*ST* II-II.92.1). In the political realm, this is the vice peculiar to the misguided believer who seeks religious solutions to what are really political problems. While this might have many of the same practical consequences as state worship, here one either literally believes the state to be divine or seeks to please God via an unbefitting political action; broadly speaking, this vice could be called theocracy. Manifestations of this could include (1) Caesaropapism (i.e., uniting the secular and religious authority); (2) viewing one's nation as holy, as the heavenly Jerusalem brought down to earth; (3) seeking to please God by using political power to force nonbelievers to engage in religious actions; (4) the failure to recognize the necessity of disobeying unjust commands under the pretense that God commands obedience to political authority.

Whether or not a people inclines more toward irreligion or superstition, the lack of religion in the citizenry leads it down the path of totalitarianism. It is absolutely critical that a people maintain a strong commitment to a transcendent measure of the common good in order to protect the true flourishing of its members. While it is true that the citizens are in some sense "parts" of the political community, in the eyes of God they are wholes. As Jacques Maritain explains, "The person as such is a *totality*, . . . through his ordination to the transcendent whole, he even surpasses the temporal society."[10] Christianity is a bulwark against tyranny, then, both in its building up of a virtuous citizenry devoted to a God who loves us as individual persons and also in its providing the proper outlet for the desire to give honor and worship. That being said, it is hard to see how Christianity can play this role given that its founder did not fight back against injustice, but submitted

10. Jacques Maritain, "Human Person and Society," in *Scholasticism and Politics* (Indianapolis: Liberty Fund, 2011), 73.

and offered up his life rather than take up the sword. An important point to take up, then, by way of conclusion to this chapter is what the Christian response to injustice should be.

In chapter 5 (§6) we discussed a situation in which the human law conflicted with natural law, and we considered the possibility of not obeying the secular authority. Here we must add the possibility of a conflict between human and Divine law. For example, if a political authority forbade the celebration of the Eucharist, one must obey God rather than human beings. It is always and everywhere wrong to disobey Divine law, even if obedience to it puts one's bodily life at risk. Whereas it is morally acceptable to obey human laws that go against natural law if this is necessary to avoid "scandal or disturbance," violating the Divine law admits of no such exception: "Laws may be unjust through being opposed to the Divine good: such are the laws of tyrants inducing to idolatry, or to anything else contrary to the Divine law: and laws of this kind must nowise be observed, because, as stated in Acts 5:29, 'we ought to obey God rather than man'" (*ST* I-II.96.4). Such is the dignity of even a single soul that the common good of the City of Man is of lower value than one's salvation.

Yet in such a case, what is the Christian to do? It would seem clear that the answer is to imitate our Savior by offering oneself up to martyrdom. But is that always and everywhere true? Is it morally acceptable for Christians to take up arms in defense of the liberty of the Church? We spoke in chapter 5 (§6) about the possibility of natural, obedient revolution, and here we wonder if there is an analogous type of revolution distinct to Christians.[11]

Divine, obedient revolution could be defined as "the rightful attempt to overthrow a political authority who has issued commands that violate Divine law." And it would seem that there is no such thing as divine, obedient revolution, for Christ does not allow his disciples to take up arms in defense of Divine law. The response to a political authority who commands Christians to go against Divine law is not to seek to overthrow, but to seek to suffer: as Aquinas says, "Martyrdom embraces the highest possible degree of obedience, namely obedience unto death" (*ST* II-II.124.3ad2). To be clear, this does not mean that Christians cannot participate in a revolution, but that they cannot do so qua persecuted Christians. For example, if a political authority commands soldiers to kill innocent people, Christian soldiers can participate in a revolution; if a political authority commands the same soldiers to worship

---

11. A further issue is how one is to respond to unjust commands given by ecclesiastical authorities. The only thing Aquinas has to say on this subject is that fraternal correction requires the Christian to correct a superior, though this should be done privately (see *ST* II-II.33.3).

idols, Christian soldiers must obey the God who exemplified true courage by giving up his life.

Another way of putting this point is that while Christians do not reject the possibility of legitimate use of violence in defense of justice, they hold that only the City of Man can authorize it. While in some situations the City of God can command the City of Man to take up the sword, she does not directly command her own citizens to do so, but rather recognizes that this is the jurisdiction of secular authority. In the case of war, it must be emphasized that Aquinas speaks of just war, not holy war. Only the secular authority can declare war, and only as a result of an injustice that threatens the common good. This does not absolutely rule out wars fought for the liberty and exaltation of the Church, but it places the decision-making and violence-commanding authority in the hands of the secular authority.

Wars are fought for the sake of peace, and thus the City of Man has a central role to play in satisfying the natural desire to live harmoniously with one's fellow human beings. Yet Aquinas would be quick to point out that, as we said at the conclusion of chapter 5, only God can establish true peace by working charity into our hearts. It is interesting to note that sedition and war, both of which we would consider to be political problems, are vices in relation to the virtue of charity. The world would consume itself were it not for the leaven of God's love that he places in our hearts. Further, though the Church does not condemn war as such, it limits both the number of available combatants from among the citizenry (see *ST* II-II.40.2) and the days of the year on which they may fight (see *ST* II-II.40.4).

There is an ancient saying that "man is a wolf to man," and, as much as Aquinas speaks of the importance of the natural common good, he is always wont to point out that only grace can satisfy our desire for justice. His description of life in the City of Man should remind us of the story of Cain: Cain founded the first city, and it was only fear of God's wrath that kept others from killing him. The City of Man is bound together by fear perhaps more than by love. Yet "the fear of the Lord is the beginning of wisdom" (Prov. 9:10), and the City of Man's radical inability to secure the conditions for happiness only points all the more clearly to the need for a Savior who alone can found a city of love and true happiness. As St. Peter so boldly told the Jewish authorities, "There is salvation in no one else, for there is no other name under heaven given among men by which we must be saved" (Acts 4:12). Only salvation will do, for the human heart's desire is for the Perfect Good; left unsatisfied, it will devour the human race itself, making of the City of Man a mortal god, a jealous god that will demand bloody sacrifices in its tyrannical attempt to create an illusory heaven here on earth. And still there is hope in all of this, for our God offered himself up to men who cried out, "His blood be on us and on our children" (Matt. 27:25), and used this perverse desire to replace God with Man as the means of our salvation. God himself offered the bloody sacrifice and continues today to offer those who "know not what they do" (Luke 23:34) the peace that can only be found in the sacrifice of the Mass.

PART 4

The Perennial Teaching of the Angelic Doctor

7

Aquinas's Moral, Economic, and Political Theory Today

1. Introduction

We have just completed an introductory tour of Aquinas's moral, economic, and political theory, showing that on his account our natural desire for happiness directs us to (1) cultivate the cardinal virtue of justice in our souls, (2) engage in economic transactions such that we value objects in light of what we owe to one another as persons, and (3) work together as members of families, communities, and political bodies in pursuit of the common good. This philosophical focus on justice must be completed by the theological recognition that charity builds upon and perfects this earthly justice, such that by the life of grace we can (1) achieve the perfect happiness for which we long, (2) value earthly goods in terms of how they contribute to reaching our heavenly home, and (3) subordinate the common good of the political community to the transcendent good of the Body of Christ. In this remaining chapter we will build upon this foundation, applying Aquinas's vision to some of the most pressing issues of our times. As we do so, we will also have an eye toward Church teaching today, showing how Aquinas is helpful in understanding as well as articulating CST.

Before we begin, let us bear in mind that it is hard enough to understand Aquinas's teachings in their own terms, much less determine how they would bear on questions that he himself did not ask. We are separated from him not only linguistically but historically as well: the more than seven hundred years that separate us from him make it necessary to "update" him on (1) the scientific and technological advances of our times; (2) the globalized, wage-based economies in which we make exchanges; and (3) the modern nation-state governing upwards of hundreds of millions of people. Since Aquinas cannot speak for himself, we must think of this in terms of what it means to be a Thomist today.

While Aquinas's central conviction that the key to human happiness is found in virtue and grace is clearly shared by the Church today, as we turn our attention to particular moral, economic, and political issues, we will come across ways in which Aquinas's understanding needs to be completed and complemented by contemporary Church teaching.[1] Most obviously, we could see this as a result of living in different societies. On the one hand, as John Paul II put it, there are "fundamental questions which pervade human life: *Who am I? Where have I come from and where am I going? Why is there evil? What is there after this life?*"[2]; and in this respect Aquinas is the Common Doctor who articulates the tradition for his time and for all times. On the other hand, the secondary questions of the thirteenth century are not the same as the questions of the twenty-first century, and so we should not be surprised to find that Aquinas either does not answer questions we wish he would have answered or does ask the questions but not in a way familiar to us.

A Dominican of our time, Serge-Thomas Bonino, speaks of a *"Living Thomism . . .* [that] strives for a living fidelity to the teaching of St. Thomas" by, first, studying the historical context in which Aquinas wrote in order to gain a deeper understanding of his thought, and second, applying Aquinas's teaching to contemporary questions and schools of thought.[3] Here we are concerned with this second "stage" of Thomism, and we will rely upon three basic principles: we can assume that Aquinas today would (1) take up the best science of our day, (2) adhere to Church teaching, and (3) engage in constructive dialogue with the last seven hundred years of social and political developments as well as philosophical schools of thought.[4]

First, advances in science necessitate updating Aquinas. While we are not concerned here with the larger questions of how to relate Aristotelian-based

1. The *Catechism* (part 3, chap. 1) discusses beatitude/happiness; the virtues, gifts and fruits, and beatitudes; sin; and so forth. This condensed presentation of Church moral teaching pretty much reads as a distillation of Aquinas's moral theory.

2. John Paul II, *Fides et Ratio* (September 14, 1998), §1, website of the Holy See, http://w2.vatican.va/content/john-paul-ii/en/encyclicals/documents/hf_jp-ii_enc_14091998_fides-et-ratio.html.

3. Serge-Thomas Bonino, "To Be a Thomist," *Nova et Vetera* 8.4 (2010): 771–72.

4. See Romanus Cessario, *A Short History of Thomism* (Washington, DC: Catholic University of America Press, 2005), 11–28, for a fuller discussion of how to delineate what makes one a Thomist, as well as a list of particular philosophical principles to which Thomists adhere.

science to modern science, we must acknowledge, for example, that Aquinas was ignorant about basic biological facts regarding the development of the fetus. Further, he was not confronted with the possibility of controlling and manipulating nature through technology (at least not to the extent that we can today), and thus we must think through how to apply his fundamental insights to these more particular issues.

Second, we must recognize that following Aquinas is not the same thing as *blindly* following him; most famously, Aquinas rejected the doctrine of the Immaculate Conception. Though we can assume that he would have accepted it had he lived after the dogma was officially declared, he reasoned to the wrong position on this issue, and one who followed him on this would be a heretic, choosing to follow Aquinas rather than the Church. As we proceed through a variety of contemporary issues, we will always take Church teaching as our starting point and show how Aquinas either is in agreement with it or could arrive at it through a development of his teaching.

Third and finally, the development of new technologies, types of social and political arrangement, and philosophical schools of thought requires a critical examination based on Aquinas's teaching. In our brief study this will be particularly important in economics and politics, for we must take up questions concerning modern, wage-based and globalized economics, as well as modern liberal democracies. In regard to philosophical schools of thought, in our discussion we will point to the work of contemporary Thomists who have engaged in dialogue with various schools of philosophy.

One more point to mention before proceeding: we must be attentive to the distinction between faith (theology) and reason (philosophy) here, for it is important to see that, by and large, the Church's position on human sexuality and economic justice is rooted in reason; the Church here is not offering teachings that only pertain to Catholics, but to all people of good will. This is why in the public sphere, as we will discuss when we turn to politics, she rightly insists that the governments of the world be attentive to the moral norms that should be observed in any society.

2. Aquinas's Moral Theory Today

The body is not meant for immorality, but for the Lord, and the Lord for the body. And God raised the Lord and will also raise us up by his power. Do you not know that your bodies are members of Christ? Shall I therefore take the members of Christ and make them members of a prostitute? Never! Do you not know that he who joins himself to a prostitute becomes one body with her? For, as it is written, "The two shall become one." But he who is united to the

Lord becomes one spirit with him. Shun immorality. Every other sin which a man commits is outside the body; but the immoral man sins against his own body. Do you not know that your body is a temple of the Holy Spirit within you, which you have from God? You are not your own; you were bought with a price. So glorify God in your body.

—1 Corinthians 6:13–20

We began our discussion of moral theory in chapter 1 by addressing a common misconception: we often think of moral life in terms of rule following, of doing one's duty as opposed to doing what one wants. As we showed, though, Aquinas helps us go beyond this, to recognizing that a moral life is a happy and blessed life, that those who freely and lovingly do what is right and just most truly do what they want. We want Truth, Goodness, and Beauty, and nothing less than a life of justice and charity will satisfy us.

In chapter 2 we began with a similar observation: religion in general, and Catholicism in particular, is often thought of as a body of rules enforced by a priestly caste which uses fear of damnation to keep us on the straight and narrow. Even if we believe the Church to be instituted by God, we may think of morality as about choosing to follow God's rules in this life so that he will reward us in the next. In this way, we think of religion as doing what God wants rather than what we want, as making a calculation of long-term self-interest: "God sees everything, and he will punish me for having a good time in this life; but if I do what he wants now, he will reward me in the next life by letting me do what I want." If we have such a view, we think that those living the life of pleasure and indulgence are right about the good life, just wrong about when to live it. We believe that those who think life is about eating, drinking, and being merry have the right idea, but they do not realize that you have to work hard in this life so that you can live the party life in heaven. What this view fails to recognize is that God wants what we want, in this life and in the next: God wants us to be happy. As we apply this general moral theory to human sexuality, we must always bear in mind this fundamental conviction that the goal is not to stifle sexual delight, but to elevate and integrate it into a life of true joy and love.

2.1 CST on Human Sexuality

Background Reading: CCC 2331–2400

The first point we should make here is that sexual intercourse is a good and beautiful means by which humans express their love for one another, come to know one another, and participate in God's creative love. People often say that sex is a "hang-up" for the Church, or mistakenly think that the Church is against sex as if it were evil. Our culture generally rejects moderation, refusing to see the legitimate difference between use and abuse: "If some is good, more must be better," we so foolishly cry. The Church has a positive and life-affirming view of human sexuality, insisting only that we understand its purpose so as to rightly use this wondrous gift. Sex is a hang-up for our culture, not for the Church. While sexuality is not just a biological fact, let us start there by way of analogy so as to understand the Church's point that "sexuality is ordered to the conjugal love of man and woman" (CCC 2360).

Why do we desire food? Most obviously, we desire food because our bodies need nourishment in order to function. Yet we also desire food because we find eating satisfying, especially when indulging in our favorite dish. This twofold reason for eating, while rooted in our biological nature, points us beyond mere biology to moral, cultural, political, philosophical, and theological questions: How much should I eat (moral)? What should we serve on a festive occasion (cultural)? How do we ensure adequate nourishment to the citizenry (political)? What is the difference between feeding, eating, dining, and feasting (philosophical)? What is the proper use of food in spiritual practices such as fasting and worship (theological)?

The desire for food is not just about the belly and its desires but also about the tongue, both because the tongue has its own desires for certain foods and because good eaters know when and how to use their tongues while eating in common with others.[5] In addition to these two bodily aspects of eating, notice that cultures try to embed a moral framework into eating rituals so as to "humanize" it, pushing us to integrate biological desires into the desire to live a good life: we eat the main courses first and save the dessert for last; we do not graze like cows but eat three meals a day with small snacks in between as necessary; if we are hosts we serve our guests first, and perhaps even deny ourselves that last piece of cake if our guests want it; and so on. As a general rule, we could say that "moralizing" eating means providing guidance for how to serve the biological needs of our bodies while also the passionate, moral, and intellectual needs of our souls.

Actions are immoral to the extent that they attend either only to the biological needs or only to the needs of the soul, to the detriment of the whole person. Humans are both body and soul, and our actions should reflect this: when we are at table it is wrong to care only about the stomach, but it is at

---

5. In this regard, it is worth noting that in most religious traditions there is no standard blessing before meals for people eating on their own: for example, Catholics say "Bless *us*, oh Lord, . . ." and my guess is that I am not alone in saying "us" even when I *am* eating alone.

least as wrong if not more wrong to only care about the tongue; humanized eating always looks to the health of the body while also prioritizing the virtues of the soul.[6]

What does all of this have to do with sex? It is so important to insist upon rooting our desires for sex in the biological but also to insist that sex is not *just* biological. First and foremost, we desire sex because we are animals that reproduce sexually, who bring about new members of the species through sexual acts. In general we must recognize that the desire for sex is first experienced with the onset of puberty; when our bodies are capable of reproducing, a corresponding desire emerges. Just as we desire food because our bodies need nourishment, we desire sex because our bodies "need" to reproduce. Of course there are people who desire sex prior to puberty, though this is a culturally induced desire as a result of the availability of information about sex (e.g., older siblings, catching parents "in the act," pornography) rather than a natural desire. Compare this to what marketers do: we do not naturally desire many of their products, but rather they "teach" us to desire them by manipulating our imaginations.

Second, while the desire for sex is rooted in our bodily needs, we also desire it because we discover it to be pleasant for a variety of reasons, from the stimulation itself to the knowledge and love we share in common with our spouse. Again, this twofold reason for sex points us beyond biology to moral, cultural, philosophical, and theological questions: When and with whom is sex appropriate (moral)? How does one go about courting a lover (cultural)? What is the difference between sexual love and sexual lust (philosophical)? Are priesthood and biological fatherhood compatible (theological)?

Recall that virtue is the mean between two extremes; we can see this here in two distortive views of sexuality: (1) the merely biological; (2) the merely recreational. The merely biological view treats sex as nothing more than a means to the end of producing children, and thus the body as an instrument for the purposes of serving personal or social needs. Such a view would lead one to accept sperm donation, cloning, stem cell cultivation involving embryo destruction, developing technologies to "grow" babies in laboratories, and so forth. The other extreme, the merely recreational, treats sex as nothing more than a means to personal gratification, usually understood as bodily pleasure. This view also instrumentalizes the body, though now as a means to pleasure. Such a view would lead one to accept contraception, prostitution, masturbation, homosexual acts, and so forth. While in some respects

---

6. I am heavily indebted to Leon Kass's *The Hungry Soul: Eating and the Perfecting of Our Nature* (Chicago: University of Chicago Press, 1999) for these observations. I cannot recommend this book enough.

these two views are opposites, both of these extremes (1) ironically enough, given that they are put forth as ways to celebrate or enhance the body, actually degrade the body, viewing it as a mere tool to be used for whatever one's purposes happen to be; (2) start with the false assumption that we can separate procreation from recreation, or the desires of the body from the desires of the soul.

Returning to the general moral principle regarding eating, we could say that sexual activity is immoral to the extent that it attends only to biological needs or only to the needs of the soul. Healthy, human sexuality celebrates the body and the soul by holding up as a model the act of a married couple seeking to know and love one another by, put simply, making babies. Stevie Wonder put this so beautifully in "Isn't She Lovely?": "I can't believe what God has done / Through us he's given life to one / But isn't she lovely made from love." Our sexual acts should seek to *make*, not *prevent* babies, and we as individuals and as a society are reaping the foul fruits of rearing children who are the result of something "going wrong" with our contraceptives; when our children come into the world as a result of an "accident" or "mistake," it is no wonder that they feel unwanted, confused about who they are, and incapable of truly loving or being loved. With this general introduction in mind, let us explore the Church's teaching on human sexuality by first providing the key passages from Aquinas on this topic and then discussing the aforementioned topics individually.[7]

2.2 Aquinas on Human Sexuality

Background Reading: ST II-II.151–153

As we discussed in the chapters on moral philosophy and moral theology, all areas of human activity must be brought under the guidance of faith and reason. In moral life, every situation requires determining the appropriate mean between extremes: to act appropriately is to be virtuous, to fail to hit the mean is to be vicious. Most fundamentally, human sexuality must be guided by a secondary virtue connected with temperance: chastity.

Chastity is the virtue that regulates the concupiscible passions in regard to sexual activity, and it is important to note that "chastity" can be used metaphorically to refer to one's relationship with God: as Aquinas explains,

7. For a fuller treatment of how Church teaching on sexual morality is compatible with and rooted in Aquinas, as well as on how the personalism of Pope John Paul II complements Aquinas's approach, see Thomas Petri, OP, *Aquinas and the Theology of the Body: The Thomistic Foundations of John Paul II's Anthropology* (Washington, DC: Catholic University of America Press, 2016).

someone who is spiritually chaste seeks union with God alone, to whom Christ weds the believer (see *ST* II-II.151.2). The restless human heart can only find delight in God, and due to original sin it is tempted to seek this delight in worldly goods and thus become guilty of spiritual fornication. Just as spiritual life requires a monogamous relationship with God as one's true lover, so does sexual life necessitate the matrimonial bond. And, further still, human sexuality cannot be understood fully without recognition of the divine gift of virginity: the woman who offers her sexuality to God as a pledge of union with him alone does this not because sex is sinful but "in order to have leisure for Divine things" (*ST* II-II.152.3).

Aquinas compares virginity to the contemplative life and matrimony to the active life, and so we must recall our discussion of this in chapter 2 (§4): the contemplative life is best in itself, and yet it is not necessarily best *for me*. Just so, Aquinas points out that Christ was himself a virgin and that he chose a virgin for his mother, for "virginity is directed to the good of the soul in respect of the contemplative life, which consists in thinking 'on the things of God,' whereas marriage is directed to the good of the body, namely the bodily increase of the human race, and belongs to the active life, since the man and woman who embrace the married life have to think 'on the things of the world,' as the Apostle says (1 Corinthians 7:34). Without doubt therefore virginity is preferable to conjugal continence" (*ST* II-II.151.4). And yet God calls some to virginity and others to matrimony, both of which are a blessing to those who are so called. In all of this we should recall the example of Maria von Trapp, who took up matrimony because this was *for her* the *higher* spiritual calling. As Aquinas points out, at times those in the married state possess a greater holiness than consecrated virgins (see *ST* II-II.151.4ad2), for, to paraphrase St. Gregory the Great, he who loves more serves God more fully.[8]

As a moral virtue, chastity involves not only following the guidance of reason in determining when and with whom one should engage in sexual activity but also regulation of the appetites. To quote John Grabowski, "Chastity represents not the elimination, but the reasonable integration, of the sexual appetites."[9] A chaste man is not simply one who refrains from adulterous acts, but one who does not desire to commit such acts. Imagine the married man

---

8. See Gregory the Great, *The Life of St. Benedict*, trans. Terrence G. Kardong, OSB (Collegeville, MN: Liturgical Press, 2009), 123–25, for this delightful story in which St. Scholastica teaches her obstinate brother, St. Benedict, a lesson about love. As St. Gregory puts it, "It was entirely right that she who loved more should accomplish more" (125).

9. John S. Grabowski, *Sex and Virtue: An Introduction to Catholic Sexual Ethics* (Washington, DC: Catholic University of America Press, 2003), 83.

who fantasizes about other women, who looks at pornographic images, who even has sex with his wife while thinking about another woman. He has an adulterous heart (see Matt. 5:28); even if he has not acted on it, he is guilty of sin. Additionally, the pleasures of the sexual act itself, even when done within the matrimonial bond, must always be directed to the purpose of the sexual act—namely, procreation. Just as love is more enjoyable than bodily pleasure, so too is chaste sex more enjoyable than "the mere bargain of a lustful love."[10] As Thomas Petri points out, "Aquinas resolutely disagrees with Gregory of Nyssa and John Chrysostom, both of whom said that there would have been no sexual activity in original innocence. In fact, Thomas goes so far as to say that sexual delight would have been greater in Eden."[11] Again, Aquinas is in no way opposed to pleasure as such, but simply to the failure to bring passion under the guidance of the virtues and thus to the inability to experience the higher pleasures that come from right living.

Finally, recall that every virtue is opposed to two vices, one of deficiency and one of excess.[12] Aquinas does not give a name, nor does he devote any direct discussion, to the vice of deficiency. It is rare to find such a person who is vicious because he or she does not desire sex. A first thought would be that someone in such a state would be called to virginity anyway, and so would not be vicious. On the other hand, Aquinas does speak of the "country lout" (agricola) who wrongly considers all pleasure to be bad and so abstains from sex in a way that is contrary to reason (see ST II-II.152.2ad2). This is an occasion to point out that Aquinas is no boor: among the virtues we find "wittiness," according to which one knows how to have a good time (see ST II-II.168), and (as discussed briefly in chapter 3, §3) "sobriety," which allows one to drink alcoholic beverages moderately (see ST II-II.149). As in the case of chastity, Aquinas points out that there is no name for someone who suffers from deficiency with respect to alcohol, and yet it is a vice: "If a man were knowingly to abstain from wine to the extent of molesting nature grievously [ut naturam multum gravaret], he would not be free from sin" (ST II-II.150.1ad1). We have already seen Aquinas's own wit on display with his example of ignorant adultery, and we can imagine Aquinas asking his students to come up with their own examples of people who so abstain from sex or from alcohol as to "molest nature."[13]

10. Augustine, Confessions 4.2, trans. F. J. Sheed (Indianapolis: Hackett, 2006), 56.

11. Petri, Aquinas and the Theology of the Body, 223.

12. See ST I-II.64 for the difficult question of how to understand the mean for intellectual as well as theological virtues.

13. Aquinas himself, in another context, provides the example of the "Aquarii," who, "under guise of sobriety, offer nothing but water in" the Eucharist (ST III.74.1).

The vice of excess with respect to sex is of course more common and is called "lust." This vice would be found among those who seek sexual activity without intending procreation as the end, either within the matrimonial bond or outside of it. This would apply to masturbation, contraception, homosexual acts, and so forth. Lust is a "capital vice" in that it tends to lead to other sins, such as in the man who murders his lover's father so that he can enjoy her body; lust can consume a man, for he can go so far as hating God and despairing of a future world "because through being held back by carnal pleasures he cares not to obtain spiritual pleasures, since they are distasteful to him" (*ST* II-II.153.5).

Aquinas takes sex so seriously because he is aware of its incredible power over people's lives; he knows that failing to integrate sexuality into love for God and neighbor often destroys individuals, families, and communities. This is why the Church today must be so focused on sex, for so many of the problems in our society stem from the loss of stable family life, and this in turn is the result of lust entering into the hearts of would-be lovers everywhere.[14]

2.3 Contraception, Abortion, Stem Cells, and Cloning

Background Reading: ST I.118; SCG 3.2.122–126

Given that human sexuality is ordered toward procreation, contraception is clearly a deviation from this natural order. Contraception is rooted in lust, in the desire to negate sexual pleasure's natural orientation toward childrearing. More broadly, we should say that sex outside of the matrimonial bond is immoral because it is incompatible with the purpose of sex; as Aquinas argues, since sex has as its aim procreation, and since the rearing of children requires the stable bond of the parents, sex outside of marriage goes against nature (see *SCG* 3.122–23). Note that this reasoning is also found in the *Catechism*, and, in addition to Aquinas's point about the procreative purpose of sex, the unitive is emphasized: "The innate language that expresses the total reciprocal self-giving of husband and wife is overlaid, through contraception, by an objectively contradictory language, namely, that of not giving totally to the other. This leads not only to a positive refusal to be open to life but also to a falsification of the inner truth of conjugal love, which is called upon to give itself in personal totality" (*CCC* 2370). There is no incompatibility between Aquinas and Church teaching here. As Petri points out, Aquinas

---

14. For an explanation of how Aquinas's views on sexuality are compatible with and complementary to the modern scientific approach, see Paul Gondreau, "The 'Inseparable Connection' between Procreation and Unitive Love (*Humanae Vitae*, §12) and Thomistic Hylomorphic Anthropology," *Nova et Vetera* 6 (2008): 731–64.

"identifies three goods [intrinsic to the marital act]: offspring, fidelity, and the sacrament."[15] Aquinas may speak of the procreative purpose of sexuality more directly, but he also emphasizes marital sex as an act of "the greatest type of friendship" (*SCG* 3.123.6). As Paul Gondreau explains, according to Aquinas "human sexuality has but one end, marriage, with two complementary, essential dimensions: the procreative (expressive of the body) and the unitive (expressive of the soul)."[16]

Whereas Aquinas's views on contraception are clearly compatible with CST, abortion presents a more difficult case, and obviously we should not be surprised to discover that he says nothing about stem cells or cloning. Beginning with abortion, let us summarize what he says and then discuss where Aquinas may fall short.

Aquinas took up the best science of his day regarding the development of the fetus in the womb, a science rooted in Aristotelian natural philosophy. According to this view, when a man's semen enters into a woman, it works upon "fetal matter" in her womb as an active power that brings into existence the soul. We could think of this as analogous to a man shaping clay, thus bringing from the inchoate matter of the clay a definitive form. Yet what is brought into being is not so much a specific shape but an intrinsic principle of organization that allows this fetal matter to receive nutrients and direct its own growth. After this takes place, "the semen is dissolved and the (vital) spirit thereof vanishes" (*ST* I.118.1ad4). In this respect we could think of semen as like a disposable tool that a man shaping clay uses, recycling it once it has achieved its purpose of establishing a definitive form. And even here we must make a distinction: the semen has the instrumental power to bring into being the vegetative and sensitive soul by which the soul directs its own growth and senses the world, but not the intellectual soul. Thus, on its own, semen can only bring into being a soul with the powers of a brute animal; were it not for a greater power that it itself does not possess, human reproduction would be frustrated, for it would lead to a beast and not a human.

Only God can provide the form of a human in this strong sense, for the intellectual soul is immaterial, and it is impossible for semen (a material agent) to produce an immaterial principle: "Since it is an immaterial substance it cannot be caused through generation, but only through creation by God. Therefore to hold that the intellectual soul is caused by the begetter, is nothing else than to hold the soul to be non-subsistent and consequently to perish with the body. It is therefore heretical to say that the intellectual soul is

15. Petri, *Aquinas and the Theology of the Body*, 297.
16. Gondreau, "Inseparable Connection," 746 (emphasis removed).

transmitted with the semen" (*ST* I.118.2). As Aquinas goes on to say, through sex humans create the material conditions that lead to a human soul, with God providing the form—namely, the intellectual soul; in this sense, we could distinguish between the animalistic parts of the soul brought about by human action and the human form brought about by God.[17]

Note Aquinas's language on God's creative act carefully: "The intellectual soul is created by God *at the end of human generation*, and this soul is at the same time sensitive and nutritive, the pre-existing forms being corrupted" (*ST* I.118.2ad2; emphasis added). This language of "at the end" suggests that up to a certain stage of fetal development there is not, properly speaking, a human being in the womb but rather an animal that will subsequently be given a human nature. In an earlier writing, Aquinas followed Aristotle's claim that the intellectual soul is not present until the fortieth day in the case of males, and the ninetieth day in the case of females,[18] for not until that point was the appropriate matter present that God could "shape" with the human soul. While it is clear that Aquinas held it to be murder to kill the fetus in the womb *after* God introduced the intellectual soul (see, e.g., *ST* II-II.64.8ad2; III.68.11), and thus for both males and females this would rule out second- or third-trimester abortions, what about abortions during the first trimester? Aquinas nowhere takes up this question, and we should note two things here: (1) a good argument using Thomistic principles could be made against abortion at any stage of development; (2) Aquinas relied on flawed embryo science, and so we should not bind him or Thomists today to this.

First, even on the false view that human life does not begin at conception, the argument could be made that just as contraception is immoral because it frustrates the purpose of the sexual act, so too is abortion immoral: the purpose of sex is to produce children, and so any act that prevents this purpose is contrary to nature and thus immoral. While this does not establish the stronger claim that first-trimester abortion is murder, it does establish that it is immoral. And in regard to emitting semen without the purpose of generating offspring, Aquinas has rather strong words: "After the sin of homicide whereby a human nature already in existence is destroyed, this type of sin appears to take next place, for by it the generation of human nature is precluded" (*SCG* 3.122.9).[19] So, even if first-trimester abortion is not

---

17. See *ST* I.118.2ad2 for Aquinas's understanding of how the intellectual soul is related to the previously existing parts of the soul.

18. See Aquinas, *Commentary on the Sentences of Peter Lombard* 3.3.5.2.

19. And, as just another example of how thorough Aquinas is, he even addresses "nocturnal emissions," or "wet dreams"; see *ST* II-II.154.5.

murder according to Aquinas, if masturbation, contraception, and the like are nearly as bad, clearly such abortions are no slight sins.[20] More strongly, one could argue that since God intends for this act of sex to lead to human life, the first-trimester abortion goes against God's providential order. While every act of sex *potentially* leads to offspring, this act of sex *actually* led to offspring; even if it were true (again, relying upon this flawed biology) that this fetus is not yet human, neither is it just semen or just a part of the mother's body. This act of sex led to this fetus, a new being that is not part of the mother's body but a distinct, self-directing being that will become a human being. God *does not choose* whether or not to let this embryo become a human; rather, he wills as a necessary effect of its development that he will cause it to be a human. If God does not choose whether or not to let this embryo live, surely we do not have a right that he does not exercise himself.

Second, as we noted in the introduction to this section, Aquinas used the best available science of his day, and it stands to reason that he would have used the best science of our day had he been alive today. Biologically speaking, there is no question today as to when human life begins: from the moment of conception, a new being is brought into the world possessing its own distinct genetic makeup. The mother's womb is not some passive recipient of the semen's active power (as Aquinas, following Aristotle, held); the mother's egg is as active in its contribution to a baby's biological constitution as is the father's semen. In this sense, to use Aquinas as an argument for abortion is tantamount to adhering to a problematic view of the mother's contribution to her own baby: there is something obviously wrong about sticking with an antiquated and demeaning view of motherhood in order to promote the dignity of women.[21] And, to make one last point on abortion, let us pause to note what should be retained from Aquinas's account of embryo development: his insistence that God commits himself to participate in a new creative act every time egg and sperm meet is a sign of just how much God loves us. To

20. We cannot go into the topic of natural family planning (NFP) here, though we must note that there is a fundamental difference between, on the one hand, the married couple who seek children as an end and yet engage in the marital act during infertile periods and, on the other hand, the married couple who do not seek children as an end and/or who use a contraceptive to prevent nature from "running its course." See CCC 2367–70 on the difference between NFP and contraception; see also Grabowski, *Sex and Virtue*, 142–54. Richard J. Fehring and Theresa Notare, eds., *Human Fertility: Where Faith and Science Meet* (Milwaukee: Marquette University Press, 2008), covers an array of topics related to NFP.

21. For a more thorough defense of Aquinas as being in agreement with Church teaching today, see John Haldane and Patrick Lee, "Aquinas on Human Ensoulment, Abortion and the Value of Life," *Philosophy* 78 (2003): 255–78.

paraphrase St. Augustine, of all the wonders of nature, none are more marvelous than man, created as and through male and female.[22]

While the moral issues concerning stem cells and cloning may seem to require a fresh discussion, at least in this respect they are straightforward: wherever there is human life present, and given that humans are willed by God for their own sake, using them for any purpose is immoral. Since human life is present whenever a cell with twenty-three unique chromosome pairs is brought into existence, any case in which stem cell or cloning research requires the creation and subsequent destruction of such a cell involves murder and is therefore gravely immoral. This is not the place to work through the nuanced distinctions between the different techniques and types of stem cell research, though in the bibliography I provide references that can guide the reader through this difficult subject. Similarly, in regard to cloning, not only is there the issue of destroying embryos in order to create the clone (a problem also with in vitro fertilization), but, even if this could be avoided, CST adds a good argument to build onto Aquinas's reasoning: children are not owed to us as a "right"; rather, they are gifts from God, who in his loving providence gave man and woman to each other as fitting partners. Children are the fruit of the unitive-procreative act of marital love, not the product of technology (see CCC 2373–79). The loving embrace of husband and wife simply cannot be replaced by the sterile hands of the bioengineer.

2.4 Homosexuality

Background Reading: ST II-II.154

Whether one experiences same-sex attraction or is a friend to one who does, it is rare today to meet somebody who does not approach this topic with some personal connection. Let us begin with the brief passage in the *Catechism* that tries both to articulate Church teaching on homosexuality and also to show sensitivity to those who self-identify as gay: "The number of men and women who have deep-seated homosexual tendencies is not negligible. This inclination, which is objectively disordered, constitutes for most of them a trial. They must be accepted with respect, compassion, and sensitivity. Every sign of unjust discrimination in their regard should be avoided. These persons are called to fulfill God's will in their lives and, if they are Christians, to unite to the sacrifice of the Lord's Cross the difficulties

22. "Man is a greater miracle than any miracle that is done through man." *City of God* 10.12, cited in Augustine, *Political Writings*, trans. Michael W. Tkacz and Douglas Kries (Indianapolis: Hackett, 1994), 75.

they may encounter from their condition" (CCC 2358). In *Gay and Catholic*, Eve Tushnet offers a personal testimony to Church teaching: as one who in the past had homosexual relationships, came to see the beauty and truth of Church teaching, and now puts her unique life experiences into the service of the Church, she offers an important witness to this topic in her book. And though she agrees with the Church here, she cautions that official statements of the Church on this topic are "not perhaps the most helpful." Advising readers with same-sex attraction who want to live out a "chaste gay/same-sex attracted life" to "look to the lives of the saints rather than the position statements of the bishops' conferences,"[23] Tushnet laments how easy it is for well-intentioned straight people to close the door to dialogue. We must be sensitive to this when we discuss the moral concerns with homosexuality, for it is part of the virtuous life to learn and communicate truth out of love for one another.[24] Still, it is also part of the virtuous life to bring our passions under the guidance of reason, to form our judgments on the basis of our intellects rather than our feelings.

We often fall prey to the dictatorship of the passions in such emotionally charged situations, saying things like, "What you are saying is hurtful, because my friend is gay," or, "You don't know how it feels to be gay, so who are you to talk?" Notice that such statements take emotions as normative for moral life: if something feels good, or people do not choose to feel it, it is therefore good. There are better and more rational arguments in defense of homosexuality, and we must take them up, but first we need to establish the possibility of moral reasoning: the man who defends homosexuality along these lines assumes that his emotions or those of his friends with same-sex attraction are trump cards, and thus that no argument is necessary in order to establish their goodness. This is precisely what is at issue here; both his mode of argumentation and his defense of homosexuality wrongly assume that gay sex is good (or at least not bad) because it is desired by certain people. With these points in mind, let us turn now to how Aquinas reasons through the issue of homosexuality.

Since Aquinas's own treatment of homosexuality is not extensive (see *ST* II-II.154.11–12), we will develop an answer to a series of questions by connecting together points from his general moral theory: (1) Is same-sex attraction present in some people *by nature*? (2) Do those who have same-sex attraction *choose* this? (3) Is same-sex attraction morally good or bad or neither? (4) Is gay sex morally acceptable?

23. Eve Tushnet, *Gay and Catholic* (Notre Dame, IN: Ave Maria Press, 2014), 178.
24. Specifically, in a situation like this, one needs the virtues of charity and friendliness.

Recall that the term "nature" can be used in at least two senses: on the one hand, nature is what is "given" or "what happens"; on the other, nature is the goal or "what things seek" (see chap. 1, §2). The tadpole that dies before becoming a frog in the first sense is more natural than the frog, though in the second sense the frog is more natural because it manifests the goal of being a tadpole. Now, with respect to the passions, Aquinas does not specifically take up the question as to whether or not some people are born with same-sex attraction, but were he to do so, he would still use the two senses of nature to examine this: in the first sense, it may be that some people by nature have same-sex attraction, while in the second sense it is unnatural for them to have such an attraction because this passion goes against the biological purpose of sexual desire—namely, procreation.

In chapter 1 (§2) we discussed the passions in relation to moral life, pointing out that (1) they are neither morally good nor evil in themselves but become so insofar as they can fall under the guidance of reason; (2) moral life consists in doing what reason commands as well as in having proper passions such that we take delight in what is morally good. While some people may have a passionate attraction to members of the same sex (and have this desire by nature in the first sense of the term), since reason indicates that the purpose of sexual attraction is to bring male and female together for the sake of generating new life, morally speaking, same-sex attraction goes against nature. Thus, our answer to the first question is as follows: while some people may be born with a proclivity to have same-sex attraction, it is *contrary to nature* to have such an attraction. In the words of the *Catechism*: "'Homosexual acts are intrinsically disordered.' They are contrary to the natural law. They close the sexual act to the gift of life. They do not proceed from a genuine affective and sexual complementarity. Under no circumstances can they be approved" (CCC 2357).

To the second question as to whether or not same-sex attraction is chosen, we can answer similarly: while it may be true that some people do not choose to experience the passion in question, they do choose whether or not to bring this passion under the guidance of reason. On the one hand, someone may experience this passion as a result of previous choices, and we could trace it back to the use of pornography or engaging in lustful, heterosexual activity: through such acts they open themselves up to other forms of sex and may come to desire them. Such people may not choose *now* to have same-sex attraction, but they made choices *in the past* that led them to have it, and for this reason we would say that they have chosen to have same-sex attraction and thus are morally culpable for it. For others, however, either because of a genetic predisposition or an environmental cause, they did not choose to have same-sex attraction. Yet, to repeat, they can choose what to do about this passion. While they may experience this passion for the rest of their lives, by pursuing homosexual acts they intensify it and give this passion control over reason; by practicing chastity they bring it under the guidance of reason and the Divine rule.

Turning to the third question, regarding the moral aspect of same-sex attraction, those who do not choose to have this passion are not immoral, and we must insist on this: we cannot praise or blame somebody for a passion that he or she does not choose. That being said, we can judge an unchosen passion to be good or bad, appropriate or inappropriate. Recall the four considerations in a moral situation: (1) genus of goodness and being; (2) the species or object; (3) circumstances; and (4) end (chap. 1, §4). In terms of its genus, same-sex attraction is evil in that it wrongly directs sexual desire to an object that cannot fulfill the natural purpose of sex. However, in terms of judging a woman with same-sex attraction to be moral or immoral, we do not simply look at the passions found in her soul but also at the other three factors, and we would conclude that she herself is not immoral unless she seeks an improper object to satisfy her sexual desire. Even if her same-sex attraction is a result of previous choices, she can freely say no to this desire. Given that she cannot both act on her same-sex attraction and will as an end the natural end of sex (procreation), she must choose between passion and reason. What this means practically is that, to the extent that same-sex attraction is not chosen, neither is it immoral. That being said, it is the moral task of the person who experiences same-sex attraction to channel and redirect this desire to acts of platonic friendship and charity; doing so would constitute a moral action. By doing so he or she is practicing a form of chastity, and even the most perfect form—namely, virginity.[25] Turning once again to the *Catechism*: "Homosexual persons are called to chastity. By the virtues of self-mastery that teach them inner freedom, at times by the support of disinterested friendship, by prayer and sacramental grace, they can and should gradually and resolutely approach Christian perfection" (CCC 2359).

Finally, as to the fourth question regarding gay sex, it should be clear from what has been said that this is immoral, for it cannot achieve the purpose of

---

25. This is a vexing topic, for it seems that, since moral virtues require proper passions, those with same-sex attraction do not have the virtue of chastity. Yet in another sense moral virtue indicates curbing our passions, as we said in chap. 1 (§5). And, to add another complication, there is the question of whether something that is a disorder in itself can actually be a good for a specific individual, a topic that we avoided in our discussion of goodness and being in chap. 1 (§2). I leave it to the interested reader to consult Aquinas, *SCG* 3.10–15, and know that this is a huge question involving such things as the possibility of evolution, the meaning of providence, and how to reconcile the presence of sin with God's desire that all be saved.

sex. Does this mean that those with same-sex attraction cannot enter into intimate relationships that, while not involving sex, may involve physical acts of
affection such as hugging and perhaps even kissing? Consider ST II-II.154.4,
where Aquinas takes up the appropriateness of "touches and kisses." On the one
hand, he says that these are not mortal sins, "for it is possible to do such things
without lustful pleasure, either as being the custom of one's country, or on account of some obligation or reasonable cause"; on the other hand, "when these
kisses and caresses are done for this delectation [of lust], it follows that they are
mortal sins, and only in this way are they said to be lustful." To the extent that
one could engage in such acts without lust, they are not sinful, though it must
be acknowledged that it would take great, perhaps infused, virtue for someone
with same-sex attraction to engage in them without doing them out of lust.[26]

Throughout all of this, it is important to bear in mind that these teachings
on sexual morality are rooted in a vision of love. It is easy to perceive Church
teaching as a legal code that places obligation above personal happiness.
Thus, the focus in communicating this teaching, and living it out, should be
on the virtues and the beauty of a life of grace. As Grabowski points out,
teaching Catholic sexual morality "would entail fostering a basic respect and
reverence for the dignity of other persons that is foundational to justice and
love in interpersonal relationships . . . [and] for the human body as the vis-
ible manifestation of the person and his or her uniqueness and transcendent
dignity."[27] What must be shown is that sexual love is a beautiful gift, and yet
that this gift can only be used rightly when it is offered up in gratitude to the
God who created us in his image and likeness out of love.

3. Aquinas's Economic Theory Today

Who then is the faithful and wise steward [oikonomos], whom his master will
set over his household, to give them their portion of food at the proper time?

—Luke 12:42

[God the Father] has made known to us in all wisdom and insight the mystery
of his will, according to his purpose which he set forth in Christ as a plan

---

26. An excellent and moving documentary on this is *Desire of the Everlasting Hills*. I struggle
to sympathize with those who could watch this and still claim that the Church's stance against
homosexuality is a result of homophobia or hatred of any sort.

27. Grabowski, *Sex and Virtue*, 158; for a fuller treatment of human sexuality aimed at
showing why homosexual sex is incompatible with the human good, see Paul Gondreau, "The
Natural Law Ordering of Human Sexuality to (Heterosexual) Marriage: Towards a Thomistic
Philosophy of the Body," *Nova et Vetera* 8.3 (2010): 553–92.

[*oikonomian*] for the fulness of time, to unite all things in him, things in heaven and things on earth.

—Ephesians 1:9–10

One of the traditional uses of the term "economy" in the Church is connected more with God's providence than with how humans use material goods. In the passage from the Gospel of Luke above, Jesus calls the one entrusted with the master's goods an *oikonomos*, which we could translate as "one entrusted to enforce the rules of the household." And in the passage from Ephesians, St. Paul speaks of God's *oikonomian* for creation, or his plan of salvation for humanity that he revealed in the Person of Jesus Christ. Through the sacramental economy, we are members of God's household. And, further, as his servants we are entrusted with the task of using well our lives and worldly goods in accordance with his plan. We participate in divine economics by practicing and preaching the gospel message that God is love and that he calls us all to the heavenly home. As the glossary of the *Catechism* puts it, the economy of salvation is "God's activity in creating and governing the world, particularly with regard to his plan for the salvation of the world in the person and work of Jesus Christ, a plan which is being accomplished through his Body the Church, in its life and sacraments."

While Aquinas does not use this term "economy of salvation," we have seen that his economic theory shares this understanding of economy as the virtuous administration of worldly goods in conformity with the vocation God has bestowed upon us. As Andrew Yuengert puts it, "The disciplinary boundary between ethics and economics makes sense only to the extent that it serves a human purpose—to the extent that it leads to a better understanding of the economy and promotes human development."[28] Economics studies how ethical living bears upon the ownership and use of the property that God has entrusted us with, to use as good stewards in accordance with his salvific plan for the whole human race (see *Compendium* 330–35).[29]

---

28. Andrew Yuengert, *The Boundaries of Technique* (Lanham, MD: Lexington Books, 2004), xiv; see also 49–61 for his discussion of three Thomistic principles that must guide the economist.

29. For an introduction to the economic teachings of CST, see Albino Barrera, *Modern Catholic Social Documents and Political Economy* (Washington, DC: Georgetown University Press, 2001), and Maciej Zięba, OP, *Papal Economics: The Catholic Church on Democratic Capitalism, from "Rerum Novarum" to "Caritas in Veritate"* (Wilmington, DE: ISI Books, 2013). For a briefer discussion of how economic claims in CST documents must be put into the context of the Church's broader moral and spiritual teaching, see Francis Russell Hittinger's "Divisible Goods and Common Good: Reflections on *Caritas in Veritate*," *Faith and Economics* 58 (2011): 31–46.

There are at least three aspects of modern life that would not be found in Aquinas's own experience and that we will discuss here: (1) wage-based economy, (2) globalized economy, and (3) ecological threats to the earth. As we acknowledged in the introduction to this chapter, it is always difficult to know what a theorist from a different time and place would say about our own situation, though we can start with the fundamental principles he or she uses and attempt to apply them to the questions of our own day. As we put it there, Aquinas answers the fundamental questions of human existence that can guide our attempts to answer the secondary questions of our own time. And, whereas with abortion we found it necessary to "update" Aquinas's biological views, here we simply need to apply what he says to issues such as a just wage, justice in transactions, and love for creation.[30]

3.1 Value in a Wage-Based Society

Background Reading: Compendium 248–251, 255–266, 301–303; CCC 2184–2188, 2426–2438

We live in a society that structures its economic life around wages, for the vast majority of people in our society are reliant upon a monetary income to provide themselves with the material goods necessary for a good life. While they may have apple trees and tomato plants out back or may jar their own pickles and even weave their own blankets, these are hobbies rather than sources of their livelihood. By and large, our daily bread is purchased with money, and the measure of our worldly wealth is how many greenbacks our labor earns.

Monetary wages were not as central to Aquinas's society as they are to ours, and so it is not surprising that he does not focus much of his attention on assessing the just value of labor. Further, medieval society is sometimes said to have had a "gift economy" given how central gift-giving was to interactions between its members. We all give gifts on occasion, but only the poorest among us depend on such free "exchanges" for their livelihood. Thus, in our own wage-based economy it is more important than ever to determine justice in exchanges of labor for money. As the Compendium puts this: "The role of financial markets is becoming ever more decisive and central. Following the

---

30. For a reflection on how Aquinas was shaped by his times as well as how his economic principles could be applied to our times, see Stephen J. Pope, "Aquinas on Almsgiving, Justice and Charity: An Interpretation and Reassessment," Heythrop Journal 32.2 (1991): 180–87. In "Uncaring Justice: Why Jacque v. Steenberg Homes Was Wrongly Decided," Journal of Catholic Legal Studies 51.1 (2012): 111–43, John Makdisi provides a thoughtful attempt to apply Aquinas's economic theory to a contemporary US Supreme Court case.

liberalization of capital exchange and circulation, these market dimensions have increased enormously and with incredible speed. . . . This is a multifaceted reality that is difficult to decipher, since it expands at different levels and is in continuous evolution along paths that cannot easily be predicted" (361). What we need to do is discuss how Aquinas's general theory of value can be applied to work. As we will see, CST's reflections of just wages can be seen as a legitimate application of Thomistic principles to our own economic situation.

According to CST, work both is a duty and, more positively, "can be a means of sanctification and a way of animating earthly realities with the Spirit of Christ" (CCC 2427). Thus, the work we do is not simply exchanging labor for wages but, more deeply, is a fulfillment of St. Paul's admonition, "Work out your own salvation with fear and trembling" (Phil. 2:12). Without undermining the traditional elevation of the contemplative life over the active life, CST emphasizes how our jobs are a central part of our practice of the virtues. We do not just have jobs, but vocations, and whether our calling is to priestly, monastic, or lay life, our job is to be Christ for others. In *The Rule of St. Benedict*, for example, we read that for monks prayer is their primary form of work, the *opus Dei* or "work of God" to which the abbot calls the monks at the appropriate times.[31] As Aquinas would put this point, charity as the form of the virtues can direct even the most menial of tasks to the glory of God.

Given this importance of work to salvation and its more immediate role in providing for daily, bodily needs, CST claims that "everyone should make legitimate use of his talents to contribute to the abundance that will benefit all and harvest the just fruits of his labor" (CCC 2429); contrariwise, society has an obligation to ensure that all who are physically and mentally capable as well as financially needy can find work and can gain enough by their work to live on. In terms of justice, this means that the value of labor must be rooted in the worker's need not just to live but to live virtuously. CST refers to this in various terms as a "just wage," "living wage," or "family wage." Each of these terms has its own merit in conveying this central point that *Gaudium et Spes* makes: "Remuneration for work should guarantee man the opportunity to provide a dignified livelihood for himself and his family on the material, social, cultural, and spiritual level, taking into account the role and the productivity of each, the state of the business, and the common good" (§67; cited in CCC 2434).[32] For our purposes, we will refer to this as a

---

31. See *Rule of St. Benedict* 47.1, in *The Rule of St. Benedict in English*, trans. Timothy Fry, OSB (Collegeville, MN: Liturgical Press, 1981), 68.

32. See also Paul VI, *Gaudium et Spes* (December 7, 1965), §67, website of the Holy See, http://www.vatican.va/archive/hist_councils/ii_vatican_council/documents/vat-ii_const_196 51207_gaudium-et-spes_en.html.

just wage in order to remind ourselves that this wage is not about liberality or charity, but about the strict demands of justice.

We often think that a contract is fair simply because the parties agree upon its terms. This reflects the way we elevate the right to choose over all other considerations. Yet as the *Compendium* points out, "The simple agreement between employee and employer with regard to the amount of pay to be received is not sufficient for the agreed-upon salary to qualify as a 'just wage,' because a just wage 'must not be below the level of subsistence' of the worker: natural justice precedes and is above the freedom of the contract" (302). Justice is an objective measure of what is owed, and thus, while consent is necessary for a valid contract, it is not sufficient for a just one. The *Catechism* goes so far as to consider an unjust wage as a kind of theft (see CCC 2409). And in regard to the social, cultural, and spiritual opportunities that work must provide, a worker is treated unjustly if he or she is forced to give these up in order to acquire enough material goods. Most importantly, work must be ordered toward leisure, especially the leisure of the one who can fulfill God's command "Be still, and know that I am God" (Ps. 46:10). As the *Compendium* puts this, "The apex of biblical teaching on work is the commandment of the Sabbath rest" (258; see also CCC 2184–88).

In terms of commutative justice, the value of one's work reflects how much one contributes both qualitatively and quantitatively, and also reflects one's needs. Recall Aquinas's stipulation that a seller can demand more for his or her goods if his or her needs are greater than the objective value (see chap. 3, §4). Thus, a worker whose needs are greater than another's is owed a greater wage. And yet the converse is *not* true: the fact that my employer is in a bad way does not make it just for me to ask for a higher wage. Nor is it the case that I may demand a just wage that is sufficient for my needs without also putting in a full day's work, day in and day out. I owe my employer the labor that will contribute to his or her ability to provide for his or her family.

In addition to the needs of the employer and employee, one must consider factors like how burdensome the work might be, the skills required to do it, the dangers it might put me in, and the "cost" to my private life as a husband or wife, father or mother, and so on. For example, if my boss calls me up and says that he needs me to work with a client in Egypt for a month and is willing to pay me extra for doing so, it is perfectly acceptable for me to factor in how hard the work would be, the fact that he needs someone who speaks Arabic, that there is political unrest in Egypt, and that my wife will need to hire a nanny while I am away. These legitimately affect the wages I receive.

Distributive justice comes into play when the company has a surplus of goods and my employer must determine how much each will receive. This distribution should factor in how great each person's contribution was as well as the needs of each. On the one hand, it is probably clear to us that an employee who improved the company's productivity or who made more sales than others deserves a greater bonus than others. On the other hand, if I am your boss and know that you are caring for your dying mother, it is no injustice to the other workers if I give you a bonus or provide you with paid leave, even if this might mean minimizing the bonus I give to the best worker. The opposite situation is true as well: if the company takes a loss and not only has no surplus of goods to distribute but even needs to cut back on costs in order to keep the company afloat, it would be just to reduce wages or even lay off workers with an eye toward justice for both employer and employee.

In practice, establishing a just wage, in terms of both commutative and distributive justice, is obviously going to be quite difficult. For example, consider the following questions that one must answer: If the company cannot pay a just wage to its employees, should it go out of business, or continue to pay an unjust wage? If two employees are hired to do the same work, should they be paid differently based on their personal needs (e.g., if one has children and the other does not)? If the just wage is what is owed to the family as a whole, should the husband whose wife is working get paid less than the one whose wife is not, so long as the salary of husband and wife combined is a just wage? The Church recognizes that such questions require economic prudence and, more generally, the practice of the virtues that each of us in our unique callings can bring to bear in our little section of the Lord's vineyard. That being said, as Kevin A. McMahon points out, "It is a requirement of [the bishops'] office that they be concerned with the welfare and security of all individuals," and thus we must acknowledge the legitimate authority of the bishops in helping societies to determine what a just wage is.[33]

One last point before moving on to justice in a global economy is that ensuring a just wage is not the sole responsibility of the employer. Society as a whole can cooperate with businesses, churches, and so on in ensuring a just wage, taking into account the unique needs of each (see, e.g., *Compendium* 250). This means that the role of an employer in providing a just wage will differ from society to society, depending upon how much assistance, if any, is provided by the government, nonprofits, churches, and so forth. As we transition to issues that arise from living in a globalized economy, we conclude here by noting that a just wage is not obtained simply by providing the minimum

---

33. Kevin A. McMahon, "Economics, Wisdom and the Teaching of the Bishops in the Theology of Thomas Aquinas," *Thomist* 53.1 (1989): 91.

wage or by following a standard-of-living index, but is the fruit of establishing a friendship, or solidarity, between the members of society.[34]

3.2 Value in a Globalized Society

Background Reading: Compendium 361–367

We live in a globalized economy: our economic transactions involve us in relationships with communities the world over. As I sit here working on my laptop, eating a muffin, and enjoying the music in the background at the neighborhood art center, I think of the complex web of relationships of which I am a part: my computer was manufactured in Southeast Asia; was purchased for me by my colleagues in IT; is connected to the art center's wireless server, which is provided by a nationwide corporation; and relies upon electricity provided by the hardworking folks at a nearby power plant, some of whom celebrate the Sacred Mysteries at a parish affiliated with my own. My muffin was made right here in town, but the ingredients likely came from all across the globe, as did the table and chair I am using, the floor upon which I place my feet, and so forth.

In our global economy, every one of our attempts to determine value, a just wage, or what is owed to each must factor in, at least to some extent, the whole human family. We can see why CST would think it necessary to speak of "new" virtues such as solidarity in order to think through what it means to live charitably and justly in a global society. Of course, Aquinas's world involved trade between communities, but on a much smaller scale and with much less complexity than in our own.

Compendium 361–76 discusses these "new things" in economic life. Here we will not work through its thoughtful presentation of the opportunities and risks provided by globalization. We will focus on just one point: "Looking after the common good means making use of the new opportunities for the redistribution of wealth among the different areas of the planet, to the benefit of the underprivileged that until now have been excluded or cast to the sidelines of social and economic progress" (363). The same principles we discussed in chapters 3 and 4 would apply here: my property is given to me so that I may serve the members of my community, especially the most needy.

---

34. Another issue that we cannot take up here is the relationship between a living wage and social norms such as how one's station in life should factor in. For a helpful discussion of these more nuanced points, John Ryan's *A Living Wage: Its Ethical and Economic Aspects* (New York: Macmillan, 1912), while admittedly dated, is a good place to start. For a more recent analysis, see Mary Hirschfeld's "Standard of Living and Economic Virtue: Forging a Link between St. Thomas Aquinas and the Twenty-First Century," *Journal of the Society of Christian Ethics* 26.1 (2006): 61–77.

Since that community is now global, at least in the sense that my possessions come to me via transactions with people all over the world, I must ensure that I am treating these members of my community justly.

That being said, the order of love still begins with God, and in my home. While I can never exploit the woman in Shanghai who makes my clothes by trading her good for that of my family, I must first look after the good of my family before looking outward. In any transaction of goods I must have a good moral object (giving what is due), but my end is to promote the good of my household before looking to the end of serving others. However, distributive justice may demand that I give my family's *surplus* goods to that woman in Shanghai. Imagine that I am about to buy my kids a copy of yet another Pixar film, and it comes to my attention that there has been a devastating earthquake in Shanghai. Now that the global economy places me in a relationship with that woman in Shanghai, and technology makes it possible to effortlessly send her money, other things being equal, I have a responsibility to share the goods entrusted to me with her.

Further, the *Compendium* quotes *Centesimus Annus* 36: we must be mindful of "the duty to give from one's 'abundance,' and sometimes even out of one's needs, in order to provide what is essential for the life of a poor person" (359). This may strike us as going too far, but at a minimum this might mean things that are "needs" in an affluent society (such as cable TV). Deeper still, though, we can never stop reminding ourselves that our model for justice and charity is the Lord, who gave his very life for us. Even my life is not a "need" in comparison to eternal life, the one thing that is truly necessary.

3.3 Charity and Care for Creation

Background Reading: Compendium 451–487; ST I.47.1; II-II.25.3

Third and finally, while Aquinas surely was aware of how human behavior could harm the natural world, he did not live in a society whose domination over nature was so great and whose reach was so global as to make care for creation a pressing concern. Aquinas did not have to reflect on the possibility that our use and ownership of the common store of natural resources could threaten the earth's natural functioning. Thus the relatively recent concern of CST with care for creation is not to be found in Aquinas.[35] And this focus of CST is not without controversy given the political implications of claiming that humans have rights to water, clean air, and so forth. In furtherance of this turn toward environmental considerations, Pope Francis

---

35. See *Compendium* 451–87 for a summary of CST's reflections on care for creation.

recently made the claim that care for creation is a work of mercy: "Let me propose a complement to the two traditional sets of seven: may the works of mercy also include *care for our common home*."[36] The Holy Father goes on to call this "new" work of mercy both corporal and spiritual. Leaving aside the theology of works of mercy, we can ask the general question of whether or not the claim that care for creation is central to Christian life can be derived from Thomistic principles.

I would argue that the responsibility to care for creation can be drawn out of three aspects of Aquinas's philosophical and theological principles: (1) to be is to be good; (2) private property is legitimate insofar as it builds up the common good; and (3) charity calls upon us to love the whole of creation as made in the image and likeness of God.

First, one of the central metaphysical principles of ancient philosophy is that to be is to be good. Plato even went further and made the startling claim that the Good is beyond Being.[37] As we discussed in chapter 1 (§2), this means that every existing thing, as existing thing, is good. From the lowly worm up to the lofty eagle, from the placid lake to the volatile volcano, goodness is all around us. Theologically speaking, God says "yes" and "it is very good" to all that he made, and humans are masters who are also stewards of this goodness. We are called upon to admire and care for creation, even when it is hard to see its beauty through the sweat of our brows.

Second, Aquinas's understanding of the common good is intergenerational: justice cannot be secured without piety toward parents, gratitude toward benefactors, and distributive justice for our children. This recognition that virtue must be practiced in regard to those whose sacrifices have made our flourishing possible and to those who depend upon our care forces us to acknowledge that our use of worldly goods must be compatible with the flourishing of those who come after us. If my use of the goods at my disposal is wasteful, destructive, or exploitative, I rob future generations of the goods owed to them.

Third, in his discussion of charity, Aquinas asks whether irrational creatures can be loved out of charity. Initially, it would appear that his answer will be "no," for the objections argue that they can be so loved. Yet in his response, after pointing out that charity is a kind of friendship and that friendship cannot be had with irrational creatures, he says, "Nevertheless we can love irrational creatures out of charity, if we regard them as the good things

36. Pope Francis, "Message for the World Day of Prayer for the Care of Creation" (September 1, 2016), §5, website of the Holy See, https://press.vatican.va/content/salastampa/en/bollettino/pubblico/2016/09/01/160901a.html (emphasis added).
37. See Plato, *Republic* 508e.

that we desire for others, in so far, to wit, as we wish for their preservation, to God's honor and man's use; thus too does God love them out of charity" (*ST* II-II.25.3). We could extend this general point to the earth and all that it contains, for we should desire their preservation insofar as this honors their Creator and shows our charity toward our neighbors, in the present and in the future, who rely and will rely upon the goods of the earth. If God loves all that he has made (Pss. 104:10–30; 145:9), surely we should too. All of creation is an image of the Creator, and so by caring for creation we are humbled in the realization that "the whole universe together participates [in] the divine goodness more perfectly, and represents it better than any single creature whatever" (*ST* I.47.1).

We could conclude our brief discussion of Thomistic economic theory today by pointing to St. Benedict's words of advice for the monk placed in charge of the monastery's goods: "He must show every care and concern for the sick, children, guests and the poor, knowing for certain that he will be held accountable for all of them on the day of judgment. He will regard all utensils and goods of the monastery as sacred vessels of the altar, aware that nothing is to be neglected."[38] Let us, in our unique vocations, follow this sage advice so that we too may become sharers in the heavenly banquet.

4. Aquinas's Political Theory Today

> Now the eleven disciples went to Galilee, to the mountain to which Jesus had directed them. And when they saw him they worshiped him; but some doubted. And Jesus came and said to them, "All authority in heaven and on earth has been given to me. Go therefore and make disciples of all nations, baptizing them in the name of the Father and of the Son and of the Holy Spirit, teaching them to observe all that I have commanded you; and lo, I am with you always, to the close of the age."
>
> —Matthew 28:16–20

> Then I saw a new heaven and a new earth; for the first heaven and the first earth had passed away, and the sea was no more. And I saw the holy city, new Jerusalem, coming down out of heaven from God, prepared as a bride adorned for her husband; and I heard a great voice from the throne saying, "Behold, the dwelling of God is with men. He will dwell with them, and they shall be his people, and God himself will be with them; he will wipe away every tear from their eyes, and death shall be no more, neither shall there be

---

38. *Rule of St. Benedict* 31.9–11, in Fry, *Rule of St. Benedict in English*, 54–55.

mourning nor crying nor pain any more, for the former things have passed away."

—Revelation 21:1–4

As we discussed in the introduction to this book, CST has its origins in the late nineteenth century as the Church began to confront the great social upheavals of that time and the political theories that gave shape to the burgeoning modern nations. The Church felt herself to be under attack by the forces guiding these "'new things' (*res novae*) typical of the modern age" (*Compendium* 3). In particular, the most powerful force shaping the development of modern political communities was modern liberalism, an approach to politics that (1) severed the tie between Church and state, (2) spoke of securing the rights of individuals rather than the promotion of virtue as the purpose of government, (3) replaced the notion of happiness as the goal of life with self-preservation and the satisfaction of desire, (4) put its faith in modern science and technology to better the human condition, and (5) replaced the organic model of politics as a union of families in various levels of society within a political body with a contractual model of politics as an agreement between individuals and a sovereign power. The modern liberal theorists and the governments formed on the basis of their ideas were often overtly hostile to the Church and had a monopolistic understanding of authority as held by the state. And the only alternative to these governments that promised moral, economic, and political freedom was socialism, an even more radical theory that, in some variations such as Marxism, rejected the very idea of private property and would found governments on an atheistic understanding of the human person.[39]

In the face of these radical changes in political thought and practice, the Church initially tried to pull back the reins, so to speak: Were not these changes an aberration? Could not Christendom and its understanding of the political community as united in the pursuit of natural and supernatural virtues under the guidance of human and Divine laws be preserved? CST could be said to begin when the Church recognized that this was not possible, that it was time for "a new beginning and singular development of the Church's teaching in the area of social matters" (*Compendium* 87).[40] If the Church was to shepherd the faithful through these monumental changes in political

---

39. For a good introduction to the quarrel between traditional political philosophy and modern liberalism, I highly recommend a careful reading of Fr. James V. Schall, SJ, *Roman Catholic Political Philosophy* (Lanham, MD: Lexington Books, 2006).

40. See *Compendium* 87–104 for an introduction to the history of CST. For a fuller treatment of CST in general, emphasizing its continuity with traditional political theory, see J. Brian

organization, she needed to develop a body of teaching that, while rooted in her great tradition, could speak to the needs of the times. In part, this would require appropriating the new vocabulary of rights, freedom, values, Church and state, and so forth, so as to enter into conversation with political leaders and their citizens. Doing so brings with it certain risks, for these new terms were themselves formulated on the basis of this flawed modern understanding of the human person and the secularist approach to politics. In order to speak to modern peoples, then, the Church had the difficult task of translating the traditional approach to politics into a new idiom without thereby distorting it. For example, as Francis Russell Hittinger explains, two of the central terms in CST's political lexicon—namely, "subsidiarity" and "social justice"—are not new ideas so much as new terms used to explain the Church's traditional teaching that societies of persons are not "outsourced" agents of state power and that general justice is not obedience to the decrees of the modern state but promotion of the common good, which both persons and the state serve.[41] In what could be seen as a twist on Jesus's saying, the Church had to be mindful of the possibility that the attempt to put the new wine of modern political theory into the old wineskins of the tradition would spill the wine and destroy the skins. As those who warned against such dangers could point out, "No one after drinking old wine desires new; for he says, 'The old is good'" (Luke 5:39).[42]

Thus, while "updating" Aquinas's moral and economic theory for contemporary issues was relatively straightforward, our task is not as easy as we come to our third and final topic, political theory. And on issues like the relationship between Church and state, it is harder to make a case for the compatibility of Thomistic political theory and CST. The difficulty in seeing a common vision stems from a difference of purpose as well as the "new things" the Church faces with the rise of the modern state. First, regarding purpose, whereas Aquinas is theorizing about the nature of politics *for all times*, CST is written *for our times*. Lest we see these two approaches as opposing one another, the *Compendium* speaks of both *continuity* and *renewal*: on the one hand, there is a "foundational and permanent nucleus of the Church's social doctrine, by which it moves through history without being conditioned by history or

---

Benestad's *Church, State, and Society: An Introduction to Catholic Social Doctrine* (Washington, DC: Catholic University of America Press, 2011).

41. See Francis Russell Hittinger, "The Four Basic Principles of Catholic Social Doctrine: An Interpretation," *Nova et Vetera* 7.4 (2009): 834–35, for a summary of his argument.

42. It should also be pointed out that these modern terms were themselves taken from late medieval political theorists who, at least to some extent, were Thomists. See Bruce Frohnen and Kenneth L. Grasso, eds., *Rethinking Rights: Historical, Political, and Philosophical Perspectives* (Columbia: University of Missouri Press, 2009), for helpful essays on this difficult topic.

running the risk of fading away" (85); on the other hand, CST is formulated as a response to the problems of each age and thus is a place "where perennial truth penetrates and permeates new circumstances, indicating paths of justice and peace" (86). *Compendium* 87–104 summarizes this tradition, from the first social encyclical, *Rerum Novarum* (1891), to what some consider to be the most comprehensive, *Centesimus Annus* (1991), showing how the various social documents issued by the Church responded to the concerns of the time. In concluding, the *Compendium* makes precisely the point that we are making here: "In the formulation and teaching of this social doctrine, the Church has been, and continues to be, prompted not by theoretical motivation but by pastoral concern" (104). While Aquinas surely had practical concerns as well—for he was a teacher—his focus is primarily theoretical and is the fruit of the contemplative life that he led.

While Catholic political theorists today are called upon to contribute to the Church's own understanding of these theoretical matters, the Church herself must look with a pastoral eye to the condition of the world and discern how best to meet the needs of the faithful as they work together with other people of good will to promote the common good. In politics, what in particular must be addressed is the rise of the modern state with its vast, centralized powers and jurisdictional authority over millions of citizens who do not share a common religion, ethnicity, culture, or even language. This may seem overstated, but we could even say that "politics" as Aquinas understood that term is dead. For Aquinas, politicians are trying to secure the common good of a relatively homogenous people with shared customs and religion. Politicians in the modern state, by contrast, are trying to provide peace and security, as well as protect the fundamental rights of individuals who have a dizzying variety of views on the purpose of human existence. Whereas Aquinas thinks of politics in terms of an organic development from the male/female relationship up to the city, and all for the purpose of the happiness found in giving one another their respective due, modern politics thinks in terms of contracts entered into by individuals with the state so that they can privately pursue what they think to be best in life for themselves and gain protection from the sovereign power. And, again, whereas Aquinas could unite these earthly cities under the City of God, the modern state sees itself as sovereign, admitting of no power greater than itself.

This change from the classical city to the modern state requires a new way of thinking about politics. CST signals that it is performing just such a task by the fact that it refers to itself as Catholic *social* thought rather than Catholic *political* thought. To call this teaching "social" is to reorient political theory *away from* the political authority and *toward* the people served by their elected officials. While this should remind us of Aquinas's point that just leaders promote the common good rather than their own good, CST is making a bigger point: since the city as a political reality no longer exists, replaced as it was by the modern state, the locus of political activity is now to be found in the private sector, in society. In other words, in the city it is the responsibility of the political authorities to look out for the common good by enacting laws, creating policies, and making prudential decisions that would promote the happiness of the citizens; in the modern state it is primarily the citizens themselves joined together as members of families, unions, sports leagues, educational institutions, philanthropic foundations, churches, and so forth who solicit the assistance of the government in pursuit of the common good. To clarify the claim that politics is dead, we could say that politics as the head of the perfect community has given way to politics as the servant of society. While both the medieval king and the modern politician serve their people, the king does so as their ruler, the politician as their representative.[43]

While in a way all of this is new and a result of the death of Christendom, in another way this is a return to the conditions of Christians living under the Roman Empire. For it was Christians themselves who "invented" the idea of a society distinct from the political body. To some extent one could find such an idea in the Roman Empire itself as it subdued non-Latin-speaking peoples and brought them under its laws,[44] yet it really is the result of the Christian distinction between rendering to Caesar and rendering to God. One of Christianity's unique features is that it is not a political religion, and thus it could conceive of two things: (1) Christians living under different regimes with unique customs yet still united together as members of the Body of Christ and (2) Christians constituting a distinct society under the secular authority of a pagan government. Whether Christians rule themselves or are ruled by non-Christians, they are called to point out the imperfection of all human things and to proclaim the good news to the City of Man. As an important early Christian testimony has it, "Christians are distinguished from other men

43. One of the central debates among Catholic political theorists today is over the nature of the common good, with the new natural lawyers (e.g., John Finnis, Robert P. George, and William E. May) arguing that this good is "instrumental" and many Thomists (e.g., Lawrence Dewan, Steven A. Long, and John Goyette) arguing that it is transcendent. In part, as I am arguing, this may be a reflection of the difference between the purposes of the modern state and the medieval city, respectively. For an introduction to contemporary debates on the natural law and the common good, see John Goyette, Mark S. Latkovic, and Richard S. Myers, eds., *St. Thomas Aquinas and the Natural Law Tradition: Contemporary Perspectives* (Washington, DC: Catholic University of America Press, 2004), esp. part 3.

44. It is worth noting that the term "law of nations" was originally used by Romans in order to think through how to apply the law when not all members of the community were Roman.

neither by country, nor language, nor the customs which they observe. . . .
As citizens, they share in all things with others, and yet endure all things as
if foreigners. . . . To sum up all in one word—what the soul is in the body,
Christians are in the world."[45]

This distinction between society and politics is enshrined in St. Augustine's
distinction between the City of God and the City of Man and was formulated
at a time when paganism was trying to reinvigorate itself as a force that could
be used to reunite the crumbling Roman Empire. By the time of Aquinas,
when kings were at least nominally Christian, one could write of a unified
Christian society ruled by earthly and heavenly authorities who shared the
same end of eternal life. Under the auspices of Christendom, Aquinas did
not need to devote much of his contemplative attention to the nature of a
non-Christian politics. And, further still, the idea of a secular politics that
did not advance some conception of the purpose of human life would have
been almost unthinkable.

It is hard to say what Aquinas would think about the modern state and
how the common good could be secured today, and it is the task of CST to
take the insights gleaned from life under Christendom and apply them to
life under a sort of post-Christian, neo-pagan Roman Empire. Whereas St.
Augustine essentially had to create Christian political theory, the Church
today has the benefit of two thousand years of experience and theorizing
from which to draw. With all of this in mind and in the limited space we have
here, we will discuss the Thomistic roots of CST's political theory as well
as the "new things" of life in the modern state. Our focus will be on some
of the key terms in political life today: "subsidiarity," "solidarity," "rights,"
"religious freedom" (and the relationship between Church and state more
generally), and "social justice."

4.1 The Principles of Subsidiarity and Solidarity

*Background Reading: Compendium 91, 160–170, 185–196, 252–254,
346–360, 417–420*

Subsidiarity is a principle that provides more guidance for the general
point that the happiness of the human person is the reason for all social organizations, for it serves as a reminder that authority is only legitimate to the
extent that it serves the needs of the members of society. More particularly,

---

45. *Epistle of Mathetes to Diognetus 5–6*, in *The Ante-Nicene Fathers: Translations of the
Writings of the Fathers down to A.D. 325*, ed. Alexander Roberts and James Donaldson, 10 vols.
(repr., Peabody, MA: Hendrickson, 1994; New York: Christian Literature, 1885–1887), 1:26–27.

subsidiarity is twofold: it insists, on the one hand, that social groups place themselves at the service of the human person; on the other hand, that there is a proper "level" of authority that must be observed in each action promoting the common good such that governmental action aims at assisting and coordinating societies rather than dominating and controlling them. Thus, CST takes a bottom-up approach to political authority: since an individual person is not an island, he or she shares responsibilities and decision-making authority with other members of the family; since the family cannot provide for every need of its members, it enters into economic arrangements with other families, businesses, and the like; since neighborhoods and local communities are in need of police forces and various forms of social assistance, they entrust local governments with certain tasks; and so forth. By the time the level of the modern state and national government is reached, a complex ordering from lower to higher levels of society has been established, with each level performing a unique, irreplaceable task. CST speaks of this in terms of participation, which is an implied aspect of subsidiarity. As Aquinas notes regarding the mixed regime, communities are healthier when their members participate meaningfully in familial, economic, and political life by putting their time and talents at the service of the other. In this sense, CST is in complete consonance with Aquinas's recognition that there should be a democratic base to political authority.[46]

While Aquinas thought participation was important for the members of a society, it should not surprise us that he did not think it necessary to connect this with a larger principle that the Church now calls "subsidiarity." Aquinas lived in a society in which, due to technological limitations and strong respect for tradition, authority always had a personal and somewhat local character. Yes, there may have been empires, but their ability to directly reach individual citizens was limited by the power of local customs and by premodern society's lack of power over the forces of nature. It is only with the rise of the modern state that it becomes necessary to warn against "certain forms of centralization, bureaucratization, and welfare assistance and . . . the unjustified and excessive presence of the State in public mechanisms" (*Compendium* 187). The "Social Assistance State," as CST calls the modern state when it fails to respect subsidiarity, in its attempt to reach all the way down to the individual members of society, supplants important societies

---

46. That being said, CST's stronger defense of democracy does not appear to agree with Aquinas's position. See John Hittinger's critical assessment of arguments purporting to derive a Thomistic defense of democracy in "Jacques Maritain and Yves R. Simon's Use of Thomas Aquinas in Their Defense of Liberal Democracy," in *Liberty, Wisdom, and Grace: Thomism and Democratic Political Theory* (Lanham, MD: Lexington Books, 2002), 35–60.

like the family or the local community and ends up harming the very people it is trying to serve.

Imagine that we as a community are trying to determine how to help the hungry members of our society. We decide to distribute surplus food to them, with the federal government using airplanes, the state government helicopters, the local government semitrucks, and various private organizations such as businesses, social clubs, and parishes using cars and getting around by foot. How do we get John Stevenson, who lives down a country lane at the edge of town, the food that he needs? Suppose that the federal government wants to do this by connecting his meal to a parachute and dropping it from the bird's-eye view of its airplane. Sure, this can be done, but with a lot of expensive equipment and with great potential for an unsuccessful drop. From the vantage point of its airplane high up in the air, the federal government can see the bigger picture of how much each community as a whole may need in relation to the needs of other communities; from the helicopter, the state can get closer to the ground and even wave at the people it serves; from the semi, the local government can stop and meet them; from the car and on foot, the members of local public and private organizations can get to know Mr. Stevenson and through such acts of justice and charity befriend him. Larger units perform the role of assisting the groups who know the particular needs of the community, so that they can prudently distribute resources with an eye toward the common good that can only be secured when John Stevenson gets what he needs as a dignified human person. And, further still, we should recognize that such air drops ideally are only necessary when natural disasters strike; a healthy community will rely on such services as little as possible in order to ensure that it does not gradually lose its independence and become a mere vassal in the Social Assistance State. The nurturing that goes on in families, the education that takes place between teachers and students, and the free acts of justice and charity between citizens cannot be replaced by a national government that is too distant to know its citizens one by one.

According to the *Compendium*, solidarity refers to "the need to recognize in the composite ties that unite men and social groups among themselves, the space given to human freedom for common growth in which all share and in which they participate" (194). While CST does not clearly delineate how solidarity is related to justice and charity, we can recognize two aspects of this principle that roughly correspond to the distinction between what reason and revelation tell us about the nature of society.

First, the *Compendium* points out that the principle of solidarity is more necessary now than ever before because "for the first time since the beginning of human history, it is now possible—at least technically—to establish relationships between people who are separated by great distances and are unknown to each other" (192). With the exception of his just war theory, Aquinas's political theory is focused almost entirely on justice within the city, offering little in the way of thinking about how to establish justice between cities, much less between nations with millions of citizens. Now that it is possible to establish permanent relationships between peoples who live on the opposite ends of the earth, and even to create a "world government" that could in theory police the whole planet, it is necessary to think about how justice between societies can be secured. And in light of the universal destination of goods, societies need to come together to determine how they can help the neediest among them in securing the material goods necessary for the dignity of their respective citizens. Yet this must be done without neglecting the principle of subsidiarity. This is a delicate balancing act, for it is important for each society to look to its own common good while acknowledging that this good cannot be pursued by harming another society and its members.

Second, the principle of solidarity is ultimately rooted in revelation, for it flows out of God's love for each one of us as a unique person and from the charity that God infuses in our hearts. In this sense, solidarity is a distinctly Christian contribution to politics, and by announcing this principle the Church is calling upon the members of the Body of Christ to put it into place and to infuse their respective societies with the leaven of charity. It is worth noting that the *Compendium* connects solidarity to integral human development and roots both of them in charity: "The Magisterium highly recommends solidarity because it is capable of guaranteeing the common good and fostering integral human development: love 'makes one see in neighbour another self'" (582).

4.2 Rights, Religious Freedom, and the Relationship between Church and State

Background Reading: Compendium 60–71, 152–159, 284–286, 384–389, 417–427

One of the most controversial aspects of the Church's attempt to "translate" her teachings into the modern idiom is her willingness to use the language of rights. While this is not the space to work through all of the controversies, let us pause briefly to discuss the difference between Aquinas's use of the term "right" and the modern understanding of rights.[47] In this context,

---

47. For a history of rights language from Aquinas up to the early modern era that argues for at least "certain threads of consistency" (97), see Bernard V. Brady, "An Analysis of the Use of Rights Language in Pre-Modern Catholic Social Thought," *Thomist* 57 (1993): 97–121.

we take up the question of how (or whether) CST's claim that there is a right to religious freedom can be squared with Aquinas's insistence that the City of Man acknowledge its subordinate status to the City of God.

In chapter 3 (§3) we explained that right is a central aspect of Aquinas's theory of justice but that this is a very different notion than the modern understanding of rights. Right is the objective measure of what is owed to each individual, and right establishes equality between the members of a community. Positive right, which establishes what is right by agreement, must be rooted in natural right, or what is right by nature. By contrast, rights are something we possess by virtue of our nature or the nature of our society and belong to us as individuals. When we speak of our right to private property, for example, this refers to the immunity we have from coercive authority as well as something that authority has a responsibility to protect or secure. Whereas the right establishes what is objectively equal and thus just between peoples, rights provide a space for us to freely decide what to do. We have rights even if we use them for immoral purposes, something that would not make sense to say regarding the right. For example, the modern understanding of the right to private property is arguably compatible with letting my surplus goods go to waste out of neglect, but one could never say that this is right in the traditional sense of that term.

The problem that those who adhere to Thomistic political theory have with the notion of rights is twofold: First, as we have just seen, rights are subjective and can be used for evil purposes, which suggests a sort of relativism. Something seems odd about saying that people have the *right* to do what is *wrong*. Second, putting rights at the heart of political theory seems to invert the way we should think about our lives: the Bible does not speak of rights but of commandments, of the obligation we have to live in accordance with God's will. Focusing on rights empowers the selfishness of fallen human beings, who would rather receive freely than give generously. But, from the biblical perspective, human beings are debtors, who are called to live out their lives by charitably returning to God the gifts they have received through acts of love of God and neighbor. By using the language of rights, CST seems to be not simply translating the tradition of Catholic political thought but corrupting it and caving in to the secularism and relativism of modern political theories.

To respond to the first point, CST explicitly rejects the idea that rights defend the viciousness of those who abuse the freedoms that rights permit. In regard to the most important kind of freedom, religious freedom, the *Compendium* says that it "is not a moral licence to adhere to error, nor an implicit right to error" (421). In the case of the person squandering his resources, CST would not consider this a right. Given that others have a right to the material goods necessary for happiness, squandering one's own property is not a right, but an abuse of a right, an act of depriving another of his rights. Thus the *Compendium* points out that one cannot claim to have rights without acknowledging one's duty to respect the rights of others (see 156). Regarding the second point, there is no doubt that the modern notion of rights can be used as a defense of selfishness, but CST rejects the primacy of rights. By contextualizing rights in the fundamental principles and values of social life and in the duties we have toward one another, CST insists that people understand their rights as gifts given to them by God by which they can freely take up the joyous task of living justly and charitably.

The importance of rights, then, is not that they give us permission to do whatever we want, but that they stop governments, social groups, and private citizens from preventing us from pursuing the happiness that we naturally desire and for which we were created (see, e.g., *Compendium* 388–89). Thus, in addition to speaking of the kinds of rights we would find in secular lists—that is, human rights, the rights of children, those of workers, those of nations, and of peoples—CST (1) points out that the right to life rules out abortion, artificial insemination, euthanasia, and the like; (2) speaks of the right of a man and a woman to marry and establish a family through the moral use of sexuality; and (3) prioritizes the right to know the truth about ourselves and our Creator, and thus the right of the Church to preach Jesus Christ as the one who reveals this truth (see 155). CST takes up the language of rights, and of values for that matter, and removes the relativistic connotations that many associate with them. Rights are the means by which we as members of society are given the opportunity to live in accordance with justice and charity, looking always to the truth that alone can set us free.

At the heart of CST's message regarding rights is that she has been entrusted with the fullness of truth and thus has a duty to preach to all nations; this adds another dimension to the theory of rights that tends to be lacking in modern formulations: communities, and not just individuals, have rights.[48] Corresponding to the Church's right to evangelize, people have a right to know this transcendent truth, and thus a duty to pursue it and live in the faith of Christ. In proclaiming a right to religious freedom, then, the Church is not relativizing religion or denying that Christ's self-sacrificial act is the only means of salvation. Rather, she is acknowledging the point that Aquinas made that religion cannot be a matter of coercion. Further, the Church has a unique right because she alone has the fullness of truth, though she has the

---

48. See *Compendium* 157. As examples of corporate rights, *Compendium* 241, 253, and 421 speak, respectively, of the rights of private schools, the family, and communities.

duty to heed the exhortation of St. Paul: "Preach the word, be urgent in season and out of season, convince, rebuke, and exhort, be unfailing in patience
and in teaching" (2 Tim. 4:2).[49] Those who reject her do not do so rightfully,
for there is no right to error, and yet she cannot force the truth on those who
"will not endure sound teaching, but having itching ears . . . accumulate for
themselves teachers to suit their own likings, and . . . turn away from listening
to the truth" (2 Tim. 4:3–4).

When Aquinas formulated his theory regarding the City of God commanding the City of Man to enforce Divine law, he spoke in the context of Christendom. At that time one had a society that by and large recognized the threat that
heresies pose to salvation, and one took it as a matter of course that religious
subverters would be punished for their spiritual forgeries. This is clearly not
true today, and, without denying Aquinas's theoretical claims regarding the
coercive authority of the Church, it would be counterproductive to insist upon
the Church's authority over all nations. In *Dignitatis Humanae*, the Vatican II
document that opened up this new way of speaking about the relationship
between the City of God and the City of Man, we read that the Church has
the same end in mind as Aquinas but recognizes the need in modern society
for a new means to that end: "Religious freedom, . . . which men demand as
necessary to fulfill their duty to worship God, has to do with immunity from
coercion in civil society. Therefore it leaves untouched traditional Catholic
doctrine on the moral duty of men and societies toward the true religion and
toward the one Church of Christ."[50]

In our times, when freedom is on the lips of all people, the most effective
way to preach the gospel is to persuade by words and deeds rather than by
law. CST is offered as a gift to the Church and to those who have ears to
hear. The Church is not calling for societies to be neutral on the question of

---

49. See, e.g., *Compendium* 426: "The Church has the right to the legal recognition of her
proper identity. Precisely because her mission embraces all of human reality, the Church, sens-
ing that she is 'truly and intimately linked with mankind and its history,' claims the freedom
to express her moral judgment on this reality, whenever it may be required to defend the fundamental rights of the person or for the salvation of souls."

50. Paul VI, *Dignitatis Humanae* (December 7, 1965), §1, website of the Holy See, http://
www.vatican.va/archive/hist_councils/ii_vatican_council/documents/vat-ii_decl_19651207
_dignitatis-humanae_en.html. For a discussion of how this notion of religious freedom taken
up in Vatican II is consistent with the tradition, see John Courtney Murray, *The Problem of
Religious Freedom* (Westminster, PA: Newman Press, 1965); Kenneth L. Grasso and Robert P.
Hunt, eds., *Catholicism and Religious Freedom: Contemporary Reflections on Vatican II's
Declaration on Religious Liberty* (Lanham, MD: Rowman & Littlefield, 2006); and Francis
Russell Hittinger's "The Declaration on Religious Liberty, *Dignitatis Humanae*," in *Vatican II:
Renewal within Tradition*, ed. Matthew L. Lamb and Matthew Levering (New York: Oxford
University Press, 2008), 359–82.

religion, but to allow her to be the leaven that will direct them beyond earthly justice's common good to the infused charity that alone can unite people to the Infinite Good. In this, she relies upon the great contribution of Aquinas to her self-understanding and applies his insights for all times to the needs of our times.

Turning now to the relationship between Church and state, CST insists upon adherence to natural law and thus to the fundamental principles, rights, and values of integral human development. Beyond that, the Church calls upon her members, in cooperation with men and women of good will, to exercise prudence in determining how to meet the common good of a particular society as it journeys in this fallen world. Additionally, the Church calls for these societies to recognize their own limitations and the need for the God of love to infuse their pursuit of goodness with the charity that transcends human justice and builds the civilization of love.

Putting all of this in the language of the virtues, we could say that the Church still calls upon human law to assist the individual persons within the community in the formation of the acquired virtues. Further, she uses her own Divine law to assist the members of the Body of Christ within any political community in growing in the infused virtues, gifts, and fruits, on the way of beatitude. In addition, guided by Christ's command to preach to the ends of the earth, she demands the freedom to preach the good news to unbelievers. While the overlap between the roles of Church and state today is not as strong as it was in Aquinas's time, this does not make for a "wall of separation" between them.

Speculatively, we could speak today of the need for the state to promote, perhaps not the virtue of acquired religion, given that it is unclear that fallen humanity can even acquire such a virtue, but what we might call "religiosity." Rooted in a proper understanding of the natural human desire for the Perfect Good but also acknowledging the inability to achieve this end without grace, political communities can promote the contemplative life in pursuit of this truth in a general sense. Such encouragement could take many forms, from promoting the arts to preserving heritage, from supporting liberal arts education to leisure activities such as backpacking, festivals, and religious observances. In terms of observances, the state need not promote Catholicism necessarily, but it can still promote religiosity in the sense of respecting the unique role of religion in building up the common good. The US holiday of Thanksgiving comes to mind as an example, for it is a national holiday that, at least in its original intention, sets aside a day for the nation to give thanks to God. While none of these promoted activities will of necessity lead to a more Catholic nation, they are the means by which the state acknowledges its limitations and the need for a higher law in order to have a truly virtuous citizenry.[51] Reading the signs of the times, CST preaches to all people the true goal of the heavenly Jerusalem; the Church does not ask the state to acknowledge the highest truth about humanity, but at least to recognize the truth that we are not made for the earthly glory of the democratic nation but for the heavenly glory of the kingdom.[52]

4.3 Social Justice

Background Reading: Compendium 182–193, 201–208, 303

Since CST speaks about the social as distinct from the political and focuses on the former in a way that Aquinas did not, it is difficult to determine how one would apply Aquinas's formulations of justice and charity to life in modern liberal democracies. CST speaks of "social justice" as a central virtue for today. This term is often seen as a new way of speaking about distributive justice, for social justice is concerned with making sure that all members of society have what they need for dignified lives, but social justice is actually another way of speaking about general or legal justice. It is worth quoting the *Compendium* in full on this point:

> The Church's social Magisterium constantly calls for the most classical forms of justice to be respected: *commutative*, *distributive* and *legal justice*. Ever greater importance has been given to *social justice*, which represents a real development in *general justice*, the justice that regulates social relationships according to the criterion of observance of the *law*. *Social justice*, a requirement related to the *social question* which today is worldwide in scope, concerns the social, political and economic aspects and, above all, the structural dimension of problems and their respective solutions. (201; see also 303)

The "old" forms of justice are not to be jettisoned, for the virtue of justice is an objective demand of human nature. Yet general or legal justice demands more of private citizens in the modern state than it did in the classical city. Aquinas often gives the impression that the citizens are like so many pawns

---

51. It should also be pointed out that Abraham Lincoln, who resurrected the national celebration of Thanksgiving, also instituted a national day of fasting. Somehow this latter "celebration" never caught on.

52. For a thorough discussion of Aquinas on the virtue of religion (though, unfortunately, without discussing the acquired/infused distinction) and on how to approach CST's understanding of religious liberty through a Thomistic lens, see Francis Russell Hittinger, "Religion, Human Law, and the Virtue of Religion: The Case of *Dignitatis Humanae*," *Nova et Vetera* 14.1 (2016): 151–76.

waiting for their orders from the benevolent ruler, that they have no initiative in looking after the common good save to direct their virtues according to the king's pronouncements on what is just. This is clearly not what he thinks, for he (1) claims that the mixed regime is best *in practice* given the importance of the citizens' participation in exercising political authority and (2) recognizes the role of virtuous people who go beyond the bare minimum of what law requires in promoting the common good. By speaking of social justice as "a real development of *general justice*," CST highlights the need to make these aspects of traditional political theory a more central focus of virtue theory. This is true not only due to the greater role of society as a whole in promoting the common good but also as a result of the complexities of modern societies both internally and externally. Given how many individual persons, families, and social groups are involved in every social decision and how the actions of one society affect the members of the other societies throughout the world, it is incumbent upon each one of us to determine how we can give one another what is due. Further and again, the turn to speaking of "social" rather than of "general" or "legal" justice is a way to combat the monopolistic pretensions of the modern state: "In view of the omnicompetent state of [the modern] era, and in view of the pressing need to articulate and defend an organic pluralism of society, it was not an unreasonable position to jettison the term 'legal' in favor of 'social' lest the common good of order be understood as exclusively the order of the state."[53]

Let us advance the following (admittedly tentative) interpretation of how social justice and another "new" virtue, solidarity, fit Aquinas's schema of the virtues: social justice is CST's term for acquired general justice; the virtue (as distinct from the principle) of solidarity is the term for infused general justice.[54] Both of these virtues are said to look after how society is structured so as to promote the good of every one of its members, and also both are said to look after how the structures of global trade, political relationships, and so forth can promote the good of all peoples on earth. Yet in the *Compendium*'s presentation of the value of justice, immediately after speaking about the centrality of social justice, we read that it is necessary "to open up also for justice the new horizon of solidarity and love. 'By itself, justice is not enough. Indeed, it can even betray itself, unless it is open to that deeper power

---

53. F. R. Hittinger, "Four Basic Principles," 833.

54. For a history of the use of the term "social justice" that reaches roughly the same conclusion I do here regarding its relation to Aquinas's theory of justice, see Edward J. O'Boyle, "Social Justice: Addressing the Ambiguity," *Logos* 14.2 (2011): 97–117, and Normand J. Paulhus, "Uses and Misuses of the Term 'Social Justice' in the Roman Catholic Tradition," *Journal of Religious Ethics* 15.2 (1987): 261–82.

which is love.' In fact, the Church's social doctrine places alongside the value of justice that of solidarity, in that it is the privileged way of peace" (203). While, again, this passage is in part addressing a "reductionist" understanding of justice that does not even meet the standards of true, acquired justice, the point here is that solidarity *goes beyond* social justice.

As a virtue rooted in charity, solidarity looks to promote the common good of all human beings created in the image and likeness of God and sharing in common a heavenly home. One particular way in which solidarity goes beyond social justice is in its regard for the poor. Christ's proclamation of the Beatitudes points us to the special love that God has for the poor. The Church, loving what her Divine Spouse loves, tries to infuse the world with this highest virtue. Solidarity, in its regard for the common good and as commanded by charity, cares especially for the poor. This teaching, encapsulated in the phrase the "preferential option for the poor," is a central aspect of CST. The *Compendium* cites John Paul II's *Sollicitudo Rei Socialis* 42 in explaining the meaning of this unique form of Christian love, and we cite it in full here given its importance:

> This is an option, or a special form of primacy in the exercise of Christian charity, to which the whole tradition of the Church bears witness. It affects the life of each Christian inasmuch as he or she seeks to imitate the life of Christ, but it applies equally to our social responsibilities and hence to our manner of living, and to the logical decisions to be made concerning the ownership and use of goods.
>
> Today, furthermore, given the worldwide dimension which the social question has assumed, this love of preference for the poor, and the decisions which it inspires in us, cannot but embrace the immense multitudes of the hungry, the needy, the homeless, those without health care and, above all, those without hope of a better future.[55]

Solidarity, or infused general justice, is that virtue by which Christians direct the particular acts of benevolence, almsgiving, liberality, and the like to the common, supernatural good. In particular, it looks to reform society as a whole, removing what CST calls "the structures of sin" (see *Compendium* 193) that prevent the poor from participating in social life as full and equal members. Solidarity is that virtue which allows Christians in modern liberal democracies to infuse society with the gospel. Christians as individual persons,

---

55. John Paul II, *Sollicitudo Rei Socialis* (December 30, 1987), §42, website of the Holy See, http://w2.vatican.va/content/john-paul-ii/en/encyclicals/documents/hf_jp-ii_enc_30121987 _sollicitudo-rei-socialis.html, quoted in *Compendium* 182.

members of society, and political leaders are called to structure society based on the gospel and to infuse political institutions, decisions, and policies with the leaven of sacrificial love.

Putting all of this together, Aquinas's fundamental divisions of the virtues of justice and charity can be "updated" for today by looking at how CST has adopted, and in some cases revised, his vocabulary in its engagement with modern social and political structures. Commutative justice demands that our transactions reflect a proper understanding of both human nature and the value of earthly goods, as well as the transcendent end of the human person. Distributive justice ensures that society looks after the needs of each, subordinating private-property rights to the principle of the universal destination of goods. Legal, general, or social justice directs the acts of the acquired cardinal virtues to the building up of the common good, a good that requires, with due regard for subsidiarity, a just wage for all as well as care for creation. Solidarity, building upon social justice, looks to direct the material goods, human work, and care for creation in a society to the common, transcendent end of its members. And, finally, charity wills all of these as a means toward glorifying God by building up the civilization of love.

The lasting peace that has been the dream of modern people and for which the modern state strives can have no other foundation than the human person whose fulfillment is achieved by life in Christ, fully God and fully Man. Only by practicing justice and charity can we satisfy the human desire for happiness, the achievement of which is the goal of every moral, economic, and political decision. This formation in the virtues and docility to the Holy Spirit is the only way to strengthen the economy and bring about the civilization of love. Building upon the insights and vocabulary of St. Thomas Aquinas, the Common Doctor, Catholic social thought is the Church's gift to the whole human family; putting it into practice is the way that we can be true disciples of the Christ, whose last prayer was that we might be one, as he and the Father are One (see John 17:20–23). The proper response to what we have learned in this introduction is to continue to study both Aquinas and CST so that we may go out into the world and proclaim the good news, witnessing to it by acts of justice and charity under the tutelage of the Holy Spirit.

Postscript

On April 26, 1336, the great Italian humanist and forerunner of the Renaissance, Francesco Petrarca, gave birth to mountain-climbing as a sport. At the youthful age of twenty-one years, "moved by no other purpose than to see what the great height was like," he climbed the 6,273-foot Mont Ventoux. When he summited the mountain, one might think that he would have found what he was looking for, a breathtaking view and the exhilaration of having achieved his goal. Yet this was not what he saw and felt; instead, Petrarch (as we English speakers call him) considered this bodily journey to serve a great purpose, growth in virtue both acquired and infused. As he tells it, shortly after admiring the view, he began to reflect on his own life and on whether or not he had accompanied his growth into manhood with cultivation of virtue: "I was happy at my progress, but wept for my imperfections." This reflection led him to take out his pocket edition of St. Augustine's *Confessions*, where he providentially read, "Men go to admire the high mountains and the great flood of the seas and the wide-rolling rivers and the ring of the Ocean and the movement of the stars; and they abandon themselves!" Reproaching himself for thinking that one could find the purpose of life in worldly things and in one's own accomplishments, he remarked that even the pagan philosophers could have taught him to look not to the world for greatness but within himself. And, beyond this, he saw that "if we were willing to endure so much labor and sweat to raise our bodies a little closer to Heaven, what cross, what prison, what rack should terrify the soul in its approach to God, treading down upthrusting pride and all man's mortal lot?"[1]

---

1. Petrarch, *Letters from Petrarch*, trans. Morris Bishop (Bloomington: Indiana University Press, 1966), 45, 49–50.

This real-life event from the journal of a lonely climber, in a remote part of France nearly seven hundred years ago, is like a fable for the journey that we have just taken: from our beginning in the philosophical pursuit of happiness to our conclusion that only by cooperating with the grace of God can we satisfy the desires of our heart of hearts, we have seen how the acquired and infused virtues and the gifts and fruits of the Holy Spirit can lead us on the path of the Beatitudes. The moral, economic, and political decisions we make can only lead to happiness if we let justice and charity be our guides. We do not need to climb mountains to see greatness; we simply need to look within to ourselves as image and likeness, and above to the God who is Love. More pointedly, we should look to Jesus Christ as the one who reveals us to ourselves and find our vocation as members of his Body, our Holy Mother the Church.

In all of this, though, we should conclude with a recognition of how difficult such a journey is and will be for each of us. Let us not go it alone. Forming ourselves in the virtues and practicing docility to the Holy Spirit must be done as members of communities and with the help of spiritual guides. Books are no substitute here, and so what we have learned should not be seen as an ending, but a beginning. Again, the purpose of studying moral, economic, and political theory is not so much to know what is good, but to be good ourselves. We must put into practice the virtues, not just talk about them. With these points in mind, let us briefly conclude with a reflection on the role of prudence in self-discernment and in acting rightly toward others. While we will not be following Aquinas strictly here, we will base our observations on his insights.

First, we could call that kind of prudence that we must have in order to judge ourselves rightly "self-knowledge." We must come to know ourselves as sinners called to be saints. To which vices am I particularly prone? What virtues are strong in me, and which weak? Self-knowledge requires a solid grasp of my spiritual state and, like other virtues, is contrasted with two vices. In terms of deficiency, we must avoid laxity, or the vice of either not knowing my vices as vices or being content with a "nobody's perfect" attitude about them. In terms of excess, we must avoid scrupulosity, or the vice of either not knowing my virtues as virtues or being obsessed with my own imperfections. The lax person is right to say that no mere mortal is perfect (in this life) but wrong to say that we should not be *on the way* to perfection. I will fail time and time again to live up to the perfection of the God whom I know and love. This is why he gave us the gift of confession and of the Eucharist, by which we become more and more like the Christ we consume.

Second, even if we gain this self-knowledge by which we judge ourselves aright, we need the kind of prudence that allows us to be good judges of the actions and characters of others. Now, to be clear, God alone is my judge and the judge of others, but I am still called upon to recognize both the virtuous and the vicious actions of my fellow children of God. And to some extent this also requires that I judge their characters, especially if I am their parent, priest, or civil judge. Opposed to this virtue that we could call "good judgment," there is the excess of judgment*alism*, a going out of my way to judge when I am not called upon to do so, or a pointing out of others' faults unnecessarily or unfairly. In terms of deficiency, there is the vice of indifferentism by which I either do not care about the souls of my fellow human beings or am blinded by the fog of relativism and unable to see sin for what it is. We are not all called to be confessors or civil judges, but we *are* all called upon to recognize virtue and vice in the world and to heed the conclusion to the "judge not" discourse of Jesus: "First take the log out of your own eye, and then you will see clearly to take the speck out of your brother's eye" (Matt. 7:5). This is the part of that teaching we rarely hear, for while Jesus is warning against judgmentalism, he is not preaching indifferentism. We must find the middle, narrow way of virtue in all that we do. Let us go forth, then, with self-knowledge and right judgment, perfecting justice with the friendship of charity.

Appendix

Schema of the Virtues

.

The schema below provides the principal distinctions between the types of virtues discussed throughout the book. While Aquinas accepts Aristotle's division between moral and intellectual virtues, he organizes his own treatise around the theological and cardinal virtues, and the schema reflects this. Thus, it does not include the intellectual virtues, except prudence. While this necessitated omitting one of the central virtues—namely, wisdom—it reflects the argument made in chapters 1 and 2 for turning our attention to justice and charity as the foci of moral life. The secondary virtues are listed (in italics) beneath the virtues to which they are annexed. This does not represent a complete list of the secondary virtues, but rather only those discussed in this book.

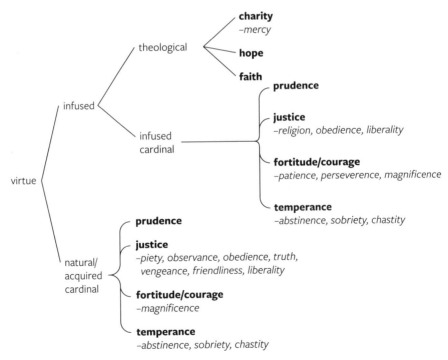

Bibliography

Introduction

Bauerschmidt, Frederick C. *Thomas Aquinas: Faith, Reason and Following Christ.* New York: Oxford University Press, 2013.

Bonino, Serge-Thomas, OP. "To Be a Thomist." *Nova et Vetera* 8.4 (2010): 763–73.

Boyle, Leonard. *The Setting of the "Summa Theologiae" of Saint Thomas.* Toronto: Pontifical Institute of Medieval Studies, 1982.

Cessario, Romanus, OP. *A Short History of Thomism.* Washington, DC: Catholic University of America Press, 2005.

Chesterton, G. K. *St. Thomas Aquinas.* San Francisco: Ignatius, 2002.

Dodds, Michael. *Philosophical Anthropology.* Oakland: Western Dominican Province, 2014.

———. *The Philosophy of Nature.* Oakland: Western Dominican Province, 2010.

Kerr, Fergus, OP. *After Aquinas: Versions of Thomism.* Oxford: Blackwell, 2002.

Konyndyk DeYoung, Rebecca, Colleen McCluskey, and Christian Van Dyke. *Aquinas's Ethics: Metaphysical Foundations, Moral Theory, and Theological Context.* Notre Dame, IN: University of Notre Dame Press, 2009.

McInerny, Ralph. *A First Glance at St. Thomas Aquinas: A Handbook for Peeping Thomists.* Notre Dame, IN: University of Notre Dame Press, 1989.

Pieper, Josef. *The Silence of St. Thomas.* South Bend, IN: St. Augustine's Press, 1999.

Torrell, Jean-Pierre, OP. *Aquinas's "Summa": Background, Structure, and Reception.* Translated by Benedict M. Guevin, OSB. Washington, DC: Catholic University of America Press, 2005.

———. *Saint Thomas Aquinas.* Vol. 1, *The Person and His Work*, translated by Robert Royal. Washington, DC: Catholic University of America Press, 2005.

227

————. *Saint Thomas Aquinas.* Vol. 2, *Spiritual Master,* translated by Robert Royal. Washington, DC: Catholic University of America Press, 2003.

Part 1

Bradley, Denis J. M. *Aquinas on the Twofold Human Good: Reason and Human Happiness in Aquinas's Moral Science.* Washington, DC: Catholic University of America Press, 1999.

Capreolus, John. *On the Virtues.* Translated by Kevin White and Romanus Cessario, OP. Washington, DC: Catholic University of America Press, 2001.

Cessario, Romanus, OP. *Introduction to Moral Theology.* Washington, DC: Catholic University of America Press, 2013.

Crosson, Frederick J. "The Analogy of Religion." *Proceedings of the American Catholic Philosophical Association* 65 (1991): 1–15.

Feingold, Lawrence. *The Natural Desire to See God according to St. Thomas Aquinas and His Interpreters.* Naples, FL: Sapientia Press of Ave Maria University, 2010.

Garrigou-Lagrange, Reginald, OP. *The Three Ages of the Interior Life: Prelude to Eternal Life.* Translated by Sr. M. Timothea Doyle, OP. St. Louis: Herder, 1951.

Harms, Arielle. "Acquired and Infused Moral Virtue: A Distinction of Ends." *New Blackfriars* 95 (2014): 71–87.

Hause, Jeffrey. "Aquinas on Aristotelian Justice: Defender, Destroyer, Subverter, or Surveyor?" In *Aquinas and the "Nicomachean Ethics,"* edited by Tobias Hoffmann, Jorn Muller, and Matthias Perkams, 146–64. New York: Cambridge University Press, 2013.

Hibbs, Thomas S. *Virtue's Splendor: Wisdom, Prudence, and the Human Good.* New York: Fordham University Press, 2001.

Inglis, John. "Aquinas's Replication of the Acquired Moral Virtues: Rethinking the Standard Philosophical Interpretation of Moral Virtue in Aquinas." *Journal of Religious Ethics* 27.1 (1999): 3–27.

Jensen, Steven J. *Good and Evil Actions: A Journey through Saint Thomas Aquinas.* Washington, DC: Catholic University of America Press, 2010.

————. *Living the Good Life: A Beginner's Thomistic Ethics.* Washington, DC: Catholic University of America Press, 2013.

Knasas, John F. X. *Aquinas and the Cry of Rachel: Thomistic Reflections on the Problem of Evil.* Washington, DC: Catholic University of America Press, 2013.

Knobel, Angela McKay. "Can Aquinas's Infused and Acquired Virtues Coexist in the Christian Life?" *Studies in Christian Ethics* 23.4 (2010): 381–96.

Krasevac, Edward L. "Can Effects That Are Inevitable and Instrumental Be *Praeter Intentionem*?" *Angelicum* 82 (2005): 77–88.

Lombardo, Nicholas E., OP. *The Logic of Desire: Aquinas on Emotion*. Washington, DC: Catholic University of America Press, 2010.

McInerny, Ralph. *Aquinas on Human Action: A Theory of Practice*. Washington, DC: Catholic University of America Press, 2012.

———. *Ethica Thomistica*. Washington, DC: Catholic University of America Press, 1997.

Miner, Robert. *Thomas Aquinas on the Passions: A Study of "Summa Theologiae," 1a2ae 22–48*. New York: Cambridge University Press, 2011.

O'Meara, Thomas F., OP. "Virtues in the Theology of Thomas Aquinas." *Theological Studies* 58.2 (June 1997): 254–85.

O'Reilly, Kevin E., OP. "The Significance of Worship in the Thought of Thomas Aquinas: Some Reflections." *International Philosophical Quarterly* 53.4 (2013): 453–62.

Osborne, Thomas M., Jr. "Perfect and Imperfect Virtues in Aquinas." *Thomist* 71.1 (2007): 39–64.

———. "The Three-fold Referral of Acts to the Ultimate End in Thomas Aquinas and His Commentators." *Angelicum* 85 (2008): 715–36.

Pieper, Josef. *Faith, Hope, Love*. San Francisco: Ignatius, 1997.

———. *The Four Cardinal Virtues*. Translated by Richard and Clara Winston. Notre Dame, IN: University of Notre Dame Press, 1966.

———. *Happiness and Contemplation*. South Bend, IN: St. Augustine's Press, 1998.

Pinckaers, Servais, OP. *The Sources of Christian Ethics*. Translated by Sr. Mary Thomas Noble, OP. Washington, DC: Catholic University of America Press, 1995.

Pinsent, Andrew. *The Second-Person Perspective in Aquinas's Ethics*. New York: Routledge, 2012.

Porter, Jean. "The Unity of the Virtues and the Ambiguity of Goodness: A Reappraisal of Aquinas's Theory of the Virtues." *Journal of Religious Ethics* 21.1 (1993): 137–63.

Rhonheimer, Martin. *The Perspective of Morality: Philosophical Foundations of Thomistic Virtue Ethics*. Washington, DC: Catholic University of America Press, 2011.

Shanley, Brian J., OP. "Aquinas on Pagan Virtue." *Thomist* 63.4 (1999): 553–77.

Sherwin, Michael S., OP. "Infused Virtue and the Effects of Acquired Vice: A Test Case for the Thomistic Theory of Infused Cardinal Virtues." *Thomist* 73 (2009): 29–52.

Simon, Yves. *The Definition of Moral Virtue*. New York: Fordham University Press, 1986.

Sommers, Mary C. "'He Spak to [T]hem That Wolde Lyve Parfitly': Thomas Aquinas, the Wife of Bath and the Two Senses of 'Religion.'" *Proceedings of the American Catholic Philosophical Association* 65 (1991): 145–56.

Part 2

Barath, Desire. "Just Price and the Costs of Production according to St. Thomas Aquinas." *New Scholasticism* 34.4 (1960): 413–30.

Bartell, Ernest. "Value, Price, and St. Thomas." *Thomist* 25 (1962): 325–81.

Biddle, Mark E. "The Biblical Prohibition against Usury." *Interpretation* 65.2 (2011): 117–27.

Burke, Joseph. "Distributive Justice and Subsidiarity: The Firm and the State in the Social Order." *Journal of Markets and Morality* 13.2 (2010): 297–317.

Franks, Christopher A. *He Became Poor: The Poverty of Christ and Aquinas's Economic Teachings*. Grand Rapids: Eerdmans, 2009.

González, Justo L. *Faith and Wealth: A History of Early Christian Ideas on the Origin, Significance, and Use of Money*. Eugene, OR: Wipf & Stock, 1990.

Harvie, Timothy. "The Social Body: Thomas Aquinas on Economics and Human Embodiment." *Heythrop Journal* 56.3 (2015): 388–98.

McMahon, Kevin A. "Economics, Wisdom and the Teaching of the Bishops in the Theology of Thomas Aquinas." *Thomist* 53.1 (1989): 91–106.

Meeks, Douglas M. "The Peril of Usury in the Christian Tradition." *Interpretation* 65.2 (2011): 128–40.

Pope, Stephen J. "Aquinas on Almsgiving, Justice and Charity: An Interpretation and Reassessment." *Heythrop Journal* 32.2 (1991): 167–91.

Schmitz, Kenneth L. *The Gift: Creation*. Milwaukee: Marquette University Press, 1982.

Part 3

Breidenbach, Michael D., and William McCormick. "Aquinas on Tyranny, Resistance, and the End of Politics." *Perspectives on Political Science* 44.1 (2015): 10–17.

Brook, Angus. "Faith: The Basis of Justice." *Heythrop Journal* 56.3 (2015): 361–72.

Coyle, Sean. "Fallen Justice." *New Blackfriars* 93 (2012): 687–709.

Cunningham, Sean B. "Aquinas on the Natural Inclination of Man to Offer Sacrifice to God." *Proceedings of the American Catholic Philosophical Association* 86 (2013): 185–200.

Farrell, Walter. "Virtues of the Household." *Thomist* 9.3 (1946): 337–78.

Ferry, Leonard. "The Framework of Deference: Obedience as a Political Virtue." *Maritain Studies / Études Maritainiennes* 26 (2010): 3–41.

Finnis, John. *Aquinas: Moral, Political, and Legal Theory*. New York: Oxford University Press, 1998.

Fortin, Ernest L. *Ernest Fortin: Collected Essays*. Vol. 1, *The Birth of Philosophic Christianity: Studies in Early Christian and Medieval Thought*, edited by J. Brian Benestad. Lanham, MD: Rowman & Littlefield, 1996.

———. *Ernest Fortin: Collected Essays*. Vol. 2, *Classical Christianity and the Political Order: Reflections on the Theologico-Political Problem*, edited by J. Brian Benestad. Lanham, MD: Rowman & Littlefield, 1996.

Gardner, Patrick M. "Aquinas and Dante on the *Duo Ultima Hominis*." *Thomist* 75 (2011): 415–59.

George, Robert P., ed. *Natural Law Theory: Contemporary Essays*. New York: Clarendon, 1994.

Goyette, John. "On the Transcendence of the Political Common Good: Aquinas versus the New Natural Law Theory." *National Catholic Bioethics Quarterly* 13.1 (2013): 133–56.

Jensen, Steven. *Knowing the Natural Law: From Precepts and Inclinations to Deriving Oughts*. Washington, DC: Catholic University of America Press, 2015.

Joseph, N. Benedict, OP. *The Virtue of Observance according to St. Thomas Aquinas*. Washington, DC: Thomist Press, 1954.

Joubert, Gerard. *Qualities of Citizenship in St. Thomas*. Washington, DC: Catholic University of America Press, 1942.

Keys, Mary M. *Aquinas, Aristotle, and the Promise of the Common Good*. New York: Cambridge University Press, 2006.

Koritansky, Peter Karl. *Thomas Aquinas and the Philosophy of Punishment*. Washington, DC: Catholic University of America Press, 2011.

Kossel, Clifford G. "Piety: The Debts Which Precede Our Rights." *Communio* 12 (1985): 33–48.

Kries, Douglas. "Thomas Aquinas and the Politics of Moses." *Review of Politics* 52.1 (1990): 84–104.

McInerny, Ralph. "The Principles of Natural Law." *American Journal of Jurisprudence* 25 (1980): 1–15.

O'Reilly, Kevin E., OP. "The Eucharist and the Politics of Love according to Thomas Aquinas." *Heythrop Journal* 56.3 (2015): 399–410.

Pakaluk, Michael. "Is the Common Good of Political Society Limited and Instrumental?" *Review of Metaphysics* 55 (2001): 57–94.

Perricone, John A. "The Relation between Justice and Love in the Natural Order." *Journal of Catholic Legal Studies* 51.1 (2012): 55–75.

Pieper, Josef. *Leisure: The Basis of Culture*. San Francisco: Ignatius, 2009.

Porter, Jean. *Nature as Reason: A Thomistic Theory of the Natural Law*. Grand Rapids: Eerdmans, 2004.

Regan, Richard J. "Aquinas on Political Obedience and Disobedience." *Thought* 56.1 (1981): 77–88.

Rhonheimer, Martin. *Natural Law and Practical Reason: A Thomist View of Moral Autonomy*. Translated by Gerald Malsbary. New York: Fordham University Press, 2000.

Part 4

Barrera, Albino. *Modern Catholic Social Documents and Political Economy*. Washington, DC: Georgetown University Press, 2001.

Benestad, J. Brian. *Church, State, and Society: An Introduction to Catholic Social Doctrine*. Washington, DC: Catholic University of America Press, 2011.

Brady, Bernard V. "An Analysis of the Use of Rights Language in Pre-Modern Catholic Social Thought." *Thomist* 57 (1993): 97–121.

Burke, Joseph. "Distributive Justice and Subsidiarity: The Firm and the State in the Social Order." *Journal of Markets and Morality* 13.2 (2010): 297–317.

Cavanaugh, William T. *Field Hospital: The Church's Engagement with a Wounded World*. Grand Rapids: Eerdmans, 2016.

———. "'A Fire Strong Enough to Consume the House': The Wars of Religion and the Rise of the State." *Modern Theology* 11.4 (1995): 397–415.

Douglass, Bruce R., and David Hollenbach, eds. *Catholicism and Liberalism: Contributions to American Public Philosophy*. New York: Cambridge University Press, 1997.

Fehring, Richard J., and Theresa Notare, eds. *Human Fertility: Where Faith and Science Meet*. Milwaukee: Marquette University Press, 2008.

Finn, Daniel K., ed. *The True Wealth of Nations: Catholic Social Thought and Economic Life*. New York: Oxford University Press, 2010.

Finnis, John. "Subsidiarity's Roots and History: Some Observations." *American Journal of Jurisprudence* 61.1 (2016): 133–41.

Fortin, Ernest L. *Ernest Fortin: Collected Essays*. Vol. 3, *Human Rights, Virtue, and the Common Good: Untimely Meditations on Religion and Politics*, edited by J. Brian Benestad. Lanham, MD: Rowman & Littlefield, 1996.

Frohnen, Bruce, and Kenneth L. Grasso, eds. *Rethinking Rights: Historical, Political, and Philosophical Perspectives*. Columbia: University of Missouri Press, 2009.

Glenn, Gary D., and John Stack. "Is American Democracy Safe for Catholicism?" *Review of Politics* 61.1 (2000): 5–29.

Gondreau, Paul. "The 'Inseparable Connection' between Procreation and Unitive Love' (*Humanae Vitae*, §12) and Thomistic Hylomorphic Anthropology." *Nova et Vetera* 6 (2008): 731–64.

———. "The Natural Law Ordering of Human Sexuality to (Heterosexual) Marriage: Towards a Thomistic Philosophy of the Body." *Nova et Vetera* 8.3 (2010): 553–92.

Goyette, John, Mark S. Latovic, and Richard S. Meyers, eds. *St. Thomas Aquinas and the Natural Law Tradition: Contemporary Perspectives*. Washington, DC: Catholic University of America Press, 2004.

Grabowski, John S. *Sex and Virtue: An Introduction to Catholic Sexual Ethics*. Washington, DC: Catholic University of America Press, 2003.

Grasso, Kenneth L., Gerard V. Bradley, and Robert P. Hunt, eds. *Catholicism, Liberalism, and Communitarianism: The Catholic Intellectual Tradition and the Moral Foundations of Democracy*. Lanham, MD: Rowman & Littlefield, 1995.

Grasso, Kenneth L., and Robert P. Hunt, eds. *Catholicism and Religious Freedom: Contemporary Reflections on Vatican II's Declaration on Religious Liberty*. Lanham, MD: Rowman & Littlefield, 2006.

Haldane, John, and Patrick Lee. "Aquinas on Human Ensoulment, Abortion and the Value of Life." *Philosophy* 78 (2003): 255–78.

Heaney, Stephen J. "Aquinas and the Presence of the Human Rational Soul in the Early Embryo." *Thomist* 56 (1992): 19–48.

Hirschfeld, Mary. "Standard of Living and Economic Virtue: Forging a Link between St. Thomas Aquinas and the Twenty-First Century." *Journal of the Society of Christian Ethics* 26.1 (2006): 61–77.

Hittinger, Francis Russell. "The Declaration on Religious Liberty, *Dignitatis Humanae*." In *Vatican II: Renewal within Tradition*, edited by Matthew L. Lamb and Matthew Levering, 359–82. New York: Oxford University Press, 2008.

———. "Divisible Goods and Common Good: Reflections on *Caritas in Veritate*." *Faith and Economics* 58 (2011): 31–46.

———. "The Four Basic Principles of Catholic Social Doctrine: An Interpretation." *Nova et Vetera* 7.4 (2009): 791–838.

———. "Religion, Human Law, and the Virtue of Religion: The Case of *Dignitatis Humanae*." *Nova et Vetera* 14.1 (2016): 151–76.

Hittinger, John. "Jacques Maritain and Yves R. Simon's Use of Thomas Aquinas in Their Defense of Liberal Democracy." In *Liberty, Wisdom, and Grace: Thomism and Democratic Political Theory*, 35–60. Lanham, MD: Lexington Books, 2002.

Jacobs, James M. "On the Difference between Social Justice and Christian Charity." *American Catholic Philosophical Quarterly* 81.3 (2007): 419–38.

———. "The Practice of Religion in Post-Secular Society." *International Philosophical Quarterly* 54.1 (2014): 5–23.

Klay, Robin, and John Lunn. "'Just Remuneration' Over a Worker's Lifetime." *Journal of Markets and Morality* 6.1 (2003): 177–99.

Krom, Michael P. "Modern Liberalism and Pride: An Augustinian Perspective." *Journal of Religious Ethics* 35.3 (September 2007): 453–78.

———. "Transcendence and Human Freedom: Modernity and the Right to Truth." *Catholic Social Science Review* 15 (2010): 153–73.

Lawler, Ronald, Joseph Boyle, and William E. May. *Catholic Sexual Ethics: A Summary, Explanation, and Defense*. 2nd ed. Huntington, IN: Our Sunday Visitor Press, 1998.

Lustig, Andrew B. "Property, Justice, and the Common Good: A Response to Paul J. Weithman." *Journal of Religious Ethics* 21.1 (1993): 181–87.

Makdisi, John. "Uncaring Justice: Why *Jacque v. Steenberg Homes* Was Wrongly Decided." *Journal of Catholic Legal Studies* 51.1 (2012): 111–43.

Maritain, Jacques. *Man and the State*. Washington, DC: Catholic University of America Press, 1998.

———. *Scholasticism and Politics*. Indianapolis: Liberty Fund, 2011.

Marzen, Chad G., and William M. Woodyard. "Is Greed Good? A Catholic Perspective on Modern Usury." *Brigham Young University Journal of Public Law* 27.1 (2012): 185–228.

McCall, Brian M. *The Church and the Usurers: Unprofitable Lending for the Modern Economy*. Ave Maria, FL: Sapientia Press of Ave Maria University, 2013.

Murray, John Courtney. *The Problem of Religious Freedom*. Westminster, PA: Newman Press, 1965.

———. *We Hold These Truths: Catholic Reflections on the American Proposition*. Lanham, MD: Rowman & Littlefield, 2005.

Novak, Michael. *The Catholic Ethic and the Spirit of Capitalism*. New York: Free Press, 1993.

———. "Democracy Unsafe, Compared to What? The Totalitarian Impulse of Contemporary Liberals." *Review of Politics* 61.1 (2000): 31–48.

O'Boyle, Edward J. "Social Justice: Addressing the Ambiguity." *Logos* 14.2 (2011): 97–117.

Pattee, Dan. "Social Justice and Catholic Social Thought." *Catholic Social Science Review* 21 (2016): 99–115.

Paulhus, Normand J. "Uses and Misuses of the Term 'Social Justice' in the Roman Catholic Tradition." *Journal of Religious Ethics* 15.2 (1987): 261–82.

Petri, Thomas, OP. *Aquinas and the Theology of the Body: The Thomistic Foundations of John Paul II's Anthropology*. Washington, DC: Catholic University of America Press, 2016.

Ratzinger, Joseph. *Truth and Tolerance: Christian Belief and World Religions*. Translated by Henry Taylor. San Francisco: Ignatius, 2004.

Ryan, John A. *Distributive Justice: The Right and Wrong of Our Present Distribution of Wealth*. New York: Macmillan, 1927.

———. *A Living Wage: Its Ethical and Economic Aspects*. New York: Macmillan, 1912.

Scarnecchia, D. Brian. *Bioethics, Law, and Human Life Issues: A Catholic Perspective on Marriage, Family, Contraception, Abortion, Reproductive Technology, and Death and Dying.* Lanham, MD: Scarecrow Press, 2010.

Schall, James V., SJ. *At the Limits of Political Philosophy.* Washington, DC: Catholic University of America Press, 1998.

———. *Roman Catholic Political Philosophy.* Lanham, MD: Lexington Books, 2006.

Schindler, David L. *Heart of the World, Center of the Church: Communio Ecclesiology, Liberalism, and Liberation.* Grand Rapids: Eerdmans, 1996.

Simon, Yves. *The Tradition of Natural Law.* Edited by Vukan Kuic. New York: Fordham University Press, 1992.

Weithman, Paul J. "Natural Law, Property, and Redistribution." *Journal of Religious Ethics* 21.1 (1993): 165–80.

Yuengert, Andrew. *The Boundaries of Technique.* Lanham, MD: Lexington Books, 2004.

Zięba, Maciej, OP. *Papal Economics: The Catholic Church on Democratic Capitalism, from "Rerum Novarum" to "Caritas in Veritate."* Wilmington, DE: ISI Books, 2013.

Index